The Young Country Doctor Book 8
Bilbury Tonic

Vernon Coleman

Dedication: To Antoinette

Without you there is darkness.

With you there is sunshine.

Copyright Vernon Coleman 2016

The right of Vernon Coleman to be identified as the author of this work has been asserted in accordance with the Copyright, Designs and Patents Act 1988.

Enquiries should be addressed to the author.

For more information about the author, please see www.vernoncoleman.com

Preface

When I finished writing *Bilbury Pudding*, the seventh in 'The Young Country Doctor' series, I did not intend to write any more Bilbury books. To be honest, I didn't think I had anything more to say about Bilbury.

But, as one incarnation of a famous spy once said: 'Never say never again'.

And here I am again, with another collection of stories from Bilbury.

Two things changed my mind.

First, the village of Bilbury, and its inhabitants, are very dear to me. Bilbury is always there; an escape from our ever troubling world; endless fears, terrorism, selfishness, deceit and ruthless disregard for decency and honour. My wife and I have never had friends as good as Thumper, Patchy, Frank, Gilly and Peter. And I have never known any place where the stories hang, like ripe fruit, waiting to be picked, as they do in Bilbury.

In recent years, I have become more of a recluse than ever. It has been said that writing is show business for shy people but these days the whole business of writing has changed. When I was younger, I used to do a good deal of television and radio and I wrote columns for many newspapers. The appearances and the columns helped attract readers to my books and I knew I could always run back to my keyboard when the frenetic multimedia world became too much for me. But the growth of social media, and the increasing acerbity in the world, and the fact that the critics never forget, never show mercy and never sleep, have combined to make life impossible for the shy and the unduly sensitive. I have now retired from everything other than writing books.

And I have found myself increasingly content to remain in Bilbury, away from the noisy hustle and disturbing bustle of the 21st century. Barking? Maybe. Do I give a stuff? Not likely.

Second, the requests for more Bilbury stories have never stopped coming and since the publication of the books in eBook format, the number of requests has increased steadily. There are, it seems, quite a few folk who share my deep affection for this quiet, isolated village in North Devon and for its inhabitants. For them, as for us, Bilbury is a stable point of refuge in an often cruel, frequently disappointing, constantly confusing and ever-changing world. It is a real joy to be able to share the village with readers who enjoy reading about it and who, I hope, might, in their hearts, like to think of themselves as honorary Bilburians.

At this point, I think I should remind you that the Bilbury books are all set in the 1970s and although this book is being written well into the 21st century I am writing about things that happened nearly half a century ago. Medical knowledge and customs were very different then.

Some older readers will remember those distant days with fondness but many younger readers will probably find it difficult to imagine living in a world without mobile telephones, computers and the mass of gadgets and conveniences which we all now take for granted.

Finally, I should also point out that I take the principle of confidentiality very seriously. None of the people or situations in this book is recognisable. Oh, and I should also remind you that real life doesn't always have nice, neat endings. It is only in fiction that things have to work out and must be in some way explicable.

Welcome back to Bilbury.

Vernon Coleman

Two Pink Gins

We most of us dream of some café or bar where we will be known and where the barman or barmaid will greet us with our favourite beverage, possibly in our own favourite mug, the moment we walk through the door. We dream that the other patrons will call out our name and smile when they see us, making us feel welcome, wanted and surrounded by friends.

It is no coincidence that the most successful television soap operas are set around bars and public houses.

Sadly, however, in most parts of the world, pubs and cafés lost their soul many years ago. They are all much the same: lots of plastic, a small choice of pre-cooked, frozen meals available to be heated up in an industrial sized microwave oven, drinks served in plastic drinking glasses and coffee made from acorns and so foul that not even British Rail would dare serve it. The staff who never recognise any of their customers and for whom English is, at best, a second or third language, seem to change once a week and their aim is for you to drink up, eat up and get out as quickly as possible.

If it didn't exist, the 'Duck and Puddle' public house would, I suppose, be the meeting place we all dream of.

Frank and Gill, the landlord and his wife, treat all their regulars like family and no one is ever asked to leave simply because they haven't ordered a drink for a long time. Lemuel Macintosh, probably the meanest man ever to have owned a wallet, once sat in the snug for a whole day after ordering just one coffee and a bag of salt and vinegar crisps. It requires a certain amount of determination and self-restraint to make a cup of coffee and a packet of crisps last ten hours.

Thumper Robinson entrepreneur, poacher and owner of the scruffiest truck south of Birmingham, Patchy Fogg, antique dealer extraordinaire and now my brother-in-law, and I were sitting in the snug.

My wife, Patsy, had gone into Barnstaple to try to find a replacement for our toaster, which had given up the ghost, and she had taken the babies with her.

'Will you manage to get something for lunch?' she asked, as she left. To us the half hour journey into Barnstaple is a trek into another world.

I said I would.

'Are you meeting Thumper and Patchy?'

I said I was.

'At the Duck and Puddle?'

'You know us too well.'

'Try to have something solid,' she said, blowing me a kiss.

And so there we were; settled comfortably into our favourite corner of the 'Duck and Puddle'.

I was drinking a modest portion of Islay malt whisky and the other two were drinking pints of Frank's best bitter, a potent brew from a small West Country brewery which specialises in supplying a small number of independent West Country public houses with beer, and a rather larger number of farmers with whisky.

The company makes a brand of whisky called 'Horse Feed' which is popular with farmers because they can buy it by the crate and be given useful receipts to show to the taxman. It is one of the least known malt whiskies but the sales figures must be very encouraging for the company concerned. There are scores of better-known malts which are far less profitable.

A medical friend of mine once went to Scotland on a course for a week. At least he said he was going on a course but I don't think he had great plans for learning anything relevant to his professional career. The word 'course' can be interpreted in a number of different ways.

My chum had booked himself into a magnificent loch side hotel which boasted a bar which claimed to stock bottles of every malt whisky made. On his arrival, my friend sat himself down at the bar and said to the barman, 'I'm here for a week. I intend to work my way through all the malt whiskies made in Scotland. Where do you suggest I start?'

The barman gave him a sad look. 'We have 274 different varieties of malt whisky, sir,' he said, 'I think you might be pushed to work your through them all in just a week. Would you not perhaps consider prolonging your stay a little?'

For lunch, I was munching my way through a couple of slices of a large, fresh, farmhouse loaf, liberally buttered, and a bowl of green and black olives while my friends Thumper Robinson and Patchy Fogg were eating pork scratchings.

The pork scratchings concerned were three months beyond something called their 'sell-by date' and had consequently been sold at three quarters of their usual price.

The introduction of sell-by dates had been something that had enraged Frank Parsons, the landlord of the 'Duck and Puddle', who regarded it as a trick introduced by the manufacturers to encourage customers, and public house landlords, to throw away vast quantities of perfectly edible food.

'How can you have a sell-by date on pork scratchings?' he had demanded incredulously when the existence of the dates had first been drawn to his attention. 'Pork scratchings are fried pig skin. They'll last forever! If there is ever a nuclear war there will be three things left: cockroaches, traffic wardens and pork scratchings.'

Neither Thumper nor Patchy seemed to think that there was anything wrong with the pork scratchings, which came from a box Frank had unearthed that morning while clearing out a cupboard. Clearing out cupboards was something which Frank tried to do once a year. It was, he once said, just below cleaning the gutters and just above filling in his tax form on his list of favourite things to do.

As I suspect people generally do when they are sitting in any public house, and as they always seem to do when they are sitting in the 'Duck and Puddle', we had been enjoying a wide-ranging discussion.

Thumper had said, not for the first time and probably not for the last for, as he once pointed out, if you think of something clever to say it is a bit of a waste to say it only once, that he couldn't understand why television news readers were treated as celebrities when all they had to do was to be able to read while sitting down.

He said he had been able to read while sitting, standing and even lying down since he'd been five-years-old.

Patchy agreed with Thumper on this but said that he was even more puzzled by the fact that fashion models are apparently paid millions of dollars a year.

'I don't mind anyone earning that sort of money,' he said, 'but I don't understand why anyone thinks they're worth it. All they have to do is walk up and down while wearing clothes.'

Thumper said he'd been told by his mother that he'd been walking around long before he was two-years-old and that he was confident that he would not have been expected to walk about without wearing any clothes.

There had then been an interval during which a good deal of chewing and sipping was done.

Patchy had then told me that he had met a man in Taunton who had a telephone fitted in his car. He said that the man, who was an antique dealer with a showroom in Bond Street, swore by the telephone, claiming that because it enabled him to make and receive calls while driving around, it more than paid for itself.

Patchy said the man had told him that while driving up to Manchester he had, as a result of a telephone call he'd received from an assistant in London, turned right and gone to Norwich instead.

The result had been that instead of attending a fairly pedestrian auction in Lancashire he had, at a saleroom in East Anglia, purchased a rare 18th century chestnut and oak table for approximately the price of a Formica topped kitchen table.

'You should get one of those car phones,' Thumper said to me. 'It would be terribly useful. People would be able to get hold of you wherever you were.'

I blanched at the thought.

'People can always get hold of me wherever I am,' I pointed out, perhaps rather defensively. 'If someone rings the house, Patsy or Miss Johnson will tell them where I can be found.'

It did occur to me, however, that it would be useful if Patsy could reach me when I was out on my rounds, or attending an emergency, if another patient in the same area required a visit.

I have on many occasions returned home from a cottage some miles from Bilbury Grange only to find that I have had to retrace my steps to visit a patient living just a few minutes away from where I'd just been.

To be honest, however, I thought that was a fair price to pay for having time away from the damned telephone; time giving me a little peace and a chance to think.

I have on several occasions managed to make a diagnosis while driving back home at 4.00 a.m.; being free to allow my mind to rifle through all the relevant signs and symptoms in order to find a solution to a particularly knotty problem.

'There wouldn't be any point in you buying one anyway,' said Patchy, still talking about the man he'd met with the telephone in his car. 'This bloke said his phone didn't work anywhere west of Taunton. I think he said it was something to do with there not being any reception.'

'You'd probably need to drive around with a fifty foot tall aerial fixed to the top of your car,' said Thumper.

I breathed a silent sigh of relief.

I really didn't want to travel everywhere with a telephone at my elbow.

Other than in the car there are few places in the world where I can relax and enjoy a little peace and quiet. I can hear the telephone ringing when I'm in the bathtub but I can't hear the phone when I'm out on my rounds in the car.

Why, I wonder, do so many people feel under constant pressure to reinvent the world, even when things are perfectly satisfactory and, indeed, usually far better the way they are?

I know that looking backwards is frowned on by some, who regard the retrospectoscope as offering an unduly rosy coloured view of the past.

But some things really were better then.

Does anyone really doubt that houses and cars were better made two hundred years ago than they are today? How many modern houses will still be standing in three or four hundred years? How many motor cars made today will still be running in another 40 years?

Service was often better too, and companies took better care of their customers.

When I was a boy in the 1950s, I remember my mother making a complaint about a box of Cadbury's chocolates. The chocolates, a rare and expensive treat, were faulty and my mother was upset enough to write a letter to the company. The next day she received a huge hamper of Cadbury's products, a bouquet of flowers and a fulsome letter of apology.

Would such a letter even receive a response today?

Things were better 20 years ago, back in the 1950s, because people were more honest, more naturally respectful of others and more concerned to do a good job and to be seen to do a good job.

I know there are many aspects of modern life which are better than they were, but we do sometimes forget that not everything modern is a wonderful improvement.

'But wait a year or two and you'll be able to buy a telephone you can carry around with you,' said Patchy, who mistakenly seemed to think that I would regard this as good news. 'This bloke, the antique dealer, said that he'd heard that they would soon be making portable phones that will fit into a suitcase – maybe even into a large briefcase. He said you'll be able to walk along the street, just like a normal person, and then there will be a brrr brrr from inside your briefcase. You'll stop for a moment, reach inside and take a phone call from someone with an important message.'

I shuddered.

'How on earth could they do that?' Thumper asked. 'You'd need miles and miles of wire! And where would you plug it in?'

'No, no!' said Patchy. 'You don't have to plug it in. It will all be done with aerials and batteries and things. This bloke I was talking to says there's all sorts of new technology coming.'

'I wouldn't have one of those,' said Thumper firmly. 'You'd probably find the call was from some bugger trying to sell you double glazing.'

'Or insurance,' I added glumly.

We sat for a while contemplating the awfulness of a future where people were expected to carry telephones around with them and be forever tormented by overbearing salesmen and saleswomen.

Thumper and Patchy chewed on their pork scratchings and I nibbled on a few olives.

'The bloke who told me about the telephones also told me that he heard that they're planning to make computers small enough to have at home,' said Patchy suddenly. 'He said that these computer things will revolutionise everything. He reckons we'll be able to do our accounts on them and keep lists of all our stuff.'

'It sounds nonsense to me,' I said, utterly unconvinced by Patchy's latest piece of science fiction. 'I've heard of medical practices which have computers but I don't have much faith in that sort of technology. What if the computer thingy breaks down? You could lose everything you'd put into it? And I don't think computers are all that clever. When I was a boy, my parents used to take me to the Science Museum in Birmingham. The museum had a computer there that could play a very simple form of draughts – fox and rabbit I think they called it. I remember that when I was about ten-years-old I could beat the computer most of the time. And the darned thing was absolutely huge. If you had one of those in your home you'd need a special room for it.'

'Well this bloke told me that he'd heard that computer chappies in America are already making computers small enough to fit on a table or a desk,' said Patchy. 'He says it won't be long before they have computers small enough to put into your suitcase along with the telephone. To be honest I wasn't really convinced myself. But you never know, do you?'

'Sounds like pie in the sky to me,' said Thumper, firmly.

I agreed with him, though this may have been wishful thinking.

'I wonder what else they'll be doing in forty or fifty years!' said Patchy.

'It's these computers that worry me,' said Thumper. 'What the devil will people use them for?'

'If you can type stuff into them you could use them for writing letters?' I suggested.

'How would you post the letter?' asked Thumper.

'I suppose you could send your computer to the person your letter was addressed to,' I suggested. 'If the new computer thingies are small enough to fit into a suitcase you could wrap up your computer, complete with letter, and pop the whole thing in the post.'

'You could use it for shopping,' suggested Patchy.

Thumper and I looked at him as if he were mad.

'Well you never know,' said Patchy defensively. 'If you can write messages on a computer then you could sit down at a keyboard, write your shopping list, some sausages or a bottle of milk for example, and send the computer round to the shop so that the shopkeeper could deliver what you'd ordered.'

Both Thumper and I thought that was very funny.

'Can you imagine Peter Marshall peering at a computer and taking orders for light bulbs and bags of spuds?' asked Thumper.

The idea of Peter doing anything with a computer made us laugh a lot more. Peter thinks a pencil with a rubber on the blunt end is a piece of high tech equipment.

'I wonder where it's all going to end?' asked Patchy, thoughtfully. 'Perhaps they'll invent a way to transmit messages from one computer to another. Or maybe we'll be able to send our messages over the radio. You ring up the radio station and give them your order for sausages and whatever, the radio station then broadcasts your order and the shop sends the stuff round.'

'I don't think that will work,' I said. 'The orders would all get mixed up. Someone else would get your sausages and you'd get their soap and toothpaste.' I thought for a moment. 'Maybe they'll make a personal spacecraft and we'll be able to pop over to Mars for the weekend?'

'Perhaps someone will invent a car which will drive itself!' said Thumper. He said he thought Dan Dare in the Eagle comic had owned something of the sort. 'You just jump into the car, tell it where you want to go, sit back, relax and pour yourself a large whisky.'

At that bizarre suggestion the three of us laughed so much that we made ourselves ill. The tears were running down our cheeks and my stomach muscles ached.

'You sit in this car,' I said, intrigued by Thumper's nonsensical thought, 'and you tell it to take you to Exeter. And off it goes, all by itself! If you get done for speeding then the car has to go to court and pay the fine.'

'Hey, I've got a good idea,' said Patchy. 'They fit a computer, a camera and a telephone into a refrigerator and when you run out of sausages the refrigerator telephones Peter Marshall and tells him to send round more sausages pronto!'

'And then,' I said, struggling not to laugh before I could put my thoughts into words, 'Peter puts the sausages into a driverless car and orders the car to take the sausages round to your place where a little robot fellow thanks the driverless car and pops the sausages into the fridge!'

We laughed a good deal more and made ourselves even more ill.

And then we sat for a while, chuckling occasionally as we remembered the silliest of our suggestions.

After a few minutes of silent contemplation of a world containing telephones that could be carried around in briefcases, computers powerful enough to use for keeping accounts, but small enough to fit into suitcases, and cars which could drive themselves, we discussed serious local topics such as Peter Marshall's forthcoming sale of the stuff he'd found in his shed and the proposed building of a new, visitors' car park on a field behind Major Porchester's ruined cottage when a couple of obvious visitors strode noisily into the pub as though they had just bought it and were planning some major changes.

The newcomers, both complete strangers, were wearing brand new walking boots (his boots still had the price tag fixed to a leather loop at the back and if it said what Thumper, with his eagle eyes, had spotted then his boots cost rather more than I had spent on clothes in the last five years), matching orange anoraks and woolly hats that had fancy logos on the front and had, consequently, probably cost an arm and a leg but which were, nevertheless, still just woolly hats. (Whatever you do to a woolly hat it will always be nothing more than a woolly hat.)

He was tall, very thin and cadaverous and although he had the look of a pompous and patronising politician about him, I could not help noticing that, quite contrary to expectations, he had the brown eyes of a Labrador puppy. He looked like a war criminal or a bank chairman and I did not get the feeling that he had any of the other characteristics usually associated with Labrador puppies. I could only assume that, if the balance of nature were to be preserved, somewhere in the world there roamed a Labrador puppy with the cruel eyes of a sadistic psychopath.

I had a strange feeling that I had seen him before somewhere. His female companion, who appeared to be his wife, had mean eyes and a pushy manner and looked to me as I imagined a ferret might look if it were suffering from constipation.

The pair looked critically at the smoke yellowed ceiling, the dusty old prints on the walls, the slightly moth-eaten lampshades on the wall lights, the scarred and well-used brown furniture and the beer stained brass topped tables. They did not spare us from their unspoken criticisms, but gave us the same critical appraisal as they had given the snug and its fixtures and fittings.

'Afternoon,' said Patchy, cheerily. Established Bilburians always welcome visitors, even ones who look like sadistic psychopaths or constipated ferrets. We tend to take people as they come, and to resist the temptation to judge on appearances or reputations. I'm delighted to say that although we all value our privacy and our peace and quiet I have never known a place more welcoming to strangers than Bilbury. It is perfectly true that Thumper once removed all the sign posts which might point motorists in our general direction but this was done after a national newspaper article suggested that Bilbury was 'The Perfect Place to Live: England's Healthiest Village' and we were, as a result, inundated with coach loads of visitors whose presence merely destroyed the peace and quiet they had come to enjoy. (This episode is described in the book *Bilbury Country*).

The two visitors stared at Patchy, as though he had spoken to them in Danish, or had demanded their money with an appropriate supply of menaces. They did not reply. Instead, the man looked around for someone on the other side of the bar. He seemed surprised and disappointed when he failed to see anyone, though this was not surprising because there wasn't anyone there.

Gilly, the landlord's wife and co-owner of the Duck and Puddle public house, was in Combe Martin buying eggs from her cousin's sister-in-law, and from the noises coming from underneath our feet we knew that Frank, the man whose name was on the plate above the door as the Licensee, was in the cellar doing something which involved a barrel of beer, a wooden mallet and a lot of naughty words.

Not being privy to the inside information about Gilly's whereabouts, and not realising that the noise coming from the cellar was being made by the only other person likely to be able to satisfy his requirements, the stranger called out, a loud voice that appeared to be accustomed to obedience, 'Service, please!'

We are all supposed to live in a liberated, classless society, where everyone is equal, but it seems to me that in some respects we are moving backwards rather than forwards. When I last went to London, I was astonished when a customer in a bookshop clicked his fingers to attract the attention of an assistant. When that didn't work, he shouted 'Oi!' in a tone of voice I would not have felt comfortable using when calling our pet sheep. I could well be wrong, of course, but it seems to me that the number of people who enjoy giving orders is increasing.

I recently examined a visitor to the area, a holidaymaker passing through who had suffered an unpleasant reaction to a bee sting, and when I checked his blood pressure, I was shocked to discover that his systolic pressure was 220 and his diastolic was 160. Those figures are dramatically high; far above the healthy normal.

'Is your doctor treating your blood pressure?' I asked the tourist.

'Oh yes,' he agreed, apparently uninterested and possibly unaware of the risks associated with a very high blood pressure. 'But nothing he prescribes seems to bring it down. I work in a legal office in London and I'm constantly under stress. We only arrived in the country today. It usually falls quite a bit when we've been away from London for a few days.'

The man was in his early sixties and so I asked him the obvious question: 'Have you thought about retiring?'

He admitted that he had thought about packing up his job and said that although he could easily afford to retire he knew that he couldn't live without having people to shout at. 'At home, when I tell my wife, children or grandchildren to do something they ignore me. But at work when I tell someone to do something they jump and do it immediately. I like that. I like the fact that I have power and that people are frightened of me.'

He liked the feeling so much, and was so addicted to the power, that he was prepared to die to keep it.

I was reminded of that man with the raised blood pressure by the antics of the cadaverous stranger who had repeated his loud demand for service several times and who was now giving an excellent impression of a small boy who has been denied a packet of sweets and is about to embark upon an attention seeking tantrum.

When no one came, Gilly being still in Combe Martin and Frank still being occupied with a barrel, a mallet and an inexhaustible supply of naughty words, the cadaverous man with the inappropriate puppy eyes took one of the horrid new, decimal 10 pence coins out of his trouser pocket and rapped it as loudly as he could on the bar counter.

You can't rap properly with the skimpy, new decimal coins. They are too light to use as rapping implements. You could rap well with an old-fashioned half crown. Even an old-fashioned shilling was better for rapping than a 10 pence piece. And so, as a result of this numismatic skimpiness, the coin rapping was, to be honest, rather pathetic.

However, Thumper, Patchy and I looked at one another.

If there is one thing that Frank dislikes more than a customer shouting 'Oi!' it is a customer who raps a coin against the bar top. It does his blood pressure absolutely no good at all and Gilly often says that if Frank ever succumbs, and has the heart attack everyone has been predicting for at least a decade, then it will be as a result of some impatient coin rapping.

Frank's attitude is that he, and he alone, decides who gets served next, and when they will be served. His attitude is that waving a five pound note in the air, clicking your fingers or tapping a coin on the counter will all send you straight to the back of the queue. (He also believes, I am pleased to say, that regular customers always get served before strangers, especially rude strangers, and that regular customers who pay cash always get served before regular customers who owe money and have thoughtlessly run up a large, unplanned amount of credit.

(Thumper, who always owes money, is exempt from this rule since he is the only person in Bilbury and, quite possibly the known world, who understands how the 'Duck and Puddle' boiler operates and the only person not in prison who has the courage and agility to squeeze through a narrow trap door into the pub's rat and squirrel infested attic whenever the cold water tank freezes over and the ice needs breaking.)

When the coin rapping produced no response, the cadaverous stranger merely rapped again, putting a bit more effort into it. Britons used to have to go to Paris to find really rude people but these days it is possible to find them anywhere in England; and occasionally they can be found wandering into Bilbury itself.

Fortunately, there wasn't a chance that Frank would hear the rapping, of course.

Frank was concentrating on what he was doing and although we could hear him well enough there was no possibility that he would be able to hear the sound of a single coin being tapped on a bar counter. The un-orchestrated combination of mallet on wood and Frank's choice of words for the day meant that he probably wouldn't have heard a thing even if the fellow had slammed a sack of coins down onto the counter.

'Is there anyone serving here?' demanded the stranger, turning and facing us. He asked the question not as one might direct an enquiry to a stranger but as one might demand a service from a servant. 'We've walked from Combe Martin,' he announced as though this were relevant.

'Our chauffeur is in Combe Martin waiting for us with the Mercedes,' added his wife. She managed to do something to the words 'chauffeur' and 'Mercedes' so that they stood out from the rest of the sentence and had little lights around them to make sure that they were properly noticed.

'Frank is down in the cellar,' said Thumper. 'He'll be up in a minute or two. He's changing a barrel.'

The man sighed loudly, shrugged his shoulders, rolled his eyes in despair and annoyance and managed to accompany these gestures with a fair amount of huffing and puffing. It seemed clear from all this that he probably worked in some dark but doubtless lucrative corner of the financial services industry and almost certainly lived somewhere in the Central London area. His wife muttered something under her breath and then turned and stared at us. She did not seem impressed by what she saw and I got the impression that, given half a chance, she would have liked to have turned us into three pillars of salt. We stared back but said nothing more.

Patchy had offered a welcoming greeting when they had arrived but he, and therefore we, had been spurned.

If the newcomers chose to ignore our presence, our availability for polite conversation and our advice on how best to get safely served, then they could hardly expect us to expose ourselves to repeated bouts of disappointment.

I suddenly remembered where I'd seen the man's picture – it had been on the financial pages of one or two of the broadsheet newspapers. He was an infamous vulture capitalist; renowned for buying up businesses, firing lots of employees, selling off the assets and making vast profits.

The two strangers, the man and the woman, were discussing whether to leave the pub and go somewhere else (we didn't like to disrupt their conversation by pointing out that whatever direction they chose, they would walk for at least an hour before they came across another pub – the King's Head public house on the road to Barnstaple closed four years ago) when Frank appeared, red-faced, damp with the perspiration engendered by unaccustomed exercise and clutching the wooden mallet with which he had been hammering the unfortunate cask. He had what looked like cobwebs draped over his hair and jacket and the sweet smell of fungus which accompanied his presence made it clear that he still hadn't succeeded in eradicating the dry rot which infests the 'Duck and Puddle' cellar and that the chances were high that what looked like cobwebs were, in fact, strands of dry rot fungus.

'I should have left it until Gilly got back,' said Frank, talking to us and pulling himself a pint of bitter. 'I don't know how she does it but she can handle those barrels far better than I can.'

'Excuse me! But we've been waiting ages for service,' said the cadaverous stranger. 'Are you the barman?'

'I'm the landlord,' replied Frank, glowering at them both. 'What do you want?'

'I'll have a glass of claret, something with plenty of body, maybe a Mouton de Rothschild. The 1970 will do nicely. And my wife will have...' the stranger turned in his wife's direction, inviting her to continue the sentence.

'...a glass of Chablis, something from one of the Grand Cry vineyards. I really don't mind which one.'

Frank stared at the two strangers as though they'd demanded fancy cocktails, topped with melon balls and served, together with a coating of blazing brandy, in a pair of Cinderella's best dishwasher safe glass slippers.

'This is a country pub,' said Frank in his firm, take no nonsense voice. 'I sell beer, whisky, gin and brandy. If you want wine, I've got red and I've got white. But you have to buy it by the bottle. The white is that German stuff because it's cheap and it's the only stuff anyone round here will buy. The red is claret from Tesco and damned good value in my opinion. But whichever you choose you have to buy it by the bottle because if I sell you a glass what am I supposed to do with the rest of it?'

Patchy, Thumper and I, who had been listening to the conversation, raised our glasses in appreciation.

Under normal circumstances, Frank would have happily polished off the rest of the bottles he had opened and, indeed, he and Gilly would often finish off a bottle of red and a bottle of white at the end of an evening. But Frank didn't like the two strangers. Maybe he had heard the man tapping on the bar with his ten pence coin. Or maybe he didn't like the colour of their anoraks. Frank is like a woodland creature in that he can be spooked by the oddest and seemingly most insignificant event. He once refused to serve a man who was wearing a Garrick Club tie on the grounds that the colours made him feel sick.

The stranger sighed the sigh of a disappointed man. 'In that case I'll have a pink gin.'

His wife paused, clearly thinking. 'I'll have one of those too,' she said at last. There was more reluctance and disappointment in her voice than there was in her eyes. I got the impression that she and pink gins were not strangers.

'Two pink gins coming up,' said Frank. He turned to the woman. 'Do you want a little umbrella in that? I think we've got some little umbrellas somewhere.' Frank is convinced that most women like a small, paper umbrella in their drink. Indeed, there is good reason for him to believe this. There are at least two women in Bilbury who don't care what they drink as long as it is blessed with a small, colourful paper umbrella.

'No thank you,' said the woman, in the tone of voice she might have adopted if Frank had asked her if she wanted to take part in a gang bang with a bunch of shepherds and farm labourers straight from muck spreading duties.

Frank plucked the gin bottle from the shelf behind him, picked up two glasses and disappeared. When he returned, a few minutes later, he was clutching what looked like two pink gins. He placed the two glasses on the counter, told the male stranger the price, took the £10 note that was proffered and slipped the change onto the bar. Most of it, I noticed, was in silver. It was clear that Frank was not trying to encourage his new patrons to become regulars.

'What on earth is this floating in my gin?' demanded the cadaverous stranger, holding his glass up to the light and pointing to something small, pink and quite unidentifiable.

Frank picked up the man's glass and examined it carefully. 'It's a bit of squashed strawberry,' he said at last.

'I've got the same thing in mine,' said the woman. She didn't seem pleased. She held the glass away at arm's length and stared at it as though it contained a mouse's head or a deadly, venomous Brazilian water spider.

'What the bloody hell is squashed strawberry doing in my gin?' demanded the cadaverous stranger.

I noticed for the first time that the man had a good deal of hair growing out of his ears and his nostrils. I wondered why a man of such self-importance did not invest in a small pair of nose and ear hair clipping scissors. My father, who had a tendency to hirsuteness in these areas, had a special pair of blunt ended scissors which he kept exclusively for this purpose. He devoted a little time each Sunday morning to mowing and trimming the areas. He became very aware of the need to keep these areas hair free when a small cousin of mine had recoiled in horror and tears when my father had tried to pick him up. 'The man's got spiders up his nose!' the youngster had complained when questioned as to why he had been so alarmed. The cadaverous stranger had a much more luxuriant growth of hair in these areas than I had ever seen on my father.

'No bad language in my bar,' said Frank puffing out his chest and speaking very sternly. 'I've got gentlemen customers in here.' He nodded in our direction. Frank has a wonderful sense of humour which is drier even than his Martinis.

'What is squashed strawberry doing in my gin?' asked the cadaverous stranger, repeating himself but excluding the modest expletive.

'I didn't have any of that stuff you put in gin to make it go pink,' said Frank. 'So I mashed up a strawberry and put a bit of the juice in each glass. Your gins are pink aren't they?'

'What sort of pub is this?' demanded the woman who appeared horrified. 'You don't sell wine by the glass and you don't have any angostura bitters!'

'I don't have any lemon either,' said Frank. 'If I had a lemon I'd have put a bit of peel on the edge of your glass.'

The man sniffed at his drink and then sipped it cautiously, as though half expecting to be poisoned.

'What does it taste like?' asked his wife, who looked horrified.

'Very odd,' the man replied. He thought for a while. 'It tastes of gin flavoured with strawberry.' He shuddered.

'Tell your friends back home and it'll be the new fashionable drink,' said Frank, with a grin. 'They can call it a 'Duck and Puddle' cocktail but don't forget I get three pence royalty on every one sold.'

The stranger stared at him. He did not appear to have much of a sense of humour and had clearly been hiding behind the curtains when the gods were handing out the ability to laugh.

'I suppose you think that's funny!' he said. 'Who owns this place? Are you part of a group? A chain?'

'We own the Duck and Puddle,' said Frank with justifiable pride. 'My wife and I.'

'Do you know who I am?' demanded the stranger.

I've only ever heard one other person say that. He was something in television and it sounded as pompous and as stupid the second time as it did the first time. It is a question which cries out for a resounding 'No'.

Frank stared at him for a moment, examining him carefully, and shook his head. He then looked at us. Thumper, Patchy and I looked at one another and then also shook our heads. 'No idea,' said Patchy. 'No idea at all. Are you going to tell us?'

'I'm Julian Blunt-Whiffle,' said the stranger, as though expecting this to mean something. 'Sir Julian Blunt-Whiffle.'

We all looked at one another and shook our heads again.

'Never heard of you,' said Patchy.

'Are you on television?' asked Thumper. 'Have I seen you on that programme for kids? *Crackerjack* I think it's called. Are you the stooge who gets the cream pie pushed into his face every week?'

'Ah yes,' said Patchy, 'I remember. All the kids hate him. They scream like mad whenever he appears.'

'I am the chairman of Stern, Rothman and Goldstein!' said the chairman of Stern, Rothman and Goldstein.

We looked at one another and, again, shook our heads.

'Never heard of it,' said Frank. 'I've got an overdraft with NatWest myself.'

'He's one of those crooked banker types,' muttered Patchy in his version of sotto voce. 'I read about him somewhere. They call him the vulture capitalist.'

'How the hell did the silly bugger get a knighthood?' asked Thumper.

'Bought it,' said Patchy. He shrugged disdainfully. 'But knighthoods don't count when you buy them with shareholders' money.'

The cadaverous stranger, who must have heard this exchange but who pretending that he hadn't, leant over the bar until his nose and Frank's nose were no more than six inches apart. 'I'm a very important man,' he hissed. 'I could ruin you!' He sounded like a pantomime villain, the sort who has staring eyes and a crooked nose and is booed by children the moment he appears on stage.

Frank, who is not easily intimidated, did not budge an inch. A couple of feet to my right I could sense Thumper tensing up. Thumper, is a tall, well-built man, now in his early thirties, who does not like bullies.

For many years I believed that Thumper (whose real name is Robert) had acquired his nickname because of a predilection for 'thumping' people who had annoyed him. This was a myth that Thumper has never done anything to expose. It was not until I had known him for some years that I discovered (from Anne Thwaites, the mother of his child) that Thumper had acquired the nickname when, as a boy, he had kept rabbits. He was, I discovered, named after a fictional character in a Disney film. I have not yet managed to find a convenient moment to let him know that I know the origin of his nickname for this is something to which I am looking forward and I do not want to waste the opportunity, or the anticipation, by hurrying it.

However, despite the fact that he had not receive his nickname as a result of his pugilistic endeavours, there is no doubt that Thumper never shrinks from thumping people who are disrespectful to his friends.

In Thumper's world there are few things which are more important than respect.

'Out!' said Frank, very softly. He opened the till and counted out some change. 'Get out of my pub. And stay out. If I ever see you here again I'll set Bismarck on you.' Frank does not have any dogs but I doubt if the cadaverous stranger knew that. Frank and Gilly do have a pet called Bismarck, but Bismarck is a goldfish and a particularly timid one at that. It spends most of its days hiding behind the weed in its tank.

Frank slammed the coins he had taken from the till down onto the bar tap. 'Refund,' he said.

'You'll regret this,' said the vulture capitalist with the Labrador puppy eyes. He slammed his gin back down on the counter. His wife followed suit, slamming her glass down so hard that a little gin splashed onto the bar top. The stranger looked at the coins for a moment, as if uncertain whether or not to pick them up. Eventually, greed overcame whatever principle was fighting for recognition and the man scooped up the change and slid it into his trouser pocket. He dropped one of the new five pence pieces and had to bend down to pick it up off the floor. It seemed a rather undignified thing to do, under the circumstances, particularly since the floor of the Duck and Puddle isn't the cleanest piece of real estate in England.

The couple then headed for the door. 'Let's head back to Combe Martin,' said the woman. Her husband agreed.

We all congratulated Frank and celebrated his small victory over the visiting Philistines by ordering a fresh round of drinks and three packs of slightly out-of-date salted peanuts.

I wandered across to the snug window and looked out. The strangers stood for a moment outside the pub, studying an Ordnance Survey Map and a small compass.

'I think they've bought one of those compasses that point south,' I said. I noticed that it was starting to rain.

Peter Marshall, who runs the Bilbury village shop, has had these compasses on offer for a year now and I have lost count of the number of visitors who have, as a result, been badly misdirected.

Our village shop owner buys most of the stuff he sells from the local supermarket (he takes his van over to Barnstaple once a week and stocks up on all the Best Buy offers and the Buy One Get One Free deals) but he also has a number of slightly dodgy suppliers from whom he purchases items which are sold as 'fire damaged' or 'bankrupt stock', though I have always suspected that many of the items he sells ought really to be described as 'fell off the back of a lorry'. Many of these items are things which Peter buys very cheaply because no one else can sell them.

In recent months, Peter has started to buy more and more of the things he sells from abroad. He describes himself as being influenced by globalisation and has a sign hanging in the shop describing his emporium as 'multi-cultural', a claim which he defends by pointing out that he has recently started to stock curry powder, purchased in bulk from a factory in Hong Kong.

The compasses he sells are sold very cheaply and were even cheaper to buy because the manufacture mounted the needles the wrong way round. Peter only sells them to tourists he doesn't like and to locals who are not his regular customers.

'They've taken the Lynton road,' I explained, watching the vulture capitalist and his wife set off on their interrupted walk. I noticed that Sir Julian was limping. His new boots were clearly causing him a little trouble.

It was immediately obvious to me that the pair were heading in precisely the wrong direction.

North Devon has many deserted areas and there are miles of open moorland across Exmoor. It would, I knew, take the vulture capitalist and his wife hours of trudging to reach anything approaching civilisation. It would be well after dark before they got anywhere with a bed and a hot meal. I wasn't even tempted to call to them to tell them this news.

Since they were both poured and paid for, and since he abhors waste of any kind, but particularly of alcohol, Frank drank both the home-made pink gins and declared them to be excellent.

When we left the pub an hour later the rain was coming down heavily and steadily. The bad weather was clearly in for the evening. The vulture capitalist and his wife would still not be more than a quarter of the way to Lynton.

I almost felt sorry for them.

Almost.

But I had an awful feeling that Frank might not have heard the last of the cadaverous stranger with the incongruous puppy dog eyes.

The Wasps

We always have lots of wasps' nests at Bilbury Grange. I have no idea why, but the wasps seem to like our company and they have been steadily chewing up our beams and soffits to make their nests. We've got enough beams and soffits to share and so we usually leave them alone and apart from the occasional sting they leave us alone too.

But this year we have a rather alarming nest developing in the dining room wall. The nest spreads up into the ceiling space and appears to have become alarmingly large. When the wasps decide to flutter together, which they do at regular intervals, it sounds just as though a very large and adenoidal cat were crammed into the wall space. And if you put your hand against the wall you can feel the heat of the nest.

None of that bothers us unduly (though the noise can be a little alarming) but when I tottered downstairs this morning I found that the wasps had started to eat their way through the ceiling. A huge crack had appeared and there was a pile of plaster dust on the rug beneath. When I pressed against the plaster, another crack appeared.

It didn't take the brain of Britain to work out that the wasps had eaten so much ceiling that it had become very thin, delicate and weak.

As I examined the biggest crack in the ceiling, a wasp's leg appeared. And then a bit more of the wasp hove into view. And then a second wasp started to wriggle through. Patsy, who has an encyclopaedic knowledge of plants and creatures of all kind, told me that it is only the female wasp that stings. That I found comforting since it meant that with every wasp, I had a fifty fifty chance of being safe. On the other hand she told me that unlike honeybees, which can sting only once, wasps can sting to their heart's content.

Patsy and I held an emergency meeting and decided that something had to be done since these wasp guests were clearly abusing our hospitality. We allow them to eat our beams, our floorboards, our windowsills and our soffits but we will not allow them to eat our ceiling.

I rang the local council, which has a department dedicated to dealing with wasps, and asked them to send a man (or woman) round as soon as he (or she) could be spared. To my surprise, the council said they would send a man round that very afternoon. It was no surprise to discover that I would receive an invoice for his services.

Meanwhile, I began the morning surgery.

The first patient was Mrs Thyme who came to have her blood pressure checked. There is never anything wrong with it but she is convinced that if she is to die of anything it will be a stroke or a heart attack caused by high blood pressure and so she likes to know that all is well in that department. When I had checked her blood pressure, and reassured her that the readings would have been perfectly satisfactory if she had been 60 years younger (she is a little over 80-years-old) she asked me if I minded if she asked me a question. I said I had no objection whatsoever and that I would answer as best I could.

'Do you know any decent men who are 105-years-old or more?'

I stared at her, thought about this for a while and had to admit that I did not know any centurions. Puzzled, I asked her what had prompted her question.

'I've decided to look for a boyfriend,' said Mrs T, as though she had decided to replace her washing machine or purchase a new handbag.

'I did meet one fellow,' she said rather wistfully, 'but he was always a perfect gentleman.' She sounded rather disappointed by this. 'And then last week I read in a women's magazine that most men over 50 only want to go out with women who are 25 years younger than they are. So, since I'm 80, it means I have to look for men who are around 105-years-old.'

I told her that I thought she could cast her net much wider, and that since she looks a good 20 years younger than her age she could quite happily look for men of her own age or even younger.

She seemed delighted by this advice and though I have absolutely no way of knowing whether or not the advice was of any value, I was delighted to have cheered her up. She left after telling me that she intended to visit Peter Marshall's village shop to see what fancy lingerie he had in stock. I assumed that her shopping expedition was inspired by the hope that her search for a male companion might soon prove fruitful. However, although I did not tell her this, I very much doubt if Peter Marshall sells anything which could be described as 'lingerie' without attracting the attention of the local Trading Standards officer. I fear that Peter's ladies' underwear department (for there is sure to be one) will most probably be well stocked with bloomers, camiknickers and whalebone corsets but little else.

My second patient, Mrs Guthrie, is in her nineties – and actually nearer to her century. She is, I suspect, kept alive by the prospect of receiving a congratulatory telegram from Her Majesty the Queen. Bilbury is a healthy village and, remarkably, I have three centurions on my medical list. I say 'remarkably' because quite a number of big city doctors, with far more patients than I have, don't have a single patient over 90 – let alone over 100.

Mrs Guthrie has so many different diseases that her medical notes have to be kept in three cardboard folders which are about three inches thick and have to be held together with a couple of large rubber bands. I keep meaning to have a spring-clean and to throw out all the old hospital letters and bits and pieces of miscellaneous information.

With younger patients, doctors always try to tie together all the available symptoms, however disconnected they might appear to be. The aim is to knit all the available symptoms into a single diagnosis. But with older patients this simply does not work, for many patients in their mature years have a number of completely disconnected health problems. Mrs Guthrie, for example, has heart failure, bronchitis, dermatitis, haemorrhoids, Meniere's disease, chronic blepharitis, varicose eczema and Raynaud's disease and I defy the brightest medical brains to come up with a single diagnostic label to fit all of those problems - other than old age, of course.

Mrs Guthrie comes to see me once a month more as a ritual than to seek advice or treatment. She once told me that she totters along mainly for reassurance that she is still alive. 'At my age things are working so badly that I worry that I might drop off the perch and not notice!' she said, with a chuckle. I wrote out prescriptions for the medicines she takes and then switched hats and dispensed the drugs from my small pharmacy.

After lunch, a very pleasant man came to deal with our wasps. He used a long tube to spray powder into the opening to the nest and told me that if the wasps are not gone in a week I should ring back. When I told him that I wouldn't have bothered if the wasps hadn't been trying to break through the ceiling, he said that it was quite common for wasps to start eating ceilings. The wasps apparently munch their way through the wood and plaster and take over a house. Nevertheless, it saddened me to see the wasps being killed. If they'd built their nest in a shed or a tree I'd have been happy to leave them there.

While I was outside showing him where the nest was situated, I spotted a dead squirrel on the ground. The poor thing had clearly been killed by a cat (a fox or a rat would have eaten the corpse).

After the wasp man had gone, I dug a hole under a hazel tree and buried the squirrel with full military honours.

I called Patsy and together we said a little prayer, asking God to welcome the squirrel. We said we hoped that wherever he went the squirrel would find a good and enduring supply of hazelnuts.

I may be mad, but at least I am my kind of mad.

The New Vet

When Bilbury's vet retired, he tried to sell the practice to another young veterinarian. But there were no takers and it didn't look as if there would ever be one. The vet's old house and surgery had been sold to a couple from Combe Martin who planned to convert it into three flats. One they would keep for themselves and the other two would be rented out to holidaymakers.

The trouble is that there simply isn't enough work in Bilbury to provide full time employment for a vet. For some years now, one of the large veterinary practices in Barnstaple has looked after most of what vets usually refer to as the 'big animal' work (cows, pigs, sheep, horses and so on) and there really aren't enough people with pets in Bilbury to keep a veterinarian occupied and solvent.

And so a female vet who has a single-handed practice in the nearby village of Combe Martin, and who is married to young George Burrows (who, like his father Harry, works in a bank in Barnstaple and is one of the few people in North Devon to go to work in a suit every day), has recently begun to hold a weekly 'small animal' surgery (dogs, cats, tortoises, goldfish, budgies and so on) in a newly painted shed behind Peter Marshall's shop.

I should, perhaps, explain how an apparently respectable vet came to be practising in a shed behind Peter Marshall's village emporium.

Peter Marshall, the Bilbury storekeeper and the most successful businessman in Bilbury or the whole of England (according to whether you are making the judgement objectively or according to Peter's own viewpoint) is always on the lookout for ways to improve his income. He is constantly aware that most villages in England have either already lost their village shop or, if shops had heads, would be, in financial terms, struggling to keep them above water.

A year ago, Peter enthusiastically welcomed the chance to become the Bilbury Post Office (a title which, in practice, means little more than that he is allowed to sell postage stamps and weigh and stamp the occasional parcel) and having successfully merged that responsibility with his own towering ambition 'to sell more variety than Harrods of Knightsbridge', decided to become Bilbury's first and only department store, offering a wide range of services to local villagers.

The wooden, felt-roofed shed behind Peter's shop had for many years served as a depository for unwanted items and when he decided to upgrade it, and turn it into a valuable piece of working real estate, Peter first had to clear out the retail flotsam and jetsam that had accumulated over the last few decades.

He discovered that the shed contained a large quantity of empty cardboard boxes (mostly mouldy), three old lawn mowers, which would not have looked out of place in a museum specialising in Victoriana, a dozen empty milk crates, a typewriter with half its keys missing, a small collection of vintage vacuum cleaners which no longer worked but which, inevitably and predictably, Peter described as 'valuable antiques of the future', a number of tins and boxes of food that would have doubtless been well past their sell-by date if sell-by dates had been invented when the tins and boxes had originally been packed and delivered for sale, and a good variety of other bits and pieces of not-quite-good-enough-to-sell-in-the-shop-but-not-rubbishy-enough-to-throw-away flimflam. (Peter, incidentally, is, like Frank Parsons at the Duck and Puddle, a fervent opponent of the new-fangled habit of putting 'sell-by' and 'best before' dates onto food products. He says he thinks that the scheme will simply lead to vast amounts of perfectly good food being thrown away. I have to say that I think he could well be right.)

Most people would have called for a skip and dumped the rubbish which had accumulated, but Peter has never been one to fit easily into the category of 'most people' and his natural and inevitable response to what he saw as a 'unique commercial opportunity' was to hold a 'shed' sale (his version of a garage sale) and to invite anyone and everyone to bid on his 'fine collection of genuine vintage retail antiques'.

If you or I had found all that junk in an old shed or barn we would have expected to pay to have it taken away but Peter was confident he could persuade people to pay him to let them take it home with them.

To the surprise of everyone present (including, I suspect, Peter himself), the sale proved remarkably successful. Peter put a small advertisement in several West Country newspapers, and dealers turned up from Taunton, Barnstaple, South Molton and Exeter.

Patchy Fogg, with whom I inspected the stuff on sale, said that apart from occasional visits to the municipal waste dump just outside Barnstaple he had never in his life seen so much rubbish collected in one place.

But, perhaps because they'd travelled some distance and didn't want to go home empty handed, and maybe because Peter's sales patter was convincing (he had put in his false teeth for the occasion – a real sign of how seriously he was taking the event), most of the items on sale found buyers.

One dealer told me that the foodstuff Peter was selling was so old that he would be able to sell it to a museum he knew which specialised in the history of food packaging. Two gross of novelty, bendy pencils with sharpeners fixed to the non-active end found buyers who would only find out in time that once you'd taken an inch off the length of the pencils, the pointy end would no longer reach the sharpener. Even the milk crates found a market. Only the mouldy cardboard boxes (optimistically labelled as 'useful storage containers') remained unsold and destined for the incinerator at the bottom of Peter's orchard.

Having cleared out his scruffy shed and sold the contents, Peter had enough cash to buy some paint and a few sticks of furniture and within a week of the sale he had completed the transformation of the shed from a derelict junk room to a 'highly desirable business rental property'. Realising that he was unlikely to find anyone prepared to rent the shed full time, Peter decided to promote the shed to individuals who wanted somewhere to run a small business for one day a week.

On Mondays the shed was rented out to a gentleman's hairdresser who travelled from South Molton, on Wednesdays the shed was rented out to a ladies' hairdresser who drove up from Exeter and on Thursdays the shed was rented out to Mrs Burrows, the ambitious young veterinary surgeon from Combe Martin. Fridays and Saturdays were available to rent for children's parties and Tuesday was available for anyone with a business needing a one-day-a-week home. It was clear to everyone in the village that Peter was making far more money out of renting his shed piecemeal than he could have ever made if he had rented out to a full-time tenant.

And, as he confided to me one day, Peter was hoping that the people who came to have their hair cut or permed, or who brought their animal to see the vet, would buy something from his shop.

On days when the veterinary surgeon was in the shed, Peter put a large board advertising cut-price pet food. On days when the barber was operating, Peter changed the board for one advertising razor blades, shaving soap, combs and 'something for the weekend'. On days when the ladies' hairdresser was in residence, there were offers on products such as artificial orchid sprays ('suitable for pinning onto posh frocks') which Peter reckoned he could sell to newly permed ladies looking forward to a posh evening out.

And so, all this explains why, one Thursday afternoon, I found myself sitting on a metal stacking chair in Peter's draughty and chilly shed with Ben, our faithful but now elderly Welsh collie bitch, lying patiently beside me. We were waiting to see Mrs Burrows, the new Bilbury vet.

Ben used to belong to a tramp called Hubert Donaldson and just before Hubert died, he asked me to look after his dog. Ben seemed to know this for he had quickly become 'my' dog; a loyal companion and canine friend.

Ben had been having difficulty in walking for some time and things seemed to be getting worse. Since I inherited him from Hubert Donaldson I had no idea how old Ben was but I strongly suspected that he had developed arthritis; a common enough problem in older dogs. He had quite a lot of stiffness in his knees and was clearly in some discomfort when he moved. I suppose I could have treated him myself, since some of the drugs used for human patients are also used for dogs, but I have no knowledge of the sort of dosages which might be suitable for a dog so I preferred to see an expert.

Mrs Burrows, smartly dressed in a crisply starched white coat, was sitting behind a small folding card table, which served as a temporary desk. We pet owners sat on chairs which were lined up in two rows. Like me, the vet did not run an appointments system; patients and their owners were seen on a simple, old-fashioned and still efficient 'first come, first served' basis. Each time someone was called, the rest of us moved up a seat. This was welcome exercise, for the chairs were not the most comfortable in the world and after three minutes I had developed cramp in both my legs.

The vet was dealing with Mrs Westbury's poodle (a friendly if rather neurotic dog called Mimi) when I first sat down.

Mrs Westbury is the wife of Reginald Westbury, a taciturn fellow who helps run Tolstoy's, the local garage, and whose skills with a spanner keep my car on the road, and I know from personal experience that she has an unusual ability to use 50 words when two or three would suffice. She does this through nervousness, for she is very shy and chatters to disguise this, but it does mean that consultations with her can stretch out for rather longer than might be strictly necessary. I realised that those of us waiting would not be going anywhere for quite a while.

I was reading a paperback copy of *Festival at Farbridge*, a novel by J.B.Priestley, which I had brought with me (I never go anywhere which might involve waiting without first stuffing a book into a jacket pocket) and Ben was snoozing quietly by my feet when Mrs Iolanthe Fielding, the pet owner who was sitting in front of me, turned round and spoke to me in what was clearly supposed to be a whisper.

'Do you have your prescription pad with you, doctor?' she asked.

Mrs Iolanthe Fielding and her husband, Bertie, live in an unsaleable house on the North Devon cliffs and their house has spectacular views. They pay just £5 a month in rent for a neat two bedroomed white-washed cottage with a decent sized garden and spectacular sea views. The rent is low because although the house had been on the market for three years, with an absurdly low asking price of just £200, there have been no takers. One or two London buyers had shown interest, thinking that they had perhaps spotted the bargain of a lifetime, but when they saw that two neighbouring cottages had already fallen down onto the rocks below they quickly withdrew their offers and hot-footed it back to the big city where houses tend to stay where they've been built and, generally speaking, show very little inclination to wander.

Bertie and Iolanthe would probably be considered by some to be an odd couple.

When they married two years ago, she was 67-years-old and he was just 20. It is, I think, fair to say that his parents were slightly surprised to find that they were nearly 30 years younger than their daughter-in-law.

Iolanthe (and that was her real name for her mother had been a great music lover) had never been married before but had what can safely be described as an interesting past. She had been a nun, a librarian, a chorus girl in a troupe of entertainers which worked on cruise ships, and a belly dancer in a nightclub in Cairo. She was an optimistic woman. When she and Bertie became engaged, she came to see me to ask if I thought she was too old to start a family. Disappointed by my pessimistic answer she founded the North Devon Belly Dancing Association and started teaching belly dancing on Wednesday evenings in the Kentisbury Village Hall. Several of my patients became enthusiastic students.

The name Bertie is not common but in and around Bilbury there are no less than four Berties and so to avoid confusion they are all known by an addition to their names. This is a practice which is exceedingly popular in Wales where it seems that 90% of the male population is called either Gareth or Dai. To help villagers identify one another, Gareth the butcher will be known as Gareth the Butcher, Dai the baker will be called Dai the Baker and Mr Evans the taxi driver will be known as Evans the Taxi. And so, the Bertie who once worked at the garden centre on the road to the village of Westward Ho! is still known as Bertie the Plant even though he left the garden centre some years ago and now works as a butcher's assistant and part time fireman.

(Westward Ho!, is incidentally, the only place in Britain which has an exclamation mark as part of its name. The village was named after a hotel which was itself named after an adventure story written by the 19th century novelist Charles Kingsley. There cannot be many authors who have had a place named after a fictitious town. Kingsley was the author of another famous book called *The Water Babies*, though as far as I know there is not yet a town called 'The Water Babies'.)

The Bertie who has been pool champion at the Duck and Puddle for as long as anyone can remember, and who is now happily married to the former Lydia Potterton, is known as Bertie the Balls.

The Bertie who delivers buns and pies for a baker who has a shop in Combe Martin and nurtures a powerful ambition to open a chain of shops throughout the South West, is known to everyone as Bertie the Pie.

Iolanthe's Bertie, who drives and operates a tanker which emptied cesspits and septic tanks is known, with searing and cruel accuracy, as Bertie the Stink. If you met Bertie dressed in his Sunday best and reeking of aftershave you would still know what he did for a living.

On the day when Bertie and Iolanthe got married, a bevy of Bertie's relatives who had motored down from Wolverhampton spent the entire day sniffing, looking at one another and sniffing again, constantly wondering where the leaky sewer could be situated. They sniffed in the church, they sniffed at the reception in the back room at the Duck and Puddle and they sniffed when they were standing on the Duck and Puddle forecourt about to get into their cars to drive home. 'Is there a sewage farm nearby?' asked a portly woman who had spent all day plucking up the courage to ask the question. 'There are a lot of cows in the locality,' explained Iolanthe, to save her husband's blushes. 'And the ones around here are an unusually flatulent variety.'

Bertie's father, who was also called Bertie and had, since the birth of his son, been known as Bertie the Fertile since he was the only Bertie in the village who had achieved the dizzy heights of fatherhood, was a specialist Stop-Go man working for Devon County Council.

A Stop-Go man holds up the metal pole which has a large disk attached to its top end. One side of the disk is painted green and has the word GO on it and the other side of the disk is painted red and displays the word STOP. The Stop-Go pole is used when work is being done on the roads and two lanes of traffic have to be controlled and funnelled onto a single lane of the highway. Bertie the Fertile's skill with the pole is legendary and whereas lesser operators would keep the traffic flowing without queues or major delays, he could, by the end of a day, have queues a quarter of a mile long and delays of an hour or more.

Bertie the Fertile, who was perpetually optimistic and who, therefore, preferred to think of himself as a Go-Stop man rather than a Stop-Go man, had always harboured an ambition that his son would follow him into the pole handling business and he had a good many tricks of the trade he wanted to pass on. He had been severely disappointed when his son chose another career but the disappointment soon passed when his son married, and although he was sad that there was not going to be any pattering of tiny feet, the fact that his son's bride was nearly a third of a century his senior did nothing to dampen his enthusiasm for this most romantic of mergers.

'Do you have your prescription pad with you, doctor?' Mrs Fielding repeated. She had turned up the volume a decibel or two.

Accustomed as she is to giving instructions to a roomful of would-be belly dancers, most of whom are old enough to have mislaid a good deal of their natural hearing acuity, she is capable of invoking a stentorian tone that would not have ashamed a parade ground sergeant major.

I agreed that I did, indeed, have a prescription pad in my inside jacket pocket. The truth is that I never go anywhere in Bilbury without a prescription pad. I would be as likely to leave the house without a prescription pad as I would be to go out without my trousers.

'I'm running out of that cream you gave me,' she said, maintaining the new, improved decibel level.

I could not for the life of me remember what cream I had given her. I asked her if she could be a little more specific.

'It's cream for down below,' she said, not lowering her voice in the slightest. 'It gets very dry and sore down there,' she told me 'when Mr Fielding and I have conjugals.'

I could not help noticing that Mr Owen, a retired postman who was holding a goldfish in a bowl on his lap, had gone a very deep red. Several female members of the small congregation seemed to be having difficulty controlling their mirth. I got the distinct impression that at least two of them would have been rolling in the aisles if there had been room between the rows of seats for any rolling to be done. Happily, Mrs Fielding seemed completely unaware of the effect her loudly voiced remarks had had upon the other pet owners.

'Oh yes,' I said hurriedly, before Mrs Fielding went into any more detail. 'I remember.' I pulled out my prescription pad and a pen and wrote out a prescription for the appropriate cream.

'Thank you, doctor,' Mrs Fielding replied. 'Bertie will be very grateful. He gets upset if he has to go without his Sunday conjugations. I'll get him to send you and your wife a dozen of his uncle's home-made spicy pork sausages.'

I did not like to remind her that Patsy and I are vegetarian but instead simply thanked her. Mr and Mrs Parfitt, our gardener and his wife, are always very happy to accept gifts of such a nature.

Before I could put away the prescription pad, another pet owner turned round. It was, I saw, Letitia Buttermilk, a plump, merry woman in her thirties who used to work as a barmaid in Bideford, but now spends her days looking after seven assorted children. Mrs Buttermilk, I remembered, has terrible varicose veins and is on an apparently interminable hospital waiting list for an operation.

'Those two-way stretch elastic stockings you prescribed for me have helped enormously, doctor,' she said, genuinely grateful. She suddenly stood up, put her right foot firmly on her chair and pulled up her dress. 'Look,' she said, showing me her leg, 'they look good, don't they?'

A stretch of white thigh was clearly visible between the straps of the industrial strength suspender belt she was using to hold up the support stockings she was wearing. If she realised how much skin she was displaying she was not concerned. I remembered that Mrs Buttermilk herself had once suggested, with more than a hint of professional pride, that her career as a barmaid had merely been the final stopping point in what might loosely be described as an adventure in the specialised branch of show business known for displays of the feminine form.

Mr Owen, still bright red, was, I noticed out of the corner of my eye, studying the roof of Peter Marshall's shed as though he had spotted something fascinating.

Mrs Buttermilk then took off the shoe and wiggled her leg round so that I could see that a hole had developed in the heel. 'But I really need another pair of the stockings,' she said. 'Two if you and the National Health Service can manage it.'

Poor old Owen had now turned so red that if he had stood alongside a London bus you wouldn't have been able to see his face at all.

Feeling rash with the nation's money, I wrote out a prescription for three pairs of two-way stretch elastic stockings.

And so it went on.

There were eight people waiting to see the vet and I wrote prescriptions for five of them, looked down the throat of one and only with difficulty persuaded another not to remove her blouse so that I could look at the rash that had appeared on her elbow. In the end, I managed to persuade her that I could manage perfectly well if she simply rolled up her sleeve.

'I was beginning to wonder who was running a surgery here,' said Mrs Burrows rather tartly, when Ben and I finally reached the top of the queue.

'I'm sorry,' I apologised, though to be honest I didn't feel that it was my fault. I explained Ben's problem and the vet examined him.

'How old is he?' she demanded.

I had to admit that I didn't know.

'He's obviously quite an age,' she said. She seemed very cold and Ben clearly didn't like her.

I agreed with the vet's assessment for it was not an inaccurate one.

'He's got arthritis,' she said.

'Yes,' I said, 'I thought that might be it.'

'It would probably be kindest to have him put down,' she said. 'If you bring him to my surgery in Combe Martin I could deal with that for you.'

'Oh, good heavens,' I said. 'I don't think he's that bad. He still gets around. He's just a little slower and stiffer than before. Couldn't you prescribe something for him?' I was very angry. I knew that Ben still enjoyed life and felt that he needed help not euthanasia. Ben is one of my closest and dearest friends. He often goes with me when I visit patients, usually staying in the car, which he guards enthusiastically, and he plays an active role in the Bilbury community. He even has membership of the Bilbury Cricket Club (so that he can sit with Patsy and me in the pavilion when we visit) and his signature on his membership card is a muddy paw print.

Mrs Burrows glowered at me and I thought for a moment that she was going to refuse to help. 'I suppose so,' she said. She bent down, rummaged in a large cardboard box that she had brought with her and took out a box of tablets. 'Give it these four times a day,' she said.

'It!'

She called my friend an 'it'!

I thanked her, paid the bill, and Ben and I then left. If my friend needs help again we will go elsewhere.

I have a strong suspicion that Peter Marshall may soon find that he has Thursdays free to rent to someone else. I really don't think that the pet owners of Bilbury are going to take to a veterinary surgeon who is so quick to reach for the euthanasia needle.

On the drive back home, the thought of euthanasia filled me with guilt for I am very conscious of the fact that we had to bring in a man from the council to destroy the wasps' nest above our dining room ceiling.

I hate killing any of God's creatures but you can't collect up wasps in the same way that you can collect up bees, and with two babies in the house I couldn't take the chance of having our home filled with insects which sting.

When I got home, I discovered that although the nest has been destroyed there are still plenty of wasps around.

I had no idea how they managed to find their way in but wasps had been coming into the house every day since the man from the council visited, and although most were dying and so not much of a threat to any of us, dealing with so many dead bodies was a sad business.

Astonishingly, in the evenings it was still sometimes possible to hear the sound of the remaining live wasps beating their wings in their nest. I couldn't believe that it was too hot for them in the roof space above the ceiling and so I could only assume that the ritualistic wing beating, ostensibly done to cool the nest, was being done more as a ritual than a practical activity. The wasps knew that something was wrong and so they did the only thing they could think of: they beat their wings to bring the temperature down. No dafter than the practice of blood-letting or many of the other things that humans do.

More worrying, perhaps, something had climbed into the incredibly small space above the dining room where the wasps' nest had been.

I had no idea whether it was a rat, a mouse or a squirrel but I was pretty sure that it was eating the dead wasps. We could hear the creature scurrying around, hither and thither and this was rather worrying since the ceiling, partly eaten by the wasps, was now perilously thin. I strengthened the area by putting long strips of sticky tape across the plasterboard. It didn't look very pretty but I hoped it would stop whatever was eating the dead wasps from falling through and landing on the dining room table.

Since the wasps were poisoned, I didn't think that eating them could do any living creature much good. I barked very loudly, very close to the ceiling, and whoever or whatever it was who was making all the noise went away.

If the intruder is killed by the wasp poison, there will be a corpse above the ceiling. And then we will, I fear, find ourselves suffering from a plague of blowflies.

Living in the country is never dull.

The Letters

'Have you seen this week's copy of the local paper?' asked Patsy.

'Nhnhnho,' I replied, through a mouthful of toast.

I know you're not supposed to eat with your mouth full but I'd had an early call out to a farmer whose foot had been trodden on by a cow.

The farmer was now sitting in his living room, with his foot up on a pouffe and a bottle of painkilling tablets on a table nearby, with the injured but not broken foot doubtless beginning the long, slow process of going from red to blue, to black and to yellow. Outside, the cow was chewing the cud and doubtless telling her friends that she'd made it look like an accident and had got away without so much as a slap on the backside with a hazel switch.

And, as a result of the early morning call, I was late for the morning surgery.

'There's a letter from a man in London complaining about the service he had when he visited the Duck and Puddle,' said Patsy, sounding astonished. 'Someone called Sir Julian Blunt-Whiffle.'

The name rang bells so loud that I very nearly developed a headache.

'Do you remember I told you about that snooty couple who came to the pub when I was there with Thumper and Patchy? It was a few weeks ago. They were walking around North Devon with their chauffeur following behind in a Mercedes.'

Patsy thought for a moment and then nodded. 'Was that the time when Frank ground up some strawberries to make pink gins because he hadn't got any angostura bitters?'

'That's it!' I agreed. I looked at the clock, decided I just had enough time for another piece of toast and reached for the toast rack. 'What does the letter say?'

Patsy found the letter again and read it out to me:

'Sir

My wife and I recently visited the Duck and Puddle public house in Bilbury. I have travelled widely throughout the world and I can safely say that I have never before been faced with such extraordinary ill manners and incompetence. After waiting an unacceptable length of time to be served, we were given pink gins which fell far below the accepted international standard for such recreational comestibles. It seems to me quite extraordinary that the landlord has a licence of any kind and it seems to me that he would be more appropriately employed in some environment where contact with members of the travelling public is not an inevitability. I would strongly advise all those who seek sustenance to seek it in some place other than the Duck and Puddle in Bilbury.

I would have written this letter sooner but after our visit to the village of Bilbury, my wife and I were misdirected by inaccurately calibrated directional equipment and we were not reunited with our support vehicle until 1.00 a.m. As a result of the delay, both my wife and I needed to spend four weeks recuperating in the Spa Hotel at Baden Baden – an institution which was, I am delighted to say, run far more efficiently and courteously than the Duck and Puddle in Bilbury.

Yours etc
Sir Julian Blunt-Whiffle

Patsy put down the newspaper and looked across at me. I finished spreading marmalade on my toast and looked at her.

'Crumbs!' was all I managed to say. 'Recreational comestibles, eh!'

My first thought was that the letter was so pompous that it was funny. I couldn't think that anyone would take it seriously. But Patsy was more practical.

'Poor Frank and Gilly!' said Patsy. 'They will be terribly upset. Do you think this will damage their business?'

I thought for a moment. 'I wouldn't have thought so,' I said. 'Most of their customers are locals. And everyone round here knows what Frank is like.'

I finished my breakfast and arrived in my consulting room with one minute to spare before the advertised starting time for the morning surgery.

But after the surgery, and during luncheon, I had a telephone call from Patchy Fogg. He told me that, as Patsy had rightly predicted, Frank and Gilly were terribly upset. They had, he said, already received several cancellations from people who had booked the pub for anniversaries, birthday parties and other celebrations.

I had forgotten this, but Frank and Gilly recently tried to expand their business by catering for individuals and groups from Barnstaple who wanted to hold their events somewhere distinctly rural. They were, therefore, offering the lounge bar as a 'function room', while keeping the snug as a bar for locals who merely wanted to consume some alcohol and nibble a few out-of-date crisps and peanuts.

With Peter Marshall having started to let out his old shed, it seemed that all our local businesses were now striving to expand and enhance their activities. I had jokingly suggested to Patsy that I should, perhaps, turn the dining room into an operating theatre and start offering breast enhancement and nose reduction operations at special prices. I pointed out that cosmetic surgery is the most profitable and commercial aspect of medical practice these days. Patsy, who had been changing one of the babies at the time, had not realised that I had made the suggestion in jest and had very nearly thrown a used nappy at me.

'But Thumper and I have a plan,' said Patchy, when he'd finished telling me just how upset Frank and Gilly were by Sir Julian Thingy-Wotsit's letter in the local paper. I winced when he told me this. Thumper and Patchy always mean well but they do sometimes come up with some very strange ideas. He wouldn't tell me what the plan was, simply telling me, with a wink, that it would be more fun if I didn't know.

I didn't hear any more about their plans for a while, but I did hear that Frank and Gilly were resigned to the fact that their burgeoning new business was ruined. They were terribly upset. Gilly had already hired two temporary waitresses and had bought them both second-hand white pinafores and black dresses from a hotel in Lynmouth which was closing. It is true that the waitresses would not have to be paid unless there was any work for them but the white pinafores and black dresses were a capital expense that seemed unlikely to be recouped. Moreover, Frank had already polished the tables in the lounge bar and, in preparation, had replaced the battered, chewed and sodden beermats with brand new ones advertising up-market drinks such as Babycham.

A week after the initial letter appeared in *The Barnstaple, Bideford and Bilbury Herald*, Patsy and I were once again having breakfast when Patsy asked me if I'd seen the local paper. I hadn't, of course.

'There's another letter about the Duck and Puddle,' said Patsy. And here is what she read out:

'Sir
I recently visited the Duck and Puddle public house in the village of Bilbury and ordered a pint of bitter. When the drink arrived a little of the fluid had spilt down the side of the glass and when I picked it up, I got my hand wet. Then, when I put the drink down onto the table provided I was distressed to find that the beer mats were quite inappropriate. How can any serious drinker be expected to put a pint of best bitter onto a beermat advertising Babycham? And why doesn't the Duck and Puddle provide beer mats which have little tricks and quizzes on the back?
Yours disgusted,
Alphonse Quiltharbour

'That's Thumper,' I said immediately.

'Wait,' said Patsy, 'there's another letter!' And she read out a second 'letter to the editor'.

'Sir
While enjoying a drink at the Duck and Puddle public house in the village of Bilbury, I decided to play a game of bar billiards. However, to my horror I found that the cue provided by the management was not obviously bent. It was indeed very nearly straight. I have played bar billiards in pubs all over North Devon and this has never happened to me before. This is an outrage. If the landlord of the Duck and Puddle cannot provide a bent cue with a decent curve on it then he should be tarred and feathered. If he repeats the offence then his remains should be hung, drawn and quartered.

I demand satisfaction.
Yours

Matt E. Mulchen

P.S. When I ordered a glass of champagne the landlord told me that he didn't have any champagne in stock but that he had some white wine and that if I put my hand over the top of the glass and then shook the glass quite a lot then the wine would get a bit bubbly and I would hardly notice the difference. I tried this but it did not prove as effective as advertised. Moreover, I had to use my own handkerchief to wipe my hand afterwards and since I had a cold at the time, I was then forced to spend the evening blowing my nose on a piece of wet rag. If the landlord persists with this suggestion then he should be obliged to provide spare handkerchiefs for customers. Or any bit of old rag would do at a pinch.

'That's Patchy,' I told her. 'Patchy always uses the name Matt E. Mulchen if he's stopped by the police. I gather Mr Mulchen is wanted by the police in three counties for various motoring offences.'

'But what are Thumper and Patchy playing at?' demanded Patsy, who is very good friends with Gilly and consequently seemed quite cross. 'Why have they written more letters attacking the Duck and Puddle?'

'These letters won't do any harm at all,' I told her. 'They'll make people laugh and they'll make people think that last week's letter was also written by some lunatic.'

Three days later Patsy told me with great delight that Gilly had reported that being in the local paper again had, to their surprise and delight, done the Duck and Puddle a great deal of good. Several local societies had telephoned with bookings for dinners and they had acquired a booking for a Golden Wedding Anniversary and one for an engagement party. 'Apparently, the people who rang said they'd never heard of the pub before,' said Patsy. 'But they all said it sounded a fun sort of place patronised by fun sort of people.'

I was not surprised when, on the following Friday, Patsy once again discovered that there were two letters about the Duck and Puddle in *The Barnstaple, Bideford and Bilbury Herald*. She read them both out to me:

'Sir,

Last week I visited the Duck and Puddle public house in Bilbury and bought a sandwich. The sandwich was very good but the chef had failed to cut off the crusts and had, moreover, cut the sandwich horizontally. I always think that sandwiches which are cut diagonally look far more classy. When I complained, the landlord took away my sandwich and refunded my money. He would not serve me any more food, not even a packet of salt and vinegar crisps, until I had promised to behave myself and to stop complaining.

I think your readers should know what is going on in our country.
Yours
Mrs Hermione Buttress

The second letter was allegedly from the captain of a touring cricket team which had played in Bilbury:

'Sir,
I am the captain of our Cricket Club and every year we tour the West Country. Last Saturday we arrived in Bilbury for our annual match and I must complain in the strongest possible tone about the way we were treated.

On the recommendation of the Bilbury Cricket Club secretary, we took our luncheon in the local public house, the 'Dick and Piddle', together with members of the home side. I now wish to complain about the way we were treated.

Throughout our luncheon, members of our team were encouraged to drink far more alcohol than can possibly be considered advisable before a sporting event. Those team members who had ordered pints of beer had their glasses constantly topped up by a landlord constantly moving around the room with a half-gallon jug of ale. As a result, every beer drinker consumed at least two or three times the amount he had paid for. And those team members who ordered spirits were given doubles if they ordered and paid for singles and trebles if they ordered and paid for doubles.

During the game, my team played as badly as you might expect of men who could not stand upright without holding onto something solid. Our wicket keeper spent the whole of the match asleep in the pavilion, and two of our best batsmen actually fell asleep while at the crease. Several players tripped over and fell while fielding. Our best bowler spent the whole match clutching an elm tree on the boundary.

No one else in the team can remember very much of what happened that day but as the captain (and a confirmed teetotaller) I wish to warn other teams not to take pre-match refreshments at the Dick and Piddle since the landlord is clearly prepared to collude with someone in the local club.

For the record, we lost the match by 139 runs – our worst defeat since 1926.

Yours sincerely
Albert Ross (Captain)

Underneath this letter there was a short note from the Editor of the newspaper reading: 'This correspondence is now closed.'

Two days later, Patsy told me that Gilly had reported that the pub was booked solid for the whole of the autumn. Several customers had already booked the pub for Christmas parties.

Sir Julian's horrid, spiteful letter had been completely forgotten, pushed out of the communal memory by Thumper and Patchy's sequence of silly letters, and the newspapers in which Sir Julian's epistle had appeared had now all been used for lighting fires or wrapping chips.

The Hairdresser

When I worked regularly on television and had to record weekly programmes at studios in Glasgow, I used to have my hair cut in the make-up department. It was a splendid perk of the job. I would sit down in a comfortable chair and nod off to sleep. Without having to give any instructions, or make meaningless chatter about football or the weather, my hair would be neatly trimmed so that it looked exactly the same as it had looked for the previous programme and for the programme before that one. Never before had my hair been so neat.

Despite the joy of free haircuts, I had retired early from my burgeoning media career when I had been able to reopen my practice in Bilbury.

There had been several reasons for this.

First, I hated leaving Bilbury and Patsy. The minute I left the village I really wanted to be back where I knew I belonged.

Second, since working as a solo general practitioner, I was really no longer able to take time off to travel around the country visiting television and radio studios.

When he had retired, Dr Brownlow was always happy to act as my locum for a day or two but after his death I had no one to turn to. I had no assistant and even if I had been able to find one, I would not have been able to afford to hire a locum doctor to stand in for me.

Third, the world of the media was becoming distinctly unpleasant and I had a feeling that things were going to get much worse. People's capacity for taking offence where none was intended seemed inexhaustible. And strangely, the same individuals who were quick to take offence seemed capable of offering abuse with no thought of the offence that they, in turn, might cause. A new innovation, radio phone in programmes where the host encouraged criticism and abuse, had probably made things worse. Local radio stations had started to encourage their listeners to express their opinions, whether or not they knew anything about the subject in hand, and much of the material broadcast seemed to be to me based more on prejudice and suspicion than on fact and reasoned thought.

The world was, it seemed, now crammed full of people who are kind enough to share their opinions on anything and everything – even on those things of which they knew nothing – with the rest of us.

To the words uttered by these public-spirited souls had to be added the trenchant criticisms engendered by lobbyists working for the pharmaceutical industry and the medical establishment.

I found that every time I put my head above the parapet, and commented on issues such as over-prescribing or the dangers of certain medical practices, I would find myself becoming target practice for professional critics who were concerned more with profits than with the truth.

I couldn't help thinking that if computers ever proved as popular as the radio as a means of communication then things might well get even worse

I had, over my years in the media, been among other things, reached the dizzy heights of being a T-shirt, a crossword clue and an answer on a radio quiz programme but I decided that it was time to bring my Z list career to an end.

I would still write books as and when I found the time. But I decided that although I would still write articles and papers for the medical journals, there would be no more television programmes, radio broadcasts or newspaper columns.

And so, having abandoned my television career and the free haircuts, I had for a year or so had my hair cut at a barber's shop in Barnstaple.

I enjoyed having my haircut there because the chap who owned the shop, and who did both the snipping and the sweeping up, had a marvellous way of talking. He cut out extraneous conjunctions and pronouns and somehow managed to sound like a series of newspaper headlines written by a subeditor trying to cram the kernel of what he had to say into the fewest possible number of words. 'Traffic Snarl Up is Result of Road-widening Project' he would start with. I would make the usual and appropriate murmur of interest and off he would go. 'Retailers Protest as Town Grinds to Halt'.

All I had to do was make an encouraging sound at the end of each headline. 'Local Football Team Destroys Opposition', 'Storms

Threaten Coastal Properties', 'Local Vicar Elopes with Girl Guide' and so on. I sometimes wondered if he had ever been employed as a headline writer.

But the last two times I visited the barber's small establishment, I had left disappointed and with just as much hair as I had when I had arrived.

My penultimate visit to this particular barber's shop happened to take place on a Monday and I had found the shop shut. The lights were off, the door was locked and one of those little cardboard signs saying CLOSED was visible through the glass. The man who ran the pet shop next door told me that although the barber advertised his shop as being open on Mondays to Saturdays inclusive, he sometimes took Monday off. He did this without warning. He did it if the weather was fine or he had enjoyed an exhausting Sunday and felt he needed an extended lie in. Towards the end of a month, he would take Monday off if he felt that he had earned enough money to pay that month's mortgage and the grocery bills.

Taking Monday off work is not an unusual practice in Devon and it used to be even commoner than it is today.

Back in the 17th century, craft workers commonly took Mondays off. Indeed, they did it so often that they called their self-appointed holiday St Monday's Day.

In his autobiography, Benjamin Franklin, the American publisher, inventor, land speculator, Governor of Pennsylvania, Commissioner to France and signatory of the American Declaration of Independence, referred to his fellow printing workers in London as having the habit of taking Mondays off.

Franklin, who was working as a printer at the time, succeeded in ingratiating himself with his employer by never following this ancient practice and by persuading his fellow printers to abandon it.

Showing early signs of his future political acumen, Franklin even succeeded in changing the chapel laws which allowed the practice of taking Mondays as a holiday. (Printing houses have been called chapels since printing was first carried on in England in an old chapel which had been converted to a printing house.)

On my very last visit to the hairdresser's establishment in Barnstaple, (it was not a Monday, for I had learned my lesson), the barber greeted me with his usual cheery smile, tucked the sheet in around my neck, and then murmured something about being away for just a couple of minutes.

Actually, I think what he said was: 'Unavoidable Incident Delays Proceedings'.

He then disappeared.

I had no idea where he had gone. I sat patiently, waiting.

When I had finished reading the advertisements for hair lotion and condoms, I picked a tabloid newspaper off a nearby chair and carefully read every word. That filled three minutes. I then pulled a book out of my jacket pocket (as I have already pointed out, I never go anywhere without a paperback book upon my person) and I read that for a while. Then I must have dozed off for a while because when I next looked at my watch I saw that I had been sitting in the hairdresser's chair for nearly three quarters of an hour.

I removed the sheet which the hairdresser had tied around my neck to catch the trimmings which were now clearly not going to come and wandered out through the back door, the exit through which the hairdresser had left. I confess that I half expected to find the hairdresser lying unconscious or even dead on the floor. Instead, the small back room was deserted.

I went out through another door and found myself in a small, sunlit courtyard.

The hairdresser was sitting on a folding chair reading a paperback novel and enjoying the sunshine. He looked up when he heard the door open. 'Hero in Jeopardy as Captivating Story Unfolds', he said. He didn't apologise or look either apologetic or embarrassed. 'Doctor Leaves with Hair Uncut,' I said, 'Work to Be Done.'

I suppose things like this must happen to everyone but they seem to happen to me more than they happen to most people.

I think that hairdresser must have been what used to be known as 'a bit of a card'.

I didn't mind him deciding to sit in the sunshine in preference to cutting my hair but I did think he might have had the decency to tell me what he was doing.

I wasn't too pleased to have travelled to Barnstaple twice without purpose and so when I discovered that a barber would be operating in Peter Marshall's converted shed I decided to try him out.

I am, and always have been, keen to support small local businesses.

The supermarkets and big out of town stores have made life difficult for small shops and although hairdressing is not yet a service usually offered by the chain stores the principle is worth observing and if a shop opens in Bilbury then I feel I should try to be a customer.

I should, I suppose, have had my suspicions when I entered the shed and found it quite empty. That was the first clue. I had never before entered a hairdressing establishment during opening hours and found it entirely empty of customers.

The second clue which should have alerted me was the fact that the man who was about to cut my hair was wearing a hairpiece which looked as if it had fallen onto his head from a great height.

When I saw his hairpiece, I was reminded of a story relating to John Wayne, the film star. Wayne regarded his hairpiece with no respect whatsoever. When about to go before the cameras, Wayne realised that he wasn't wearing his toupee. He picked it up and plonked it onto his head with about as much care as you or I might take when carelessly tossing a cushion onto a chair.

'Is that real hair?' asked one of the film crew, rather rudely. 'Of course it's real,' replied Wayne. 'But it's not mine.'

One might, however, reasonably expect an experienced barber to take a little care with his own tonsorial appearance.

The third clue which should have forced me to find an excuse to turn round and leave was the fact that even from twelve feet away it was clear that the man had quite a very severe tremor in both hands. Indeed, his hands were actually shaking. This was not a mild case of Parkinson's Disease (in which case the tremor would have disappeared when he started cutting hair) but a severe neurological problem which was not going to disappear when he started snipping away around my ears with a pair of sharp scissors.

Now, I am all for people with disabilities being employed in whatever capacity seems appropriate but I have never before come across a hairdresser with a distinct hand tremor.

I am not particularly bothered about losing a bit of an earlobe (though I confess I would rather hold onto as many of my bits and pieces as possible, on the grounds that if God put them there he wanted them there for a purpose) but I really don't fancy having the point of a scissor blade poked into one of my eyes. God gave me two eyes and that is definitely the number I'd like to continue with.

Still, for one reason or another, I ignored all these signs and I sat down in the man's chair and put myself at his mercy.

Forty five minutes later I left, shaking and grateful to be still alive and in possession of my eyes and most of both ear lobes. I had lost a little blood but as long as the barber washed the blood off his scissors between patients this was probably nothing to worry about. I was still alive and that was something for which I felt enormously grateful.

I popped into Peter Marshall's shop before I went home.

'Where did you find that new hairdresser?' I asked him.

'You've got blood on your collar,' said Peter.

'I was stabbed with a pair of scissors,' I told him. 'Where the hell did you find that new hairdresser?'

'Oh, he lives in a cottage near Kentisbury,' said Peter who was unpacking cardboard boxes which appeared to be full of spectacles. 'He used to work in a car factory. Nice chap.'

'Nice chap,' I agreed. 'But where did he learn to be a barber?'

'I don't think he learnt it anywhere,' said Peter, putting a double handful of spectacles into a box on the shop counter. 'I think he's self-taught. Said he had to give up the car factory job because of the shakes but he always wanted to be a hairdresser.' Peter looked at my hair and asked me to turn round so that he could examine the back and sides too. 'Did he do the back too?'

'He did,' I said.

Peter shook his head. 'I don't think I'll be letting him near my hair,' he said. 'Yours looks a bloody mess.'

'Bloody being the key word,' I said. Peter picked up another double handful of spectacles. 'What are you doing with all those spectacles?' I asked.

'I bought them from a wholesaler who got them from a chain of opticians which went bust,' said Peter. 'They're spectacles which they made for customers but which were never picked up or, if they were picked up, weren't quite right and were rejected.'

'How many pairs have you bought?'

'Twelve boxes,' said Peter. 'I bought them by weight.' He looked at the number of spectacles he'd taken out of the one box he'd opened. 'There are about 500 pairs in each box, I'd guess.'

I looked at the boxes of spectacles. There were enough pairs of spectacles to provide the entire population of Bilbury with eyewear for seven or eight generations. 'How on earth are people going to pick out which spectacles they want?'

'Easy enough,' said Peter. 'They just try 'em on and see if they suit. I reckon these will go like hot cakes.'

'Or compasses,' I suggested.

'Oh, the compasses have all gone,' said Peter. 'I sold the last six to a group of tourists from Japan.' He grinned. 'I told them that over here, on this side of the planet, 'north' is the other way round.'

I left him unpacking spectacles.

When I got home Ben ran away from me and when she'd finished laughing, Patsy spent half an hour sticking plasters onto my lacerations and re-cutting my hair so that I didn't look as if it had been cut by a man with a neurological disorder.

By the time she'd finished, I had a pretty good idea of how I'll look like when I go bald.

'Did you have that done for a bet?' she asked.

I thought that was unnecessary.

The Sheep Shearing

Our five sheep have a warm, dry stable in which they can spend cold winter nights but some modern farmers don't seem to bother providing their animals with any protection from the elements. Indeed, many farmers have chopped down all of their trees (a decent sized tree can be sold to a timber yard and turned into a number of fence posts, or, at the worst, sold as firewood) and so livestock such as sheep which are kept out of doors all year round suffer enormously.

The sheep's fleece will provide it with some protection, and the animal's natural oils help to make the woollen coat waterproof, but I know from observation that sheep hate getting cold and wet. Our sheep can sense a storm coming a quarter of an hour before the first raindrop falls and they will run for shelter in good time. Knowing this, Patsy and I had a splendid barn built especially for our tiny flock.

Of course, although a sheep's fleece will keep it warm through the coldest of winters and will provide it with some protection from wind, rain and snow, a fleece which can be life-saving in December can become a deadly burden during the summer months.

Carrying around seven or eight pounds of wool can be exhausting, and the sheep's thick coat will push up its temperature to a dangerously high level. If you don't shear sheep before the hot weather starts they will suffer enormously.

Many farmers now shear their sheep twice a year, the small amount of money they receive for each fleece, just exceeding the cost of having the animal shorn. But to me that seems rather cruel. Shearing twice a year means that the sheep will be without its protective coat during some of the colder months and, without the shelter provided by trees and bushes, sheep have to suffer and shiver when the weather is wet and windy.

But the weather was becoming warmer and our four sheep needed to be sheared. As usual, I asked Mr Kennett, Patsy's father to arrange for of our sheep to be shorn.

Normally, the process of collecting sheep together in order to shear them is a fairly easy job. The farmer, the shearer and the farmer's dog can usually round up a flock of sheep in a few minutes. But our sheep don't respond to a sheep dog in the same way that normal sheep behave.

Our five sheep, Lizzie, Petula, Cynthia, Sarah-Louise and Miss Houdini, are all pets, and consequently they have never learned that a sheep dog Must Be Obeyed. Instead, when they see a dog approach they simply stand and stare at it as though saying, 'Who might you be? And what, precisely, do you want?'

When the sheep dog barks, the sheep stand their ground. If they move, it is not to retreat but to move slowly forwards to inspect the rude intruder who is making so much noise.

After having a dog turned into the canine equivalent of a nervous wreck by our confident sheep, Mr Kennett no longer brings his sheep dog with him when he and the shearer come to give the animals their annual short back, top and underneath.

Instead, Patsy or I usually call the sheep, sometimes offering a digestive biscuit or two as an incentive, and then when they come running we leave the shearer to his work.

But on the day of the shearing, Patsy was working at Dr Brownlow's old home, helping Bradshaw and a couple of volunteers redecorate the kitchen, and I had been called out to see a patient called Humphrey Todcaster who had told my receptionist, Miss Johnson, that he had developed very severe jaundice. He had, reported Miss Johnson, told her that he had probably developed a deadly liver disease that might require an urgent liver transplant.

I was leaving the house as Mr Kennett and the sheep shearer and the sheep shearer's young assistant arrived. I hadn't seen either of the shearers before. The previous man who had sheared our sheep had retired and was now living in a small cottage overlooking the river Lyn in the famous and picturesque village of Lynmouth.

Mr Kennett explained to me that the new shearer and his workmate, who is his son, spend the summer travelling around Devon and Cornwall, going from farm to farm and shearing sheep for 12 hours a day. The two men sleep rough. The shearer sleeps in the Dormobile in which they travel and his son sleeps in a tent or, if the weather is fine, in a sleeping bag under the stars. They spend the winter in Southern Spain, recovering from their exertions and spending their hard-earned money. The duo had been shearing Mr Kennett's large flock and had turned up to shear our five sheep before moving on to the next farm.

I apologised to the three men and explained that I had just received an urgent call to visit a patient.

'Don't worry,' said my father-in-law. He was squinting and was wearing a pair of new spectacles. They had jet black frames and if he hadn't been wearing manure-stained jeans, a jumper with more holes in it than a chicken wire fence and a pair of elderly rubber boots with the tops turned down, they would have given him a very business-like look. My father-in-law was on the grumpy side of bad tempered and explained that he was angry because two loose dogs which had been allowed to roam the countryside had killed two of his sheep and badly mauled several more. No one had identified the dogs or their owner but one sighting had suggested that the bigger of the two dogs was either a Rottweiler or a Doberman. Farmers loathe having dogs loose on their land and some, Mr Kennett included, will shoot to kill if they see a dog worrying their stock. One local farmer goes further and if he shoots a dog he hangs the corpse on the nearest tree 'pour decourager les autres' (though it is possible those aren't the words he would use himself). Another local farmer has let it be known that he will shoot errant dog owners as well as their dogs.

'We'll be done by the time you get back,' said the senior shearer, confidently. He had the voice of a man who is accustomed to shouting instructions over long distances.

When he spoke, the sheep in a field half a mile away suddenly started baaing like crazy. They had undoubtedly heard, and recognised the shearer's voice. Sheep can be very sensitive and these, having just been shorn, weren't keen to repeat the experience. The baaing flock sounded just like politicians 'debating' important issues of State in Britain's House of Commons. Actually, the sheep were probably making just as much sense as the politicians.

'I've got a couple of bottles of new parsnip wine in the car,' said Mr Kennett. I'll leave them in the kitchen if you're not back before we leave.'

I was, to be honest, astonished at Mr Kennett's confidence since as far as I could remember neither he nor the previous shearer had ever managed to get hold of the sheep without assistance from Patsy or myself. Our sheep are, like all creatures of their species, naturally nervous. Unlike most other creatures of their species, they are unnaturally disobedient.

But the call from Mr Todcaster had sounded urgent and I didn't have time to hang around and make sure that all went well with the shearing. So I left the three of them to it and drove off to visit Mr Todcaster in the cottage which he shares with his mother, two goats, a collection of cats and a stuffed armadillo.

'He's in bed but you're wasting your time, doctor,' said Mrs Todcaster, who celebrated her 80th birthday some time ago and who looks considerably older. She was sitting in the living room staring at a television which was switched on but without the sound.

'Why is that?' I asked.

'He'll be dead in a week,' replied Mrs Todcaster, apparently without concern or regret. She stated it as baldly as she might have told me that it was due to rain later, or that they had run out of milk.

'I'd better take a look at him then,' I said.

'He's in bed. But you won't get any sense out of him. He rambles.'

'Rambles?'

'Just witters on and on,' said Mrs Todcaster, clearly irritated at having to explain herself. 'He is a very boring man. He was a boring boy. His father was boring. If you asked his father how he was, he'd take half an hour telling you everything about him. He was very boring. He used to tell people the history of every piece of furniture we owned. 'That dresser came from an auction at Lower Petherbury farm,' he would say. 'They bought it from a store in Exeter. It was made by a firm that went bankrupt in 1839.' On and on he'd go. He couldn't make a cup of tea without telling you the history of the pot, the cup and the tealeaves. John is the same as his father. He just goes on and on about his health. He's a health freak. He wanted me to take euthanasia tablets when I got a cold.'

'Euthanasia tablets?' I asked, slightly concerned. It occurred to me that young Mr Todcaster might, perhaps, have wanted to get rid of his mother. It would have been difficult to blame him. Living in the same house as Mrs Todcaster could not have been fun.

Mrs Todcaster picked a plastic bottle off the mantelpiece and showed it to me. The bottle was marked 'Echinacea tablets'.

'I don't need tablets to get rid of a cold,' she said. 'I'll either get better or I'll die. And at my age it doesn't much matter which.'

'Maybe I'd better go on up and see your son now,' I suggested. 'Is he in the front bedroom?' I hadn't known Mrs Todcaster's husband but it occurred to me that if he rambled more than she did he must have been painful to listen to.

'Of course he's in the front bedroom. He's not going to be in my bedroom is he?' She peered intently at the television set. The picture, which was in black and white, was fuzzy and it was difficult to decide what was happening on the screen.

Leaving her to the television, I pulled aside the curtain at the bottom of the stairs and made my way up the steep, narrow staircase. There were two rooms downstairs and just two rooms on the first floor. There was no bathroom in the house. The toilet was in a wooden hut at the bottom of the garden. On the rare occasions when they wanted to wash, Mrs Todcaster and her son used the kitchen sink. For their quarterly bathing they used a tin bath which hung on a nail in an outhouse.

'I've got liver cancer,' shouted Mr Todcaster when he heard me climbing the stairs.

He was lying in a huge brass bedstead which Patchy Fogg would have loved to have got his hands on. Patchy is always looking for old brass bedsteads. There is, apparently, an insatiable market for them. Interior designers in the posher parts of London adore them. And American householders also seem to find them attractive. Patchy is always trying to persuade me to tell him when I spot valuable old pieces of furniture so he can call in and buy them. He tells me what to look out for but I always refuse to cooperate. Acting as a furniture scout for an antique dealer would make me feel more than slightly uncomfortable – particularly since I know that Patchy is always eager to underpay for the items he buys. An old oak commode stood in the corner of the room and there were oak tables on either side of the bed. Both tables were covered with bottles of herbal remedies, alternative medicines and heaven knows what else.

There was no chair in the room and I didn't fancy sitting on the commode so I put my black bag down on the floor and remained standing. 'What are your symptoms?' I asked.

'I'm jaundiced,' replied Mr Todcaster. 'I'd have thought you'd have been able to see that. You're supposed to be the damned doctor.' Other than the obvious change in his skin colour he looked perfectly fine to me. But he wasn't jaundiced. His skin was orange rather than yellow.

'Strictly speaking, jaundice is a sign not a symptom,' I said. I was feeling a little crotchety myself by now. 'A symptom is something you feel; something you're aware of; a pain, a discomfort, a change in your bowel habits. A sign is something that can be observed – a discolouration, a rash or a twitch. Have you noticed anything other than the change in the colour of your skin?'

Mr Todcaster thought for a moment. 'No, I don't think so,' he admitted.

I looked closely at his skin which, on close examination, was clearly far more orange than yellow. The whites of his eyes, the conjunctival membranes, were still white. In jaundice they turn yellow.

'Any change in the colour of your urine?' I asked him.

He shook his head.

'Not exceptionally dark?'

'No.'

When a patient has jaundice their urine will usually be much darker than usual.

It was already pretty clear that Mr Todcaster was not jaundiced. And I strongly suspected that I knew the cause of his strange skin colouration.

I opened my bag, took out my stethoscope and listened to his chest. His heart and lungs were fine. I examined his abdomen. I could feel nothing amiss. His liver was definitely not enlarged.

'What medicines are you taking?' I asked Mr Todcaster.

He waved a hand over the pills on the two tables.

I looked at the pills on the table nearest to me and then walked round the bed and looked at the pills on the other table. I could see nothing that would explain the skin pigmentation.

'Have you changed your diet recently?' I asked.

'I put myself on a vegetable juice diet,' he told me. 'Drinking lots of juice helps strengthen the immune system and fight off cancer.'

'Lots of carrot juice?' I asked.

'Oh yes,' he agreed. 'I drink several pints of fresh carrot juice every day. It's good for the eyes.'

Carrots contain a substance called carotene which is the chemical which gives them their colour. Actually, carotene is the chemical which gives all sorts of plants and animals their colouring. Pink flamingos are pink because their usual diet includes shrimp which are rich in a carotenoid. A rich man whom I once knew had a lake which he stocked with pink flamingos. He thought the birds would add a splash of colour to his estate. He was very disappointed when his flamingos all turned white because they were fed a carotene free diet.

Carrots have a reputation for enabling people to see in the dark because the carotene they contain can be converted into a form of vitamin A and without vitamin A, human beings develop night blindness. This is a scientific fact but although people who are deficient in carotene can be helped if they eat carrots, a surfeit of carrots won't improve normal eyesight. The myth that eating carrots improves the eyesight of healthy people was made popular during the Second World War when the British Air Ministry put out press releases claiming that British fighter pilots were able to shoot down enemy aircraft in the dark because they had better night vision. The Ministry releases claimed that the marvellous night time vision was a result of them eating lots of carrots. The story was a deliberately concocted fiction designed to disguise the fact that British aircraft were equipped with a new-fangled invention called radar.

The whole thing got out of hand and when sugar rationing meant that sweets became pretty well unobtainable, children were encouraged to put their pennies into slot machines which served up carrots on a stick. The myth that carrots improved eyesight became established.

Decades after the end of the Second World War, enthusiasts were still encouraging one another to eat vast quantities of carrots and it was widely believed that carrots were a 'good thing' and that it was impossible to have too much of this particular 'good thing'.

Sadly, this was nonsense and many people were made seriously ill by eating too many carrots. At least one man died as a result of drinking too much carrot juice.

Fortunately, it didn't seem to me as if Mr Todcaster had done himself any permanent harm.

Carotenemia, the condition in which the skin turns orange as a result of eating too many carrots, or drinking too much carrot juice, is reversible and in most patients the condition causes no long-term damage.

'Your skin has turned orange because of all the carrot juice you've been drinking,' I told him. 'There's nothing wrong with you.'

He stared at me in disbelief. He actually looked disappointed.

You might have thought that a man who thinks he is dying and then finds out that he has simply been consuming too many carrots might be overjoyed.

But Mr Todcaster moaned a good deal about having to give up his carrot juice.

'What happens if I carry on with the carrot juice?' he demanded, rather aggressively. 'Carrot juice is very good for you.'

'If you carry on drinking so much carrot juice then your skin will stay orange and you will die,' I told him.

He said he would think about what to do.

I left him and gingerly made my way back down the steep and narrow staircase. It was so steep that it was more like going down a ladder than going down a flight of stairs. As I descended, it seemed to me to be a miracle that neither Mrs Todcaster nor her son had fallen down the stairs. It was also a miracle that they had been able to resist the temptation to give each other a good push.

'How long has he got?' demanded Mrs Todcaster when I finally reached the bottom of the staircase and, relieved, stepped back into the living room.

'Probably another thirty years,' I told her.

'He's not dying?'

'Not at the moment.'

'Well, bugger me,' said Mrs Todcaster, sounding very disappointed that she wouldn't be able to attend her son's funeral, do a good deal of wailing and bathe in assorted sympathy and commiseration. She sniffed and turned back to watching whatever it was that she could see through the interference on her elderly television set.

I was away from the house for just over an hour and when I returned to Bilbury Grange, I thoroughly expected to see our five sheep standing in the field, bald and cool and looking very summery without their winter coats.

But that was not what I saw.

The five sheep were spread around the field and they all still possessed their winter coats. They were lying down, chewing the odd blade of grass.

As they lolled about, quietly chewing blades of grass and occasional daisies, the five sheep carefully watched the two men standing in the middle of the field.

The shearer and his assistant had clearly been doing a good deal of chasing around. They were both now red-faced, sweating heavily and breathing with some difficulty, and they were standing with their hands on their knees. I could hear their heavy breathing from the spot at the fence where I met Mr Kennett. He was standing some distance from the five-barred gate which provided access to the field and was far too sensible to get involved with chasing five very independent-minded sheep around a ten acre field on a hot day.

The shearer and his assistant had set up their shearing equipment, powered shears and a diesel engine, in a corner of the field close to the gate. I looked across at their impressive looking equipment. Sheep shearers have moved with the times and no longer use the old-fashioned hand powered shears. I don't blame them. The last time I saw a man who sheared sheep by hand he had thick calluses on his palms and fingers and had, over the years, lost two fingers to his own sharp shears. Modern shearers can usually shear a flock of sheep without spilling a drop of blood.

'Things are going according to plan, then,' I murmured.

Mr Kennett, chewing on a long piece of grass, nodded. 'Good entertainment,' he said. 'They thought they'd nearly got one of 'em a few minutes ago but she slipped through their fingers like a wing three quarter avoiding a couple of clumsy forwards. They were never even close.'

I couldn't help noticing that Patsy's father was now wearing a different pair of spectacles to the ones he had been wearing when I'd left him. This second pair had tortoiseshell frames and gave him a vaguely academic appearance.

I immediately guessed where the two new pairs of spectacles had come from.

Half of my patients seemed to be struggling to cope with new spectacles which they had bought from Peter Marshall.

Since the glasses which they had purchased had all been made for another pair of eyes they were, not surprisingly, having some difficulty in finding a pair which actually improved their eyesight.

'Have they been chasing the sheep around since I left?' I asked.

'They have,' said Mr Kennett. He moved the new spectacles down his nose an inch and tried looking over them. He pushed them back and tried looking through them. Finally, he took the spectacles off his nose and held them a few inches away from his face. Then he put them back on his nose and tried squinting. 'There has been a lot of chasing, a lot of diving, a lot of very poor tackling and absolutely no catching. The sheep are winning hands down at the moment and I don't expect that to change at any time in the future.'

We stood for a few minutes and watched the shearer and his son.

The funny thing was that the sheep seemed to make absolutely no real effort to evade the men – they slid past them with the greatest of ease.

For a moment, I thought the two men were going to catch Miss Houdini but she sidestepped them very neatly and was, within a moment, back chewing grass while the two men, thwarted, lay flat on the ground.

'If I were choosing the England rugby team she'd be my first pick,' said Mr Kennett, nodding towards Miss Houdini, who had been given her name because she seemed capable of escaping from virtually any situation. He took off the spectacles he was wearing and put them into his left hand jacket pocket. From his right hand pocket he took another pair of glasses. This third pair had simple steel frames in the style made famous by John Lennon.

'I needed some new glasses,' he explained unnecessarily. 'And the last lot I bought from the opticians in Barnstaple were damned expensive. These were a bargain. I bought three pairs for £1.'

'From Peter Marshall's shop,' I said. Mr Kennett is a cautious, sensible man who does not throw his money around. But not even he is immune to one of Peter Marshall's marketing schemes.

'They were ridiculously good value,' he said. 'You just pick out any three pairs from a huge box. I paid nearly £80 for my last pair.' He paused and thought about it again. 'Three pairs for £1! Amazing value.'

'I was there when he took delivery of the damned things,' I said. 'He's got boxes full of them.' Mr Kennett was just one of many who had been unable to resist Peter's offer. I'd spotted our local postman climbing out of a ditch. He had been riding around the village on his bicycle while wearing his new spectacles when he'd become dizzy and fallen off his machine.

It had not occurred to any of the buyers that a bargain is only a bargain if it does what it's supposed to do. Nor had it occurred to them that the chances of finding a pair of spectacles that matched their requirements were somewhere between slim and non-existent.

'It's just a question of finding a pair I can see through,' said Mr Kennett. 'I don't care what they look like as long as I can see and they don't give me headaches.' He scratched his head. 'It looks as if I might have to go back to Peter's shop and buy myself another pound's worth.'

Mr Kennett is a farmer, and so hates spending money unnecessarily. He always says he's simply careful with his cash but his wife and daughters, who love him dearly, all describe him as being firmly and permanently settled on the mean side of generous.

While we had been talking, the shearers had come up with a plan.

The senior shearer stood in the middle of the field and ordered his assistant to get behind Sarah-Louise and to shout at her until she started to move. The shearer then tried to position himself directly in front of her so that he would be able to grab her as she trotted past.

Naturally, this plan proved as ineffective as all the others.

Sarah-Louise walked forward until she was about six feet away from the shearer and then suddenly, without any warning, she turned sharp right and started to run. She was having great fun and doubtless thought that the 'catch me if you can' game she was playing with the shearer had been organised entirely for her benefit. A ewe, even quite a large one, can accelerate at an extraordinary speed and it can probably run far faster, and for longer, than any human athlete. It can certainly run faster than an out of condition sheep shearer who has spent too many lunchtimes eating steak and kidney pie and too many evenings drinking beer. A grown ewe can run at 30 miles per hour and it can keep that speed up for a surprising length of time. Moreover, its four foot drive configuration means that it can change direction without apparently losing speed and no human can do that.

I stood and watched the shearer and his pal for a few minutes longer and then I took pity on them. I called them over to where we were standing.

'I think it's time to get on with the shearing,' I said. The two men were red-faced, soaked with sweat and out of breath. They also looked embarrassed.

'You two are out of condition,' said Mr Kennett.

'Why didn't you bring the dog?' asked the shearer's assistant.

'They won't take any notice of him either,' said Mr Kennett. 'The last time I brought a dog over here the sheep terrified the life out of him. It took him a month to recover and he was never the same again.'

'If you can catch those darned sheep I'll shear 'em for free,' said the shearer.

'Get your clippers ready,' I told him. 'I'll have all five ready and waiting before you've started the generator.'

The shearer looked at me and did his best not to scoff. But he and his assistant strode off quickly towards the spot by the gate where they'd left the clippers and the rest of the equipment.

'Come on, you lot!' I called, climbing over the fence into the field.

The sheep, hearing my voice, turned and looked in my direction.

'Come over here,' I said.

The sheep started running towards me.

I walked towards the spot where the shearer was busy trying to start his generator. Mr Kennett, who prefers to go through gates rather than to climb over fences, walked along the other side of the fence.

The five sheep and I arrived a minute or so before the shearer managed to start his generator.

'Ready and waiting!' I said.

'Well, bugger me if that ain't the strangest thing I've ever seen,' said the shearer. His son just stared in astonishment.

'It's just a knack,' I said modestly. I didn't think it necessary to point out that there were only five sheep in the whole world who would respond in such a way to my voice.

With me standing next to them, the sheep didn't even move when the generator eventually started to hum. They stood there, patient and obedient, knowing that they were safe and would probably receive a couple of digestive biscuits each if they behaved themselves. It took the shearer less than ten minutes to shear all five. There wasn't a nick or a scratch on any of them.

Afterwards the shearer refused to let me pay him. 'I thought I'd seen everything where sheep is concerned,' he said, shaking his head. He even offered me a job as their travelling sheep dog. 'With you calling in the sheep we could get through twice as many as we do now,' he said.

As the two men drove away in their battered Dormobile, Mr Kennett wrapped up the five fleeces and bundled them into the back of his truck. He then presented me with two bottles of his parsnip wine; as potent a brew as has ever been made with the aid of the humble parsnip.

I fetched a packet of digestive biscuits from the kitchen.

Our fleeceless sheep deserved a reward.

The Brownlow Country Hotel

My predecessor and mentor Dr Brownlow had lived in a wonderful old house in the centre of the village of Bilbury. You can walk to it easily from the Duck and Puddle. You turn right, follow the road around the village green and take the first lane on the right (it's signposted to Combe Martin). Dr Brownlow's old house is a hundred yards on the right. The black painted iron gates, the largest I've ever seen, hang from two huge stone pillars upon each of which rests a massive stone griffin. On either side of the pillars is a nine foot high stone wall which separates the road from the gardens. The wall must have cost a fortune to build. Fortunately, it was built well and shows no sign of disrepair. A long driveway, flanked by seventy foot tall poplars, leads up to the house which is built entirely of grey stone, softened slightly by several acres of green ivy.

Dr Brownlow who lived in the house for many years is now buried in the garden in a splendid stone vault which was paid for not out of his estate but by a subscription raised by the villagers. I was very proud that it was Dr Brownlow's patients who paid for his tomb. He would have been proud too.

The house has towers, battlements and mullion windows and a Union Jack flag flies from a pole standing to the front of the central tower. Directly underneath the flag, and flanked by two huge stone lions, is a front door which is 12 feet high and decorated with scores of solid metal studs. These were designed, I have always assumed, to give battering rams a hard time. The roof, like the roofs of all old houses, is made with tiles which taper in size from the top to the bottom: with the small tiles at the ridge and the larger tiles towards the eaves. It wasn't until around 1850 that builders in Britain started to build house roofs with tiles of a uniform size.

The inside of the house is, as you might expect from the outside, unmistakeably gothic. A long corridor, around ten feet wide, runs through the centre of the building, with the walls on either side decorated with huge old oil paintings which are hung in massive gilt frames. The dining room is dominated by a great stone fireplace and the oak panelling in the billiard room is richly decorated with wooden carvings. The whole place costs a large fortune to heat.

Dr Brownlow has a son who works as a GP in Barnstaple but the two had not been on good terms for many years and when he died Dr Brownlow left the house to me with the suggestion that it be turned into a small hospital.

'Nothing elaborate,' he had said. 'Somewhere friendly and local for patients to be looked after when they're too ill to stay at home but not really ill enough to be in a proper hospital.'

Long before the Industrial Age, hospitals were built like cathedrals, in order to lift the soul and ease the mind; hospital buildings were decorated with carvings, works of art, flowers and perfumes. The ancient Greeks had musicians playing in hospital corridors.

Dr Brownlow felt (as I do) that modern hospitals are built with no regard for the spirit, the eye or the soul. They are bare, more like prisons than temples, designed to concentrate the mind on pain, fear and death. Where there are windows they are positioned in such a way that patients can't see out of them (though even if they could they probably wouldn't be able to see anything more enthralling or uplifting than the refuse bins or the air conditioning units).

In most hospitals, it is difficult to believe that the staff understands the meaning of the word 'dignity' – not, at least, when applied to patients. Patients are talked to as if they were infants, invariably being addressed by their first names. In many hospitals, patients are given revealing little gowns to wear. These awful gowns hide nothing from general view but patients are instructed that they must be worn without underwear. Patrons in the seediest type of nightclub would be arrested if they wore such attire. Where is dignity in such circumstances?

And, of course, big, proper hospitals are dangerous places.

There are many hazards but the greatest danger is that a patient may catch a hospital infection. As a result of worsening hospital hygiene (there is clear evidence that in British hospitals neither doctors nor nurses wash their hands properly or often enough) infections are now a significant health threat. In some hospitals, these days the sheets aren't changed when patents leave and when patients arrive. Instead, to save money, the sheets are just turned over. Top to bottom. That sort of practice is frowned upon in the sleaziest of seaside boarding houses but hospital staff find it acceptable. It is, of course, the administrators who decide that this will be done. But it is the nurses who supervise its doing. In a State-run health service, the staff become institutionalised. They work for the Government and they are too afraid for their careers to speak out when they are told to do things which they know are wrong.

'I fear that things are just going to get worse,' Dr Brownlow said to me a few months before he died, 'I hate to think how dangerous hospitals will be by the 1990s and the end of the 20th century.'

To all this must be added the fact that modern hospitals tend to be bureaucratic and dangerously overstaffed with administrators. Most modern hospital administrators seem to be convinced that hospitals will only run smoothly and efficiently when there are no patients at all.

And so Dr Brownlow, who understood just how bad hospitals had become, and who spent his final weeks at home, being cared for by his faithful butler Bradshaw, wanted his permanent legacy to be a small, friendly hospital run by people who genuinely cared about the sick and the weak and the frail. He knew that we couldn't build a hospital equipped with operating theatres and intensive care units. But he believed that with the correct intentions we would be able to create a cottage hospital that would provide the villagers of Bilbury with a haven and a refuge at their time of need.

And so, in addition to leaving me his house, Dr Brownlow also gave me £50,000 in cash (via a simple ploy which I described in Bilbury Village and which could, I suppose, be loosely described as entirely justifiable tax avoidance) to spend on converting his former home into a cottage hospital.

Although he was a charitable man, Dr Brownlow himself had never had much faith in big, formal charities – the ones with posh offices in London and battalions of highly paid executives. He always said that he would rather give his money direct to the needy rather than simply put it into a collecting tin and allow some city based charity to spend it on administrative, salaries and expenses. Many of the biggest charities spend more than three quarters of the money they receive on salaries, pensions and similar costs. Patsy and I could see no point in that sort of charitable giving and agreed with Dr Brownlow's philosophy.

Our attitude on this matter had been hardened when, a week or so earlier, Patsy and I had been in Barnstaple buying linen for the new hospital when we had been approached by a young man collecting money for a charity which claimed to look after people who had fallen on hard times; he told us that the charity specialised in caring for the homeless, the weak and the elderly.

'If I give you £1 how much of the pound will go to the homeless?' Patsy asked the man.

He had looked at her as if she were mad.

'How much will go on administration?' I asked. 'How much will be spent on advertisements, marketing and producing leaflets?'

The young man didn't know any of the answers to those questions.

'Are you being paid a salary to collect money?' I asked him.

He said that he was being paid and he said that he and the organisation for which he worked would prefer it if I signed a direct debit form so that my bank could give them money every month.

Across the street there was an elderly man wrapped up in a blanket.

'If I give you £1,' I said to the young man, 'how much of it will your organisation give to that old fellow over there?'

The young man stared at me as if I were in need of strong medication. (This is a look which I know well.)

We left the charity employee and went over and talked to the old man. He turned out to be not as old as he appeared. His name was Tim and he was, he told us, in his fifties. His decline had been swift. His wife had died and his world fell apart. He lost the love of his life and he lost his partner in life too.

Together they had run a small business. He had been a chimney sweep and had done odd jobs. During the summer he had done a bit of gardening. He'd cut people's lawns, trimmed hedges, pulled up weeds and generally tided things up for them. She had done the accounts and booked the appointments. Without her, the business had folded. He had no inclination for paperwork or for collecting the money he was owed and within a year he had lost his van, his house and his possessions. Now he had nothing but an old anorak, a woolly hat and a filthy blanket. And he had, he admitted, a growing tendency to try to forget his predicament by drinking alcohol.

'How much alcohol do you drink?' I asked him.

Nearly all tramps and homeless people over 40 are alcoholics. Nearly all the homeless under 40 are drug users.

He said that he got through a bottle of sherry a day but that sometimes one bottle wasn't enough and that if it was particularly cold he needed one and a half bottles to get through the day. He admitted that he also smoked 20 cigarettes a day. He said he was confident that he could give up the sherry if his circumstances improved but was honest enough to admit that he might have more difficulty giving up the cigarettes.

Patsy and I each gave him one of the new £1 coins. To us it seemed better to cut out the middleman and give the money directly to someone who needed it.

As we carried on our way we agreed that we would look out for him whenever we visited Barnstaple and that he would be our moral, 'direct debit' obligation. We both desperately wished we could do more.

The big charities boast of changing the world but all most of them really do is enrich themselves.

Maybe we could find a way to do more to help him.

We both remembered Mr Parfitt, our gardener. He had been sleeping rough when we'd first met him. Today, he was a happily married man with a loving wife, a beautiful home and reliable employment.

But miracles like that don't happen often.

Meanwhile, we continued on our shopping expedition.

Patsy chose the linen and the other things we needed for our new hospital and I stood and nodded wisely. From time to time I carried bundles back to the Rolls Royce.

As far as I could discover, Bilbury had never had a hospital of its own and villagers who needed nursing care, palliative care, had always had to go into hospital in Barnstaple or Exeter. Most, if not all villagers, disliked this idea very much. Their relatives and friends all lived in Bilbury and it's quite a trek from the village to Barnstaple. People who have to rely on public transport find the journey next to impossible. There are no trains, of course, and buses are almost as rare as black swans.

After Dr Brownlow had died, I had appointed his former butler, Bradshaw, as my district nurse but I also decided that he would be the only person suitable to take on the responsibility as the Matron of the new cottage hospital.

To my astonishment and delight, Bradshaw had, within less than two days, found enough volunteers to staff the hospital without our having to hire any professional nurses. Most of the people whose services Bradshaw enlisted had no academic nursing qualifications but they were women of a certain age and they all had a quality which is far more important than any number of diplomas: they were all intrinsically kind people.

They wanted to help because it pleased them to be able to help people. They realised that people who are sick will get better quicker (or, if there is to be no getting better, reach the end of their days in greater peace and contentment) if they feel that they are among friends, and feel that the people around them genuinely care for their physical, mental and spiritual well-being. The people Bradshaw recruited all understood that people who are ill need to be cared for. They understood that a good nurse knows when to be attentive and when not to be fussy. They knew that providing a patient with a clean nightie, or doing her hair, or helping her put on a little make-up, can all do far more for her state of mind and her spirit than wearing a well-starched bib, putting on a cap at the correct angle or knowing how to fold a neat hospital corner when making a bed. And they understood that people who are ill or convalescing or dying are all helped if they can be cared for and treated within a community they know. When people fall ill abroad one of the first things they want to know is 'when can I go to a hospital back home?'

Britons who fall ill in Germany want to be cared for in Britain. People from New York want to be in New York if they must be ill. And the people of Bilbury were no different: if they had to be poorly then they'd rather be poorly in Bilbury than anywhere else.

Of course, they knew very well that if they needed to have an operation or to undergo extensive tests and investigations then they would need to be in a large hospital in a large town. But if they just needed to be looked after then they would, all things being equal, prefer to be looked after in Bilbury.

Our plans to provide Bilbury with its own small hospital did not go completely according to plan, of course.

Indeed, in my life, 'things' seem to prefer to avoid going anywhere near to plan.

Right from the beginning the local health service administrators were obstructive, it sometimes seemed deliberately so, and it quickly became apparent that converting Dr Brownlow's home into a hospital was going to be far more difficult than we had thought.

The health authority staff, of whom there were enough to form two full rugby teams with enough left over to make the teas and to stand on the touch lines and cheer, had enough red tape to wrap up Bilbury ready for posting off to Timbuktu.

As soon as we had solved one problem they thought of another problem.

For every answer we found they had another question.

The whole thing had begun to remind me of a fairground game which has recently become popular; the one where you hit one springy, toy mole on the head and find that as soon as the one you've hit disappears another one immediately pops up.

It seemed to me that we would never be able to defeat the doubters and the pessimists at the health authority. You cannot ever win against such people because there are always far more questions than there can ever be answers.

There were endless questions about staffing and about the type of beds we would use and the size of the staff dining facilities and, most of all, about the administration. How would we recruit and train our staff? What uniforms would they wear? What pensions would we offer our staff? How big an office would the chief administrator be given? What forms would we have and how would we ensure that their forms were filled in correctly and distributed, at the appropriate time intervals, to the appropriate departments in the appropriate parts of the National Health Service? There were even questions about the size, shape and weight of the filing cabinets we would use for storing the forms.

It was Bradshaw who thought of the solution. And the utter simplicity of his good-sense solution delighted me.

'Are we going to be performing major surgery on any of our patients?' he asked me.

'Good heavens, no!' I replied. I know my limits as far as surgery is concerned. I can sew up a wound and remove the sutures when they have done their job. I can remove a small cyst without too much effort. In a dire emergency I could probably remove a misbehaving appendix. But major surgery? No thank you! Despite my jokey suggestion to Patsy about opening a cosmetic surgery clinic I prefer to leave surgery to the masked professionals; the men and women who can murmur 'Scalpel, nurse!' in the certain knowledge that when they are given one they will know exactly what to do with it.

'Am I right in thinking that our aim is to provide the sick, the elderly, the frail and the dying with pleasant surroundings where they can be looked after properly?'

'You're absolutely right in thinking that,' I said.

'Then we really don't need to be registered as a hospital, doctor. We don't need to have anything to do with the health authorities. Why don't we simply call our establishment a hotel,' suggested Bradshaw.

I stared at him, in absolute awe.

'We could refer to our patients as 'guests' and we could still provide them with the sort of care they require,' continued Bradshaw. 'But the health service people would have no authority over our plans. We would probably have to satisfy the busy body authorities who regulate hotels but their requirements are relatively simple. We would need to have a fire extinguisher on every floor and clean surfaces in the kitchen. Compared to the hoops we would have to jump through to run a hospital there would be very little red tape to worry us.'

I had to work hard to suppress the desire to hug the old man. 'You are,' I said to him, 'a genius.'

But although he originally trained as a nurse, Bradshaw had spent many decades as a butler. You don't hug butlers. It simply isn't done.

So instead of hugging him, I held out a hand and we shook hands to confirm and celebrate our change of direction.

'Instead of being matron at the Brownlow Cottage Hospital you will, I hope, accept the position of Manager of the Brownlow Country Hotel.'

To my delight, the brilliant, the incomparably inventive Mr Bradshaw enthusiastically accepted the appointment.

'I was worried about what uniform would be appropriate for a matron,' he confessed. 'I am not a matronly type. But as a hotel manager I shall wear tails and a white tie. I think that would be appropriate.'

'Absolutely,' I agreed. 'Tails and a white tie at all times. And perhaps, if I might be so bold, a fresh carnation in the button hole?'

'A green one, I think, sir,' said Bradshaw.

Jeremy the Cat

We have for some years shared our home with two cats; one is called Emily and the other is known as Sophie.

We acquired both animals when they were kittens. They came from the home of a pair of spinsters called Miss Phillips and Miss Tweedsmuir.

But we acquired our third cat in a very different way.

Winifred Arnott-Toynbee had been married to a British diplomat who had served in embassies all over the world. She lived alone in a cottage overlooking the Bilbury village green, the centre of our small community.

Traditional English villages, the ones which have existed for a thousand years or more, rather than the artificial ones created more recently by unholy conspiracies founded by builders and local planners, tend to fall into one of three main types.

First, there is the village which exists around a central square or a green (the 'village green' which is famously used for cricket matches, maypole dancing and fairs).

Second, there is the village which is strung out along a single street.

And third there is the village which, although it clearly exists as a collection of houses, cottages and farms, appears to have been created in a haphazard fashion and to have no pattern whatsoever.

The archetypal village green, the feature which defines the first type of village, invariably has two features.

First, there is usually a church, which either stands upon the green itself or is situated close by, and which usually has a simple tower rather than the sort of impressive spire which only started to appear on churches built in the 13th century and later. If there is any seating at all in the church it will consist of just a few oak pews although other embellishments might be added much later, as the village grows and some of its inhabitants grow wealthy and become benefactors.

Many Devon churches have been rebuilt or enlarged as the centuries have rolled by but the church in Bilbury has changed very little.

Other churches had bells put in their towers and new windows put in – some with stained class. But Bilbury's church has remained steadfastly untouched.

The chapel which is attached to Dr Brownlow's old house, and which was built in the 16th century using blocks of granite, is larger and more impressive than Bilbury church.

And, of course, all self-respecting village greens always have a well.

Of the two ingredients, church and well, the well was, of course, always considered to be the most vital for it was the availability of a water supply which made the village possible. A church might help provide for the spiritual comfort of the villagers but without a reliable well the villagers would have either moved away or died.

Apart from a church, and some sort of stonework around the well, it has always been the case that the only buildings allowed on the village green were a smithy and a school.

Bilbury's green has never had anything built upon it, though the well, now disused, is currently covered with a low stone wall and has a heavy wooden lid which is chained into position to prevent children falling in and drowning. In the 19th century two small brothers, one aged six and the other eight-years-old, fell into the uncovered well and drowned. The village didn't need a health and safety official to decide what had to be done and the wooden lid was put on top of the well as quickly as it could be made.

Actually, Bilbury is rather unusual in having a proper village green.

Most villages in Devon exist around a central square, rather than a green, and although some squares have been built on, visitors to Devon can still find many villages (some of them have grown into towns, of course) which still retain their square.

A century or so ago, the square would have had houses all around it, some small and some large and very elegant, and it would have been the site of the weekly or twice weekly market where stallholders from miles around would arrive to sell their wares. It would also have been the site favoured by travelling fairs and circuses. Some squares were huge because they were the site of the local sheep market.

Today, the majority of village squares are given over to car parking and the houses which once stood around the square were long ago turned into shops and offices. The baker, the ironmonger and the banker now work alongside the local solicitor, the pharmacist and, unless he has moved out into a brand new health centre in some inaccessible part of the town, the local doctor too.

With the square surrounded by shops there is little need for market stalls to appear once or twice a week, and though in some towns the markets still take place, the stall holders are usually selling bags and jackets made by Peruvian peasants rather than home-made bread or sausages.

Whether a village has a square or a green, the principle purpose was much the same: to enable the villagers to defend themselves against attack – either from marauding bands of bandits or from wild animals.

There was originally often very little space, if any at all, between the individual houses around the square and the openings which did exist could easily be closed at night. With the gaps between properties closed off it would be easy to defend the village and livestock could be driven into the village square to protect them from marauding bandits or from wolves.

(The same sort of basic pattern exists in countries such as Africa where huts are grouped around a circular pound wherein animals can be kept at night, to protect them from lions.)

We often forget just how few people used to live in England in the days when Bilbury was a 'new' village.

Just a thousand years ago, the total population of England was about a million and a quarter people.

The whole of Devon, including the city of Exeter, was then home to no more than 70,000 people – that's only twice the population of Barnstaple today.

Devon was at something of a disadvantage compared to many other English counties in that there was very little stone for building. As a result, many of the older houses, cottages and bridges were built not of stone but of wood. Even bridges were built largely with wood and the vital bridges at Barnstaple and Bideford were built of timber when they were first erected in the 13th century.

That's the end of the scene-setting digression.

Bilbury, of course, has a village green, rather than a square, and the village has changed very little for a thousand years or more.

A peasant, transplanted by time machine from the Middle Ages, would perhaps stare shocked at the items for sale at Peter Marshall's shop, but he would recognise the village as home. There probably weren't many plastic combs, aerosol cans of deodorant or suspender belts on sale a thousand years ago.

I never met Mr Arnott-Toynbee because he died of heatstroke in some very hot country long before I qualified as a doctor and so when Mrs Arnott-Toynbee came to Bilbury, and bought a cottage facing the village green, she came alone – although she did bring with her several trunks full of mementoes, photographs and furniture which she and her husband had collected. Her arrival in the village pre-dated mine by some years.

Most of the many photographs which she brought with her were of him, her or both of them posing alongside local and visiting dignitaries.

There were several photographs of them with various ambassadors and one of them posing, along with half a dozen other people, with Sir Winston Churchill when he was the British Prime Minister. These pictures, each one carefully presented in a silver frame, were clearly considered to be the cream of the collection, and sufficient to represent the apogee of Mr Arnott-Toynbee's career.

Mrs Arnott-Toynbee was not a warm person; she was not the sort of old lady with whom one could chat or even share a joke. She wrote poetry and, for some reason best known to herself, wrote poems where the first words of each line rhymed. She wrote poems about slavery and pollution and I believe she disapproved of both, though I was never entirely sure of this and it was not possible to draw a conclusion from the poetry.

Years working in the diplomatic service had made her very conscious of her position. Even though it had been her husband who had been the diplomat she had allowed herself to acquire all the mannerisms usually associated with minor royalty. As a country doctor I was clearly considered to be a rather inferior sort of person;

probably fitting into her social hierarchy somewhere between one of the gardeners and an assistant cultural attaché. She was not exceptional in this. I remember once having a couple of former diplomatic corps employees as my patients. She had been a senior housekeeper but he had been a lowly security guard and decades after they had retired, she still treated him as though he were a minor functionary. She ordered him about as though she were royalty and he were a junior footman. She treated me as a servant. He, on the other hand, treated me as an equal.

Mrs Arnott-Toynbee had been ill for almost all her time in Bilbury but she had not been very ill.

She had most of the ailments usually associated with ladies of a certain age.

She was a little deaf, a little blind and a little dizzy on occasion. She had varicose veins which resulted in her ankles swelling and she had osteoarthritis in her hips and her knees. She had slightly raised blood pressure for which Dr Brownlow had prescribed medication (and which she would not allow me to change) and she suffered from chronic constipation which she herself treated with a daily bowl full of prunes. I tried on many occasions to explain to her that she had, over the years, eaten far too many prunes and that the dried plums had by now probably damaged the muscles of her bowel and created a new type of constipation. I suggested that she tried to wean herself off the morning bowl of fruit, perhaps simply cutting down the number of prunes per serving, but Mrs Arnott-Toynbee was a keen believer in the value of the prune as a digestive aid and she was not about to accept advice from a young doctor on the subject. What could I possibly know about the value of prunes? The laxative value of the prune can probably be traced back two thousand years.

These minor ailments were not threatening but they were inconvenient and Mrs Arnott-Toynbee rather leant on them; they were, in their way, essential to her because they helped explain her inability to do as much as she had done when she had been younger.

It was no longer her fault that she could not run everything as she had once run the social group for the diplomatic wives, it was the fault of her silly physical frailties. The illnesses were, it seemed to me, essential to her well-being. I suspected that if they were not taken seriously then she would probably go into a steep and serious decline for then she would have to come to terms with the fact that she was simply getting old. And so I always treated her as an invalid and I think that reassured her.

At the age of 93, Mrs Arnott-Toynbee developed cancer of the bowel and eventually it became clear that this was the condition that was going to kill her. Had the prunes damaged her bowel? I have no idea. Had the prunes masked her condition and delayed the point at which she consulted me for advice? Possibly.

She refused to go into hospital, or even into the Brownlow Country Hotel, and so that she could stay at home during her final weeks and days she hired a nurse from an agency in London. She had no relatives to call on since although Mrs Arnott-Toynbee had a daughter called Loki (named after the Norse god of Mischief, since she was born when Mrs Arnott-Toynbee was being terribly important in one of the Scandinavian countries) Loki had had nothing whatsoever to do with her mother for years and I had never seen her. The nurse, a sour woman in her forties, was hired to provide constant care and to this end she lived in a room in the house.

I visited the old lady two and sometimes three times a week and although there wasn't much I could do, I prescribed whatever medicines might ease her symptoms and help her through the final stage of her condition.

She was very near the end when she told me to sit down on the chair which had been placed beside her bed. She said she had something very important to tell me. I obediently sat down and waited.

'My cat Jeremy is twelve-years-old,' she told me. 'I have had him for all of that time and now that I am dying I do not want him to go to live with anyone else.'

I looked at her, frowning. I did not understand what she was telling me. Or, perhaps, I did not want to understand.

'I want you to give him an injection to put him to sleep,' she said. 'When the Viking kings died their servants were buried with them. I don't have any servants anymore and so I want my cat to be buried with me.'

I was given instructions to take the cat away, to inject him with something suitably lethal, to arrange for him to be cremated and to bring back the ashes in a small wooden box. Mrs Arnott-Toynbee had the small wooden box ready and waiting and she handed it to me when she had finished giving me my instructions.

I was as horrified as I think most people would be.

I took Jeremy, in a bamboo cat carrier, and the wooden box for his ashes and headed back to Bilbury Grange feeling very angry. How dare this damned woman decide to have her perfectly healthy cat sacrificed for her own vanity?

When I got back home I undid the catch on the door to the cat carrier and Jeremy strolled out, a little timid but nevertheless curious about his new surroundings. Jeremy was a short-haired cat, mainly black with white socks and a patch of white on his tummy. He looked like a feline gentleman ready for a night out on the tiles.

'Who's this?' asked Patsy.

I explained.

Patsy was as appalled as I had been.

We watched as Emily and Sophie walked around Jeremy and inspected him. After a few minutes they wandered over to their eating area. Jeremy followed. To our astonishment Emily and Sophie stood quite still while Jeremy lapped up some milk.

'They like him!' said Patsy, delighted.

It was clear to us both that whatever else happened, Jeremy would not be going back to Mrs Arnott-Toynbee in the little wooden box she had provided. Jeremy was now our third cat.

'What are you going to do about the box?' asked Patsy. 'Mrs Arnott-Toynbee is expecting to have Jeremy's ashes in her little box. You have to put something into there – she might take a look.'

That bit was easy. I walked up the garden and was gone no more than five minutes.

'She'll never know,' said Patsy, examining the box, when I returned.

'She'll have no idea,' I agreed. 'Ashes are ashes are ashes.'

Mrs Arnott-Toynbee died three days later and was buried clutching a small wooden box containing ash from our bonfire site.

The Old Railway Station

I have always had a fondness for trains in general and for branch lines and small railway stations in particular. You can sit quietly on a train and read a book. You can think, talk or work. You can eat and you can sleep if you are tired. Or you can, of course, look out of the window. Everywhere in the country has a view but some places have better views than others. A train journey gives the traveller a chance to look at all the available views without having to worry about road signs, traffic policemen or dangerous corners.

Moreover, it has, for many years, been my belief that the best way to see the heart and soul of a town is to arrive by train. The railway lines invariably run through the back part of the town, the scruffy bits, the engine of the town if you will.

From the carriage it is usually possible to see the rows of back to back terraced houses, the second-hand car lots, the small garages where grease-stained mechanics do clever things with recalcitrant engines and battered bodywork, the small industrial units where unseen workers produce Christmas crackers, plastic shoe horns, parts for motor cars and shop signs. Each small factory will have grown up out of some entrepreneur's ambition, enthusiasm and imagination and will have survived, and perhaps thrived, as a result of years of hard work and determination. When I see these small businesses I am always reminded that it is not easy to create a business and that the men and women who have built a new enterprise with their bare hands deserve more recognition than they receive.

Travellers who left a station in the great days of the railways would have invariably found a station hotel nearby; it would have been the smartest local hostelry. In the early decades of the 20th century, the local gentry would have their dinners and dances at the hotel. Organisations such as the Round Table would hold their meetings there. Wedding receptions, silver wedding celebrations and Christmas parties would all be held in the function room where remnants of burst balloons and streamers which had long ago been torn down and discarded would be visible; still tied to light fittings and attached to walls and beams with drawing pins. Successful travelling salesmen would stay at the local railway hotel as would a wide variety of visiting dignitaries.

Today, most of these once great hotels are a mere shadow of their former selves. Grubby, fading and declining they are now rather sad.

If there is still a railway station the hotel will probably be surviving. If the railway station has gone then the hotel will probably be on its last legs.

Either way the area near to the railway station will probably be rather run down.

Near the station there will be the sad remains of once-proud shops, formerly representing the posh end of the town's commercial possibilities, and, still visible, there will be beautifully made signs for the local pharmacy and drug store, a haberdasher's, a gentlemen's outfitters and so on. The shops will now be struggling to survive in a world which favours department stores and chain stores.

Close by there would be a junk shop, with old chairs and broken down washing machines displayed on the pavement in front. And there will be a record shop, with brightly coloured posters in the window and several empty shops which are awaiting 'development'.

Shoppers who have money to spend will take their purses, wallets and their shopping bags to the High Street, half a mile away, where they can find chain stores and shoe shops, jewellers and maybe a pet shop and an ironmongers.

The houses near to the railway station will be Victorian or Edwardian since most railway stations were built during the feverish years of Victoria's reign and very few railway stations were built after Edward VII's death. Each house, whether detached, semi-detached or terraced will have a pillared front gate and a few square feet of stained glass above the front door. The front garden will have been laid to lawn, with a few rose bushes standing to attention beside a crazy paving path and if a stable was required it would have been approached from a lane at the back of the house. The lane and the stables will have long ago disappeared and been replaced by a modern housing development, together with a school.

There will be a pub as well, of course. Probably called the Railway Inn or the King's Head and not as posh as the station hotel, it will cater for thirsty railway workers and for the men who worked in the factories situated alongside the railway lines into the town.

By the 1960s the pub would have been already declining; the red brick facade chipped and scarred and blackened with railway soot. By the 1970s the end would be in sight.

In my mind the railway station in any town is an important focal point; probably the most important focal point, certainly more vital than the town hall, the statue to a long-forgotten hero ('But what did he do in the Boer War, Daddy? And what was the Boer War?'), the ornamental fountain that has not worked since 1957, the floral clock which looks like all the other floral clocks in the world or the council buildings that look as if they were designed by a six-year-old architect using a cardboard box as his inspiration.

And so when a railway station closes, loses its purpose, and no longer reverberates to the sound of approaching trains, there is an inevitable sadness accompanying the death.

Some towns never recover from the loss of their railway link to the rest of the world; sinking slowly into a permanent state of lethargy, as though the absence of the rumble and hiss of trains approaching and departing has resulted in the place losing its life, its reason for living and its identity.

For those towns the closure of the railway station invariably marks the beginning of a long, slow, painful end. It is as though the town, having been symbolically cut off from the rest of the world, feels rejected; unworthy of a place in the greater scheme of things.

Bilbury had lost its railway station many years earlier but it was a village not a town and the loss had not had any damaging effect on the village or the community.

Indeed, visitors could be forgiven for not realising that Bilbury had once been served by a railway line at all. Many probably didn't realise that there had ever been a railway station in Bilbury at all.

Bilbury, and the surrounding area of North Devon, was one of the last districts in England to use wheeled vehicles. Up until the start of the 18th century, people in North Devon who wanted to be somewhere that they were not simply walked. And goods were transported by pack horse and by horse drawn sledge.

But in Victorian times, the enthusiasm for railway transport finally spread to North Devon and a line was built between

Barnstaple and Lynton. A narrow gauge line was built across the fields and a specially formed train company purchased some engines and a supply of coaches. As a result, trains had chugged into and out of Bilbury and some of them had actually stopped in the village for there had been a railway station too.

The station, which looked rather like one of those small railway stations which are used to decorate model railway layouts, had been called 'Bilbury Halt' because, like most smaller railway stations, the train only stopped there on request. Bilbury Halt was so small a station that it did not even appear on some of the railway maps of that period but it was, nevertheless, real enough and important to the villagers and to travellers and tourists. The stations between Barnstaple and Lynton were, in no particular order: Snapper Halt, Chelfham, Bratton Fleming, Bilbury Halt, Blackmoor, Parracombe Halt and Woody Bay.

If a passenger wanted to alight he would tell the conductor and the conductor would send a message to the driver. If a passenger wanted to board he would inform the station master who would 'halt' the train with the wave of a flag. The driver would look out of his cab to see if anyone wanted to board his train. Washing out the station master's green flag in a bowl of hot, soapy water was the nearest the rural railway station got to technology in those days.

The Lynton to Barnstaple railway, which served Bilbury Halt, first opened in 1898 but there were problems right from the start. Miscalculations meant that there were massive cost overruns and the money paid out for land, and as compensation, was four times the estimated budget. Worse still, the wise burghers of Lynton and Lynmouth insisted on having the Lynton railway station put in a position where it would not be visible either from Lynton or from the lower, twin village of Lynmouth. This was partly through a feeling that a railway station might mar the natural beauty of the locality and partly a result of the fact that a local landowner steadfastly refused to give permission for the line to be continued across his land to a more accessible spot. Sadly, the fact that the Lynton railway station was invisible from the twin villages also meant that it was pretty well inaccessible. Visitors who arrived on foot, as most did, either had to hire a carriage or else walk down a rough path known as Shamble Way which mostly consisted of rough stones, kept that way so that the ponies which carried luggage could find a foothold. The path, which was measured as having a 1 in 4 gradient, was hard work for anyone, let alone the elderly or the infirm, and it was considered so difficult that a handrail was fitted to help locals and travellers haul themselves up and steady themselves when going down.

The original aim was that travellers would be able to get from Barnstaple to Lynton in much less than the three hours that the mail coach took. But things didn't work out quite as planned. The train managed to travel from Barnstaple to Lynton in under two hours but it then took around an hour to travel from the station down to the beautiful village of Lynmouth, which was where most of the travellers and all of the holidaymakers wanted to go.

An attempt to bring holidaymakers from the resort of Ilfracombe to Lynton failed miserably. In 1903, a very early motorised charabanc service to Parracombe was abandoned when one of the drivers was arrested for driving his vehicle at 8 mph on a public road. The official speed limit on public highways had just been raised to 20 mph and it was widely thought that the local police and magistrates were simply trying to kill the railway in order to protect the business activities of the man who ran a coach and horses between the two towns and the company which, on calm days in summer, took holidaymakers by steamer from Ilfracombe to Lynton and back again.

When motor cars and charabancs started to appear in North Devon the death of the railway was inevitable. The death of the railway was pretty much confirmed when a meeting was held at Barnstaple to oppose the closure and all the delegates from Lynton arrived by car because it was faster and more convenient. Their arguments opposing the closure were easily dismissed.

The last train from Lynton to Barnstaple ran on the 29th of September 1935 and immediately after the train had passed through the intermediate stations the track was torn up. The engines, rolling stock, line and equipment were all sold in a sale held on the 15th of November 1935. All but one of the engines was sold for around £50 each and turned into scrap: the metal was salvaged, the wood was burned. The exception, an engine called Lew, went to Brazil to work on the plantations. Coaches were sold for as little as £9 each and covered wagons went for £4 apiece. One assorted lot consisting of signal boxes, lamp posts and telegraph wiring raised the unprincely sum of £7. The railway stations did not do much better. Blackmoor Station was sold for £700, Woody Bay station fetched £405 and both Bratton Fleming and Bilbury Halt were sold for £100 each.

Much of Britain's railway system, including many of the stations, were closed during the Beeching blitz in the 1960s, when a man called Dr Beeching, hired by the Government to rationalise the railway system and to ensure that only those stations which offered commercial profit were allowed to remain, decided that many lines and stations were surplus to requirements.

It is sometimes believed that it was Dr Beeching who was responsible for the closure of Bilbury Halt. Not guilty. Unhappily, Bilbury Halt did not even last as long as the 1960s. It died in 1935 with the rest of the railway line from Lynton to Barnstaple.

Many towns which lose their railway station, and which are removed from the railway network, allow themselves to sink into a deep and permanent depression. Bilbury, however, hardly noticed the loss of its railway station or its railway connection.

Although I was not living in Bilbury when the station was closed, I believe that the closure was, after a short period of mourning, met with celebration rather than dismay, relief rather than despair.

The fact is that Bilbury had never relied upon the railway and its loss was regarded by the villagers as a welcome rupture of an unnecessary link to the outside world. Bilbury has always stood alone, proud and independent, and if London no longer wanted to be connected to Bilbury then that was perfectly fine with Bilbury.

Frank Parsons, the current landlord of the village pub, the Duck and Puddle, remembers that his father, who ran the village pub in the 1930s, was unable to shed a tear when it was announced that the twice a day trains from Barnstaple to Bilbury would run no more.

As the village's only serious representative of the tourist industry, Mr Parsons might have been expected to regard the railway as an essential source of tourists; forever waiting for waves of potential new customers to bring freshly minted pound notes into the local economy. But, like the rest of the villagers, the old Mr Parsons was not terribly keen on the outside world and nor was he over keen on strangers who came to the village out of idle curiosity or because it was something to do on a dull or rainy day.

Things haven't changed much.

Today, the people of Bilbury are enormously welcoming to people who come to the village because they want to be in Bilbury, but they do not much care about people who arrive because they have nowhere better to be.

After I'd lived in Bilbury for a year or two I understood their attitude.

The good folk of Bilbury think of themselves as living in their own version of paradise.

If people want to come into the village then the villagers will welcome them with open arms, a crackling log fire in the grate, a plateful of steak and kidney pudding and a foaming glass of ale.

But if people prefer other versions of paradise then that is absolutely fine, too.

The Bilburians don't really want strangers wandering through their village just for the sake of it. They don't want them wandering about and alarming the wildlife in their brightly coloured kagools, discarding their sweet wrappers and crisp packets and generally making the place look too busy and untidy, when they would have just as soon been in villages such as Chipping Sodbury in the Cotswolds or Three Cocks in Wales.

Like thousands of other railway stations, the redundant and unwanted Bilbury Halt had been sold on the open market, auctioned off at a mass sale in London, offered and bought for a song and duly converted into a bijou holiday residence by a property developer who specialised in such projects and who swept into and out of the village without anyone knowing he'd been or gone. The new residence was duly photographed and advertised in *Country Life* magazine at a price that would have bought any three ordinary Bilbury cottages.

The now unnecessary railway tracks had been torn up and sold to scrap metal dealers from the North, who had carted them away on lorries, melted them down and sold them on to be turned into washing machines and garden gates.

The wooden sleepers, almost as thick and as heavy as tree trunks, were sold to a smart garden designer who wanted to use them for garden steps and for path edging. And the railway signs, including the 'Bilbury Halt' signs themselves, had been torn down, sold to indiscriminate railway memorabilia collectors, and duly dispersed to the far corners of the world where they would, no doubt, be displayed in garden sheds or tucked away at the back of overcrowded garages.

The new owners of Bilbury's former railway station were a couple who worked in London and who had purchased the station from the developers.

He was called Boris and he was a senior executive employed by a large, well-known charity with offices in central London; it was one of those charities which is more famous for its luxurious offices and expensive advertisements and marketing programmes rather than for any good work it might purport to do. This was, apparently, a post which required him to wear Italian silk suits when he was travelling to and from London (and, presumably, when he was in the capital) and to wear expensive, three piece suits in loud checks when he was 'down in the country'. When decked out in one of his checked suits he doubtless thought he looked like a country gentleman. Sadly, he looked more like a crooked bookie – the sort who will take the punters' money but disappear to Lanzarote when a big bet goes sour and it comes to paying out.

She was called Doris and she worked for the Home Office and apparently favoured tweed suits at all times.

Their surname was Hardley-Fitzwalter and they had two children, both girls, who were called Cello and Viola. They also had a small, very yappy dog, a Jack Russell terrier, whom they had, with a surprising lack of imagination, named Jack, and a Doberman Pinscher who was called Karl and looked as if he ate two postmen for breakfast every weekday morning and got through three a morning at the weekends.

The family drove to Devon in a large, green four wheel drive motor car called a Range Rover, which was, so Thumper told me, a posh version of the traditional Land Rover and which had apparently been on the market for a few years though no one in our part of Devon had ever seen one before. The Range Rover had already proved to be very popular with financially successful folk who spent most of their time in London and who took their car along to the car wash if they had to drive through a puddle. Country folk either couldn't afford them or considered them to be far too 'flash'; like green Wellington boots and two tone brogues. Not even Thumper had ever seen one before the arrival of the Hardley-Fitzwalter family.

The Hardley-Fitzwalter family did not usually consult me on medical matters, or indeed on any other matters. Nor, indeed, did they have much need for any other locally based services.

When the couple remodelled the railway station to suit their requirements they used a smart London architect, who also drove a Range Rover (his was a mustard coloured yellow) and a team of builders, carpenters, electricians and plumbers who drove down in convoy from somewhere called Islington and who stayed at a hotel in Barnstaple because the Duck and Puddle wasn't big enough to accommodate them all, smart enough to cater for their gentrified tastes or sufficiently important to have been awarded rosettes for culinary excellence. The villagers were amused by the fact that men who cut wood and mended leaky taps for a living required food that had been blessed with rosettes.

Since they never consulted me, I had never actually spoken to any members of the Hardley-Fitzwalters, though I had seen and recognised them from afar for their motor vehicle was easily recognisable, but I gathered from Patchy Fogg that although they did not come from Yorkshire, a county which is known to produce folk who pride themselves on their plain speaking, they nevertheless had absolutely no qualms about pointing out to strangers the precise extent of their shortcomings.

(The fine folk of Yorkshire, who exhibit many of the finer qualities of the English nation, do this proudly, generously and with unbridled enthusiasm and it is widely believed in southern England that anyone who is complacent, smug, over-confident, or suffering from hubristic tendencies, should be sent to Yorkshire for a week or two in order to bring him or her back down to earth. The Hardley-Fitzwalters had the Yorkshire straightforward way without the innate Yorkshire grit, honesty and decency which give that bluntness a fine quality.)

Patchy was the first to have met the Hardley-Fitzwalters for he had been consulted by them in his role as local antiques expert. The couple were keen collectors of objects d'art.

When they first called at his shop, Patchy had been delighted. He thought that he might be able to unload some of his 'sticky' stock – the stuff that discerning buyers do not want to buy and which hangs around for years, tying up capital. He had not long earlier taken delivery of a mixed lorry load of freshly made antiques, each one carefully hand finished by a team of skilled Chinese craftsmen, and the Hardley-Fitzwalters, who were awash with money but clearly had no taste or style, were just the sort of people he'd had in mind when he'd bought the stuff.

Ever since I've known him, Patchy has been selling quite remarkable antiques to discerning clients. He has sold the desk upon which Shakespeare wrote Hamlet at least seven times. He has also sold Shakespeare's best bed (not the second best bed which the playwright left to Anne Hathaway), the very chair Queen Victoria often sat in when discussing world affairs with Benjamin Disraeli and an ebony walking cane used by Lord Byron.

Patchy had, however, been more than slightly miffed, not to say offended, when the Londoners had sniffily announced that they didn't want to buy anything from him because, they told him bluntly, the quality of his merchandise would certainly not be up to their standards. (Patchy said that he had detected a shudder in Mrs Hardley-Fitzwalter's demeanour at the very thought of buying anything from a dealer operating in a tiny Devon village). Their sole reason for calling into his shop was to commission him to pick up some garden furniture which they had bought in Hungerford and which was too large, too heavy or too dirty to fit into the back of their Range Rover.

When Patchy had, not unreasonably, asked why the dealer in Hungerford hadn't been prepared to bring the pieces to Devon, Mrs Hardley-Fitzwalter told him, with undisguised disdain for Patchy, that the man in Hungerford was a proper antique dealer (she apparently managed to put inverted commas around the words 'proper antique dealer' when she pronounced them) who couldn't possibly be expected to go traipsing around the country delivering things. Patchy had immediately doubled his price for fetching the garden furniture, two oak benches and an oak table, which he later described as looking like Victorian stuff but nowhere near as well made. 'I could have sold them exactly the same furniture for less than the fee they paid me to bring the stuff from Hungerford,' he later told me, with a grin.

I met the Hardley-Fitzwalters when I was called in to see their daughter Viola.

When I arrived, I found that I could not manage to park the Rolls Royce in their parking area because the Range Rover was so badly parked that there was no room at all for any other vehicles. I had to leave my car in a gateway on the other side of the lane.

I was not invited into the main part of the house, or to sit down, but was allowed only into the hallway of the converted railway station.

'Viola suffers from asthma,' said Mrs Hardley-Fitzwalters. She was, as had been advertised, wearing a ghastly tweed suit. Underneath it she wore a cashmere sweater in a rather muted, earthy colour. A single row of pearls was visible. She wore comfortable, chunky, flat shoes which fastened with laces. I think she probably thought she looked like a country lady but to me she looked like a social worker who was stuck in the 1950s and had absolutely no interest in escaping. Looking at her I couldn't help wondering if she had ever been a carefree little girl, playing with dolls who took afternoon tea and hugging a teddy bear when she went to bed at night.

'I'm sorry to hear that,' I said politely.

'She requires regular treatment with an inhaler called Ventolin which is normally prescribed by our physician in Harley Street. Unfortunately, her inhaler has expired and she forgot to bring a replacement with her. We therefore require a replacement inhaler which, of course, we will need you to prescribe.'

'Where is Viola?' I asked. It seemed to me not entirely unreasonable that I should take a look at the patient for whom I was being asked to prescribe.

'She is doing her French homework,' said Mrs Hardley-Fitzwalters.

'May I see her for a moment, please?' I asked.

'Can't you just write out a prescription,' sighed Mrs Hardley-Fitzwalters, who was obviously not accustomed to having tradesmen talk back to her. 'We will, of course, pay you for a private prescription.' She paused and lifted her head a degree or two. 'We aren't health service patients.'

'I'm afraid I don't see patients privately,' I told her, though strictly speaking this was not entirely true since there are two elderly patients in the village who still regard the National Health Service as an unacceptable form of welfare and who insist on still being charged for consultations and medicines. I usually send them a bill once a year, charging £1 for a consultation and £2 for a home visit, and I give them the drugs they need. They never pay me and I never chase them for the money. 'But I will need to see Viola if I am going to prescribe for her.'

Mrs Hardley-Fitzwalters huffed and puffed, and tutted a bit too, as though I was being entirely unreasonable, but turned and disappeared, leaving me still standing in the hallway. I was beginning to feel like a boy scout trying to rustle up business for Bob-A-Job-Week.

A couple of minutes later Mrs Hardley-Fitzwalters reappeared, followed by a little girl who looked about six or seven-years-old. She was dressed in a dark blue dress, dark blue socks and black patent leather shoes. Her hair, which was cut short, was as neat as if she'd just come from the hairdressers and she was as perfect and as spotless as a brand new doll just taken out of the box.

'This is Viola,' said Mrs Hardley-Fitzwalters.

I said hello to the little girl and introduced myself. The little girl, who seemed very self-assured, said hello back and held out a hand for me to shake. I shook it.

'How are you?' I asked.

'I suffer from bronchial asthma,' said the little girl. We were still standing in the hall. I thought about asking if we could go somewhere a little comfortable but decided that if Mrs Hardley-Fitzwalters wanted to continue in the hallway then that is where we would stay.

'How long have you suffered from asthma?' I asked.

'For two years.'

'What symptoms do you have?'

'I wheeze.'

'How often do you wheeze?'

'Quite a lot of the time,' replied Viola. 'But it only happens when we are at home.'

'In London?'

She nodded.

'Our doctor in London has asked all these questions,' said Mrs Hardley-Fitzwalters, impatiently. 'He is a very eminent physician. He treats quite a few titled people and looks after guests, including foreigners, at some of the large London hotels.'

'Does your doctor think that Viola's asthma might be stress related?' I asked. 'Is Viola more relaxed when you're down here in Devon? Is she more anxious in London?'

'Good heavens, no!' said Mrs Hardley-Fitzwalters. 'Viola doesn't suffer from anxiety in the slightest.'

'No school problems?'

'Absolutely not! Viola and Cello go to a very exclusive private school near our home.'

'But Viola doesn't suffer from asthma when you're staying in the country?'

'She doesn't,' admitted Mrs Hardley-Fitzwalters, reluctantly. 'But she might. Are you going to prescribe a Ventolin inhaler for her? Or do we have to call someone else? Viola has to use her inhaler three times a day. Every day. If I have to call someone else to provide us with what we need, I will certainly make a formal complaint about you. I believe even doctors in the country are obliged to provide treatment for their patients, are they not?'

'They certainly are,' I replied. 'But treating patients unnecessarily is frowned upon in some circles.'

Much to her mother's annoyance, I then listened to Viola's chest. I could hear nothing abnormal. There wasn't even the slightest wheeze. Despite the mother's demands I was reluctant to hand out another prescription for an inhaler for although enormously helpful when they are needed these things can easily do more harm than good – particularly when used unnecessarily. Over the years, countless millions of patients have been made well by having their prescriptions for addictive drugs such as bromides, barbiturates or benzodiazepines slowly withdrawn. The side effects produced by such drugs can be infinitely worse than the symptoms which triggered their use in the first place. Asthma inhalers probably aren't addictive in the way that psychotropic drugs can be, but psychological addictions can easily develop – sometimes in a relative as much as the patient. An anxious mother or father sees that a child's wheezing is banished with the aid of an inhaler and so assumes that the inhaler should be used three, four or five times a day in order to keep the wheezing at bay. And thus the addiction develops and the child, and its parents, feel they cannot exist without the drug.

Suddenly, something occurred to me.

'Who does your laundry when you're here in Devon?' I asked.

I have no idea what made me ask the question. A combination of intuition and experience, I suppose. I'd seen a similar case sometime in the past.

Mrs Hardley-Fitzwalters blushed. 'I do,' she said. 'We have a very expensive machine. We did try to find a woman to help but it is very difficult down here to find such people with the appropriate references.'

'And in London?'

'I have a woman to do the housework,' she announced as if it would be absurd for me to think otherwise.

'Do you use the same washing powder in London as you use here?'

'Sadly no,' said Mrs Hardley-Fitzwalters impatiently. 'In London we use a special biological washing powder but the local store here in Bilbury doesn't stock it and the man there refuses to order it in for us. We have to buy the detergent he sells to the other people.'

'You don't bring your detergent with you from London?'

'We bring most of our food with us,' she said. 'But I thought we ought to be able to obtain basic necessities locally – soaps and such like.' She paused. 'Maybe we should bring all our things from London,' she sniffed. 'Harrods deliver our groceries,' she told me inconsequentially.

'I certainly don't think you should bring everything from London,' I said. 'If Viola only suffers from asthma when you are in London then there's a very good chance that it is the washing powder you use there which is causing the problem.'

Mrs Hardley-Fitzwalters looked at me and frowned. She seemed startled at the suggestion.

'Ventolin is a powerful drug,' I told her. 'It would be much better for Viola if she could manage without it.'

'You mean that you're suggesting that Viola's asthma could be caused by our washing powder?'

'It happens quite often,' I told her. I'd read about it in one of the medical journals.

'Why didn't our London doctor tell me that?'

I wasn't quite sure how to answer that.

'If that is the case then I shall instruct our solicitors to take action against the manufacturer of the washing powder,' she said.

'I'm not sure that will do much good,' I said. 'Soap powder manufacturers often warn that their products can cause these problems. It's in the small print.'

'So, if you're right, what do we do?'

'Change your washing powder in London. Use the powder you use down here in Devon. See what happens over the next few days. If Viola starts to wheeze, call me and I'll listen to her chest again. If she doesn't wheeze then she can probably stop using the inhaler if you just change your powder in London.'

Mrs Hardley-Fitzwalters looked at me suspiciously, as though concerned that I was tricking her in some way.

Just then the door opened and a man I assumed to be her husband burst in. He was accompanied by two dogs and carrying two unframed paintings. The dogs, which were not on leads, ran up to me barking and growling. I stood still and glowered at them. I hate dogs which do that but I hate the owners even more.

'Just look at these!' said Mr Hardley-Fitzwalters to his wife. He sounded very excited and ignored me completely. 'I got these from that dealer in the village. The man is an idiot. He didn't realise what these are!'

Mrs Hardley-Fitzwalters examined the paintings her husband had brought home. 'They're both by Chagall!' she said, very excited. Her daughter's problem was now forgotten.

'The chappie in the shop, Fogg I think his name is, didn't have the faintest what he'd got. He sold me the pair for £500 each. He wanted cash, as these chappies always do, so I drove into Barnstaple and went to the bank.'

Mrs Hardley-Fitzwalters was examining the pictures. 'They're not signed,' she said.

'Doesn't matter,' replied her husband. 'You can tell who did them just by looking. The colours, the content and the brushwork are all absolutely unmistakeable. They're pure Chagall – he didn't always sign his stuff – especially the early work.'

The darned dogs were still barking and snarling. They were very unpleasant creatures.

'What do you think they're worth?' Mrs Hardley-Fitzwalters asked her husband.

'Heaven knows. Millions! The big auction houses will be falling over themselves to sell these. I must go back to that Fogg's place next time we come down. I bet he's got more good stuff hidden away in his scruffy little shack.'

I coughed and picked up my bag. 'I'll be going,' I said.

Mr Hardley-Fitzwalters, who still hadn't acknowledged my presence, looked at me, puzzled. 'Who are you?'

'Oh this is just the village doctor,' said Mrs Hardley-Fitzwalters dismissively. 'He's going.'

I couldn't help noticing the way she had added the word 'village' in front of the word 'doctor'. Village idiot, village doctor.

'That's not your Roller parked outside, is it?' asked Mr Hardley-Fitzwalters.

I admitted that it was my Rolls Royce.

'Our doctor in London has got a brand new one,' said the charity boss dismissively. 'Latest model, packed with all the gizmos. He has a new one every year.'

The Doberman, which had been staring at me and merely growling suddenly started barking again and bared its teeth. I instinctively flinched and moved back a few inches.

'Oh, he won't hurt you,' said Mr Hardley-Fitzwalters, 'he never bites.' He patted the Doberman on its back. The dog then turned its head and growled at him. 'Both the dogs love it down here,' he told me, 'we let them go a bit wild because they can go for long runs across the fields.' He turned to his wife and laughed as he told her how the dogs had chased a flock of sheep around one of the fields they'd crossed.

'I don't think the local farmers like dogs chasing their sheep,' I commented.

'Well they can just jolly well lump it!' said Mr Hardley-Fitzwalters.

I thought of telling him that farmers have the legal right to shoot dogs which worry their livestock but I really didn't want to be there any longer so I told them to call me again if Viola had any wheezing and then I left.

Part of me felt that I ought to tell Mr Kennett, my father-in-law, that I thought I knew whose dogs had killed his sheep. But I had acquired this knowledge as a doctor and I have always taken the principle of confidentiality very seriously.

I hadn't expected them to be grateful but I hadn't expected them to be quite so dismissive; contemptuous almost.

As I walked to the car I could hear the badly behaved dogs still barking inside the house; they had no better manners than their owners.

When the family left to go back to London a few days later I hadn't heard from them again, so I assumed that Viola's asthma had disappeared.

The Old Hoover

Patsy and I were in the kitchen having a quiet lunch. The babies were both fast asleep, the telephone had been quiet for so long that I had twice lifted the receiver from the cradle to check that it was still working and that we hadn't been cut off (an eventuality which sometimes happens in the country, where a falling tree can result in downed lines and no telephone service for days) and we were contemplating a pleasant hour or so in the garden before the evening surgery was due to start.

Suddenly, the peace of the day was shattered by a hammering at the back door.

Before either of us could speak, the door was flung open and Adrienne, Patsy's sister and now Mrs Fogg, was standing beside us looking for all the world as though the end was considerably closer than nigh. She was red-faced and had clearly been crying. Patsy and I jumped up. Patsy gave her sister a hug. I stood there feeling, and doubtless looking, useless. After a few moments I sat down again.

It took two cups of tea, a large piece of apple and rhubarb pie (with both custard and ice cream) and a medium sized sherry before Adrienne, who is, at the best of times excitable and who can occasionally wander onto the hysterical side of over-reaction, had calmed down enough to tell us what had brought her crashing through our back door.

'For as long as I can remember I've always kept my jewellery and my savings in an old vacuum cleaner,' she told us. 'The hoover hasn't worked for years and years but when I lived at mum and dad's place they never threw it out and it lived at the back of the cupboard under the stairs. I always thought it was a good place to store my valuables because no one used it and what burglar would think of stealing or looking inside a clapped out old hoover?'

It occurred to me that this was indeed an excellent hiding place for valuables.

'What jewellery?' asked Patsy. 'I didn't know you'd got any valuable jewellery.'

'Well, it's perhaps not valuable to anyone else,' admitted Adrienne. 'But it's valuable to me. There's an old brooch that used to belong to grandma, a bracelet Mum and Dad bought me when I was twelve, a ring I got in a cracker when I was six, a necklace you bought me for my 21st birthday and a few bits and pieces Patchy has given me over the years. And there was £57 in cash in there. It was my sort of safe deposit box.'

'So what's happened?' asked Patsy.

'When Patchy and I got married and I moved into his house I took the old vacuum cleaner with me. Mum and Dad didn't want it because it didn't work so they didn't mind my having it. I kept it with Patchy's old hoover in the cupboard under the stairs. That's where everyone keeps their hoover isn't it?'

'We keep ours in a cupboard in the boot room,' said Patsy.

Inwardly I winced.

Adrienne is rather competitive, particularly with her sister, and doesn't like the fact that Patsy and I live in a bigger house which, now that we have got rid of the woodworm and the dry rot, has a boot room, a butler's pantry and a flower room rather than just a cupboard under the stairs. My wife and her sister get on well most of the time, and love each other very much, but Adrienne can be a little explosive, and perhaps a trifle potty, at times. At her wedding she managed to poison most of the guests by serving up mushrooms she'd picked herself. I have just the faintest suspicion that there may, occasionally, be a tinge of mild jealousy in the relationship between the two sisters.

'Well, we haven't got a boot room,' said Adrienne, in a huffy, why would anyone want one of those, sort of way. 'So we keep our hoover under the stairs.'

'You've got a conservatory and we haven't,' Patsy pointed out.

'You've got stables,' said Adrienne. 'And a lake.'

'You've got four garages,' said Patsy.

'Yes, but Patchy uses them to store antiques. They're really just for business. They're his shop. You've got a Rolls Royce.' Adrienne was clearly feeling a little better.

'It's a very old Rolls Royce,' said Patsy. 'It was Dr Brownlow's. It only does about eight miles to the gallon so it costs a fortune to run.'

I thought I ought to intervene before the competitive conversation got completely out of hand. I did not think it worthwhile pointing out that after the local garage had done something inexplicable to the carburettor I had managed to get nearly ten miles a gallon out of the old car.

'So,' I said, 'what happened to the hoover containing all your jewellery?'

'And £57 in cash,' added Adrienne.

'And £57 in cash,' I agreed. 'What happened to the hoover? Has someone stolen it?'

'No. Why would anyone steal an old hoover that doesn't work? That would be daft.'

I agreed that it would be a daft thing to do. It occurred to me, but I did not say, that people seem to do daft things all the time.

'Patchy got rid of it,' said Adrienne, and burst into tears again.

'Why on earth did he do that?' asked Patsy.

'He threw out both of the old ones. The one he had when I married him, and which sort of worked, and which I've been using, and the old one which I brought from Mum and Dad's and which didn't work.'

'Why did he throw out the one which worked?'

'It didn't work very well,' admitted Adrienne. 'It made a bit of a funny noise and there was a sort of burning smell. So he bought me a new one as a sort of early birthday present.'

I closed my eyes and wondered if Patsy would say anything about Patchy buying her sister a vacuum cleaner as a birthday present. Patchy isn't mean but he can be careful. And he's not what I would call a natural romantic. It took Thumper and me three hours to persuade him that an ironing board, complete with second hand iron, would not make an acceptable substitute for an engagement ring.

'What sort of funny noise?' asked Patsy. I gave thanks. It seemed that she hadn't noticed that Patchy had bought the cleaner for Adrienne's birthday.

'I don't know. Just a funny noise. Smoke came out of it and sometimes there were little flames and sparky things. Patchy said he thought the motor was tired and over-heating.'

'Do motors get tired?' asked Patsy.

'Patchy probably meant it was worn out,' I explained.

'And Patchy didn't know that you stored your jewellery, and £57, in your Mum and Dad's old hoover?'

Adrienne shook her head.

'What did he do with it?'

'I don't know,' admitted Adrienne. 'Most people would have probably thrown them out into the rubbish but Patchy...'

She didn't need to finish the sentence. Patchy, like many of the people I now know, does not easily throw things away. He prefers to sell his rubbish. He stores his old newspapers and sells them to a man who takes them to a factory where they are pulped and turned back into useful paper. He has a large boxful of old light-bulbs which he firmly believes he will one day be able to sell to someone. Patchy was a trifle sneery when Peter Marshall sold the contents of his old shed but behind the sneer there was a good deal of admiration.

'Haven't you asked him what he did with them?'

'I'm too embarrassed,' said Adrienne. 'I did ask him where it had gone and he said he'd got rid of it and then he showed me the new one he'd bought.' She bit her lip and looked down. 'He'd think I was daft if I told him I kept all my valuables in an old hoover. He's always telling me that I should keep all my valuables in the safe.'

'Well at least he bought you a new hoover for your birthday,' said Patsy, who had noticed after all. 'As a present,' she added unnecessarily.

'It's not actually new, new,' said Adrienne. 'It wasn't in a box or anything like that. He got it from a house clearance sale. But it's as good as new and Patchy said he got it for a very good price. And there are lots of things to attach to it if you want to clean under sofas or behind the fridge. We got all those bits in a plastic bag.'

'The attachments,' said Patsy.

Adrienne looked at her.

'That's what they call them,' said Patsy. 'The bits that you fix onto the vacuum cleaner so that you can clean under sofas and things are the attachments.'

I couldn't help wondering why anyone would want to clean under a sofa but I kept quiet about that. I've always thought that what is under the sofa is better kept under the sofa.

'I also kept our wedding papers and my driving licence in there,' said Adrienne. 'And the flower Patchy wore in his button hole when we got married. It's in a paper bag to keep it safe. The inside of the old hoover is quite clean. I brushed it all out before I started using it as my hiding place.' She started to cry again. 'This is the most awful thing that could ever happen to me,' she said through her sobs.

I was tempted to point out that if this was the worst thing that ever happened to her then her life would have been a breeze. I decided some years ago that real pressure is having to decide whether to choose chemotherapy or radiotherapy for yourself or a loved one. Most other problems are hardly worth a damn; they can probably be ignored or else they will go away with time. But I didn't think that either Adrienne or Patsy were ready for my brand of philosophy.

'Well, we need to find out what Patchy did with the old hoovers and then we need to get them back,' I said firmly, standing up. The quiet afternoon in the garden was now a forgotten dream.

'Would anyone like a home-made scone?' asked Patsy, who has a talent for avoiding problems, a talent for delaying action and a talent for baking which puts everyone else's talents into the shade.

'Oh yes,' said Adrienne instantly. 'But don't forget to put the jam on first.'

One of the first things Patsy taught me when we got married was that when making a Devon cream tea it was vital to put the cream onto the scone before adding the jam. In Cornwall, they do things the other way round: putting the jam onto the scone before the cream. Adrienne has no Cornish roots, and as far as I know has only been there once when she went to Padstow for a slightly discoloured weekend with a tractor salesman from Liskeard, but she has always been rebellious and has insisted on having her scones the Cornish way since she was sixteen.

And so Patsy took some scones and a pot of strawberry jam from the cupboard and a pot of cream from the fridge, put the kettle on and made us a huge Devon cream tea. It was only twenty minutes since I'd had my lunch but who can turn down a Devon cream tea – especially when Patsy made the scones?

You can't talk about things like missing vacuum cleaners and lost valuables when you're eating scones with cream and jam (I think there is probably a by-law forbidding such behaviour within the boundaries of the county of Devon) so we ate in silence.

Actually, it wasn't complete silence because Patsy and Adrienne talked about our babies for a while. It's strange having two young babies because when you mention 'babies' to strangers they assume they must be twins whereas, in fact, our oldest is eighteen months older than our youngest. I am well aware that in the blink of an eye they'll be starting school, climbing trees and sticking posters up on their bedroom walls but for the moment they're still babies.

In the end, of course, the pleasant delaying tactics came to an end, the plate contained no more scones and the cream seemed to have evaporated. There was jam left in the pot but nothing upon which to spread it.

'So,' I said, 'where do you think the vacuum cleaner could be?'

It was immediately apparent that neither my wife nor my sister-in-law welcomed this reminder of the awful reality which had brought Adrienne to our door. They looked at me, looked at each other and sighed.

'I think he might have sold both of them to 'Jack' Ladd,' said Adrienne.

I groaned but tried not to make a sound as I did so.

Jack Ladd, whose real name is Ivan Ladd but who is known as 'Jack' (as in Jack the Lad) calls himself a dealer but he is the biggest crook in North Devon and that, believe me, is no mean compliment.

Jack is convinced that the world is desperate to rip him off and is determined that if there is going to be any ripping done then he will be the one to do it. The last time I saw him he was in Ilfracombe selling seaweed to tourists. He had the seaweed bagged up and was selling it by the pound as a cure for arthritis. Each pound of seaweed came with a leaflet containing enthusiastic quotes from sufferers who had been able to throw away their crutches and put their wheelchairs into the garage as a result of just a few weeks' treatment. Jack told his customers they had to boil the stuff and inhale the vapour, and he was doing surprisingly good business. The funny thing was that the power of the placebo effect is so great that Jack's seaweed cure probably did more good (and less harm) than most of the dangerous pills doctors prescribe. Having said this it is, I think, only fair to point out that Jack is a patient of mine and he readily accepts the regular prescriptions for anti-inflammatory drugs which I give to him for his own arthritis. I once had to give him a medical examination for an insurance policy. 'Can you touch your toes without bending your knees?' I asked him. 'I haven't the foggiest,' he said, looking puzzled, 'but why on earth would I want to do that?'

'You're not sure he sold them to Jack?' I said to Adrienne.

She shook her head.

'I'll ring Patchy,' I said. I didn't want to drive all the way to Jack Ladd's place only to find that he knew nothing about the vacuum cleaners.

I left Patsy and Adrienne alone and went into my surgery to call Patchy. He was where I thought he would be – at the Duck and Puddle, having rehydration therapy.

I was in a bit of difficulty, of course, because I wasn't supposed to tell Patchy that Adrienne had hidden her jewellery and £57 in her old vacuum cleaner.

'Patsy has an old vacuum cleaner that she wants to get rid of,' I said when Frank had handed the phone to Patchy. 'It seems a pity to throw it away. Do you know anyone who's likely to buy it? It might be worth a couple of quid.'

'Try Jack Ladd,' said Patchy immediately. 'He'll probably buy it. I sold him two clapped out old vacuum cleaners this morning. He paid me £2 for the pair. Haven't got the foggiest what he's going to do with them. One of them works a bit so he can probably flog it on to some poor punter.'

I thanked him, went back to the kitchen and told Patsy and Adrienne the good news. 'I forgot to ask where Jack works these days,' I added, cursing myself.

'He has a workshop in Blasting Daily now,' said Adrienne.

Patsy and I looked at her. 'Where did you say?' asked Patsy.

'Blasting Daily,' repeated Adrienne. 'It's a village on the road to Exeter.'

'Blasting Daily isn't a village,' I said.

'Of course it is,' insisted Adrienne. 'There's a big sign.'

'That's just a warning sign telling people that the quarry does blasting every day,' I explained.

'Well, it looks like a road sign,' said Adrienne indignantly. 'It's a big sign with lettering on it, just like a road sign.' She frowned and thought for a while. 'I thought it was a funny name for a village,' she admitted, 'but there's a village down near Sidmouth called Cat and Fiddle and there's a place in the Cotswolds called Loose Chippings.'

'There isn't a place called Loose Chippings,' I said, rather wearily. Patsy's sister is a lovely lady but when she was made, I think the Great Creator got all her wiring mixed up. 'There's a Chipping Campden, a Chipping Sodbury and Chipping Norton. Chipping is an old English word for 'market'. But there isn't a village called Loose Chippings.'

'I've seen signs for Loose Chippings,' said Patsy, supporting her sister. 'I think it is a village. We used to go through it often when we were girls. We had an aunt who lived in Bourton-on-the-Water.'

'It's just a sign they put up when they've been repairing the road,' I said, with commendable patience.

Patsy looked unconvinced. 'Are you sure?'

'Pretty sure.'

'So that probably explains why the village always seems to be in a different place?'

'It probably does,' I agreed.

'Ah,' said Patsy. 'I had noticed that it seemed to move about. One day we would see it when we went to Cirencester and then another day we'd see it when we went to Cheltenham. But the Cotswolds are very confusing. I never know where I am or where I'm going.'

'I'll buy you a compass from Peter Marshall's shop,' I promised.

'Don't you dare!' said Patsy, laughing. 'The last lot he sold all pointed the wrong way. They put the magnet bit on the wrong end of the needle so the little arrow thing always seemed to point south.'

'I went to Peter Marshall's to buy a toasting fork last week,' said Adrienne. 'All the toasters that we got for our wedding stopped working and so I thought I'd make toast in front of the fire. But Patchy was quite cross and made me take the fork back. He said it was just an ordinary fork and that you'd get your hands burnt if you used it to make toast.'

'All those toasters stopped working?'

'All of them,' said Adrienne with a nod. 'They caught fire, one by one. Patchy said he thought there was a fault in the wiring.'

Just about everyone in the village had given Adrienne and Patchy a toaster as a wedding present. We'd bought them cheaply from Peter Marshall. We gave the happy couple proper presents later, for the toasters were a joke. Still, I hadn't thought they'd all break down so quickly.

'I'll go and see Jack,' I told them.

'We were just kidding about there being a place called Loose Chippings,' said Patsy.

I looked at her. I didn't think I believed her but I wasn't entirely sure. 'What does your vacuum cleaner look like?' I asked Adrienne. 'The one with all the stuff hidden inside it.'

'It's an upright which is sort of grey and has a long lead attached to it,' Adrienne said. 'It's dusty on the outside but quite clean inside.'

I sighed. 'You'd better come with me,' I told her. 'If Jack is collecting vacuum cleaners he's probably got a hundred that match that description – apart from the 'clean inside' bit.'

So Adrienne and I (together with Ben) climbed into the Rolls Royce and headed off for the picturesque Devon village of Blasting Daily in the hope that we might be in time to rescue the missing vacuum cleaner and its assorted contents.

Jack Ladd, the new owner of Adrienne's vacuum cleaner, is somewhere between 30 and 100-years-old. His medical records are incomplete and I doubt if any official body has any record of his existence, let alone his date of birth. He is the sort of man who shaves once a month, last bathed a week last Wednesday and keeps his dog on a piece of string rather than a leash not because he spends all his money on beer and cigarettes but because he cannot see the point in spending money on a dog lead when a piece of string will serve the same purpose perfectly well.

Actually, I don't know what it is about the dog owners of Devon but hardly any of them ever seem to buy proper leads for their animals. Mrs Marigold Stickers (whose husband was christened Cedric but is, inevitably, known by one and all as Bill) has been seen using an old stocking as a lead and Peter Marshall once told me that Mrs Felicity Dingle, Bilbury's world renowned shoe designer, once came into his shop with her dog at the other end of a substantial, black, lacy brassiere. She told him that she had come out without a dog lead and then realised that the field through which she intended to walk was full of sheep and lambs. Rather than test her dog's good reputation, and her own reputation as a caring county woman, she decided that she would need to create a lead out of some article of clothing. Since she was wearing socks rather than stockings or tights, and her coat was fastened with buttons rather than a belt, she decided that she had to sacrifice an item which, in a quiz at the Duck and Puddle, she once described as her most valuable possession (and the one item she would grab if her house caught fire) in the cause of dog control and good neighbourly relations.

We found Jack spraying artificial rust onto an ancient perambulator.

'Hello, Jack,' I said, thinking it probably best if I did the negotiating. Jack is a well-known misogynist and I felt certain he would take advantage of my sister-in-law if she attempted to negotiate with Jack herself. Besides, I have often fancied that I could wheel and deal as well as anyone in Bilbury if I had the chance. Thumper, Patchy and Peter Marshall always seem to think that they're the only ones who can make a few bob buying and selling things. But how difficult can it be?

'The Germans love these old prams,' he explained. 'But they like them rusty so that they can restore them and feel they've done something useful. Putting rust on doubles the price I can get.'

'Patchy Fogg sold you a couple of vacuum cleaners this morning,' I said, 'but he didn't know that they'd got sentimental value. Adrienne would like to buy them back.' This hadn't come out quite as I had intended and I immediately realised that I had put myself into a hopeless negotiating position.

Jack grunted something incomprehensible.

'They've been in her family for a long while and she didn't want to get rid of them,' I explained, making things worse.

'I've got a buyer,' said Jack, stopping what he was doing and standing back to examine his handiwork. 'There's quite a market for old vacuum cleaners. People collect them.'

I looked at him disbelievingly. 'Who on earth collects old vacuum cleaners?'

'You'd be surprised,' he said, 'I sell a lot of stuff to museums of household appliances.'

'You're kidding!'

'Not at all,' said Jack. 'Collecting old vacuum cleaners and washing machines is all the rage these days. In Germany there's a Museum von Haushaltsgeraten. And in Sweden there's the Museet av Hushallsapparater.' He pronounced these names as though he really knew what he was talking about. I can never, ever tell when Jack is having me on. He's such a good liar he would have made a great politician.

'How much do they pay for a vacuum cleaner?' I asked him, knowing that the answer was going to upset me.

'Oh £40 or £50 each,' said Jack with an unconcerned air.

'What?' I demanded. 'That's crazy! You can buy a brand new vacuum cleaner for far less than that.'

'It's age and patina they're buying,' said Jack, wagging a knowledgeable finger. 'These old cleaners are rare, you see.'

I sighed. I always know when I am defeated. I turned to Adrienne. 'Which is the one you want?' I asked her quietly.

Adrienne pointed to one of the vacuum cleaners.

'How much do you want for that one?' I asked Jack.

He looked at the vacuum cleaner, picked it up, and examined it. '£60, since it's you, doctor.'

'How much for anyone else?' I asked.

'£50,' said Jack. He laughed. 'No, go on, I'm teasing you,' he said. 'You can have it for £50.'

'That's crazy!' I said.

'Take it or leave it,' said Jack with a shrug.

'We'll take it,' I sighed. I took out my wallet and found that I only had £30. I turned to Adrienne. 'Can you lend me £20 to buy back your vacuum cleaner?'

Adrienne opened her handbag, took out her purse and gave me two £10 notes. 'Congratulations,' she said drily. 'Your negotiating skills are awesome.'

I glared at her and handed the £50 to Jack. He handed me the vacuum cleaner. 'Do you want to buy an old washing machine?' he asked. 'I've got one that was made in 1952. It doesn't work but it would make a great talking point in your new museum.'

I glared at him. 'One of these days,' I warned him, 'you'll cut yourself and need stitching up.'

'Don't worry about me,' said Jack, laughing.

'My stuff isn't here,' said Adrienne. She had opened up the vacuum cleaner and looked inside.

I turned to Jack. 'Did you find anything inside the hoover?'

He shook his head and seemed genuinely puzzled. 'Why on earth would I bother looking inside it?'

'I'll give you another £50 for the things that were inside,' said Adrienne desperately. 'The jewels are all paste. Nothing is valuable. But they're worth that much to me.'

'Honest, love,' said Jack, 'I haven't looked inside and I haven't taken anything out.'

Strangely, I believed him. 'Can I sell this damned thing back to you?'

He looked at me and looked at the vacuum cleaner. 'It doesn't work,' he said.

'I know,' I said. 'But you can sell it to a museum.'

He laughed. 'You're kidding! Who is going to buy this piece of rubbish?'

'But you said…'

'That was when I was selling it,' said Jack, 'now you want me to buy it. I'll give you a quid in the hope that I can get it working.'

I stared at him for a full thirty seconds and then handed him the cleaner. He gave me a £1 in coins. 'Let me give you a tip, doctor,' said Jack, 'and you can have this for free.'

I looked at him and waited.

'Stick to doctoring,' he said.

Adrienne and I drove back to Bilbury in silence. She asked me to take her home.

As we drew up in front of their home, Patchy came out to see us. He was smiling and carrying a plastic bag. When Adrienne got out of the car he handed her the bag. She looked inside and her expression changed dramatically. 'My jewels!' she cried.

'And £57,' said Patchy. 'And our marriage licence. Everything is there. If you want to put them somewhere then I suggest you put them into the floor safe in the bedroom. Hiding them in an old hoover is daft.'

Adrienne threw her arms around his neck and kissed him. She then ran indoors to put her treasures away.

'I paid £50 for that damned old hoover,' I told Patchy.

'Teach you a lesson,' said Patchy, with a wink. 'Stick to doctoring.'

I drove home.

'Someone put this through the letter box,' said Patsy, handing me a grubby brown envelope.

I opened the envelope. There was £50 in notes inside.

'Did you see who left it?' I asked. I put £20 aside to give back to Adrienne.

'It was someone on a motorbike. He had a helmet on but he looked like Jack Ladd,' said Patsy. 'I recognised the jacket. He's had that jacket since I was a little girl.' She looked puzzled. 'What's this all about?'

'Oh, nothing much. Adrienne and I have both been taught a lesson, that's all,' I told her, feeling rather embarrassed.

A Small Victory

I was examining Mrs Pearce's left knee when the noise of a jet hurtling overhead made both of us jump. The noise also made Mrs Pearce scream in alarm and sit upright. She had been reclining while I examined her and was so startled by the noise that she lost her balance and very nearly rolled off the couch.

Startled by the noise of the jet and my patient's scream, I jumped back rather suddenly and knocked over the screen which stands near to the examination couch in order to give patients privacy when they undress and dress themselves. Mrs Pearce's voluminous outer garments, festooned over the screen, fell with it. Mrs Pearce feels the cold and knows that the best way to keep out the cold is to wear several layers of clothing.

Mrs Pearce is a spiritualist who is famous for her ability to see into the past. We've had one or two of these in North Devon in recent years. In addition to holding meetings and providing private 'readings', Mrs Pearce grows, nurtures and admires a small but impressive collection of cacti. It is, she has told me several times, the most extensive cacti collection in North Devon. She also attends Iolanthe Fielding's belly dancing classes which are held in Kentisbury Village Hall.

I once attended one of Mrs Pearce's meetings in a hall in Combe Martin. It was very well patronised and at 50 pence a head entrance fee, she probably did well for herself.

'Do I have anyone in the room for whom the letter E has meaning?' she asked.

About two dozen people put their hands up.

'A male,' said Mrs Pearce and half the hands went down.

'He was quite old when he died.' A third of the remaining hands disappeared.

And by this simple, logical method she narrowed down the possibilities to a woman who lived in the village of Berrynarbor.

'There was a connection to the railways,' said Mrs Pearce firmly. Her eyes were now closed and she was clearly 'channelling'.

I thought that the business about the railways was a safe bet since a huge number of people of that age worked on the railways, travelled by rail or had a connection with someone who did.

But, disappointingly, the woman from Berrynarbor shook her head.

'Ah. There should have been,' said Mrs Pearce. She thought for a moment. 'You perhaps didn't know of the connection,' she said sagely. 'There may have been a family secret. Something no one talked about.' This seemed to me to be pushing it a bit. I couldn't see why anyone who worked on the railways, or who travelled by rail, would need to keep the connection a secret.

The woman from Berrynarbor looked confused.

'Maybe he used the railways for assignations,' said Mrs Pearce.

And I have to admit I thought that was a brilliant way to wriggle out of her potential embarrassment.

The evening continued in much the same way and at the end of it everyone seemed very satisfied. Some took it seriously, others regarded it as entertainment.

Mrs Pearce also predicts the future and her words of wisdom sometimes appear in the national press. She has forecast that Prince Charles will marry a nice Swedish Princess and that the royal couple will have three children – all daughters. She also says that Scotland will win the football World Cup in 1982 and that by the year 2000, American astronauts will have colonised Mars.

I confess that I never had much time for Mrs Pearce.

It has always seemed to me that she gives vulnerable people false hopes and expectations, with the inevitable, but tragic, result that she ends up distributing nothing but copious quantities of disappointment.

'What in the name of Hades was that?' I asked my receptionist Miss Johnson, who, having heard the scream, had rung through to the surgery to check that all was well. 'Are we being attacked?'

Miss Johnson does not feel entirely comfortable with bad language and in her book the words 'What in the name of Hades was that?' would probably necessitate my putting one of the new-fangled 50 pence pieces into the surgery swear box if we had one.

'I think it was an aeroplane,' replied Miss Johnson rather stiffly. 'Probably one of those little ones which go quite quickly. Would you like your morning coffee before the next patient?' I didn't know whether she was upset by my bad language or by the fact that I had allowed or caused a patient to scream.

I am very fond of Miss Johnson but she can be a little stiff at times.

I persuaded Mrs Pearce to lie down again, put back the screen, re-draped her clothes over the top of it, marvelling at the vast number of hooks and eyes and press studs which seemed to be involved, and re-examined the errant knee. 'You've twisted it,' I told her. 'You need to wear a support bandage for a while. It will get better.'

'It's arthritis is it?' she said.

'No,' I said patiently. 'It isn't arthritis. You've twisted a ligament. You just need to rest for a while and wear a support bandage.' I smiled and made a foolish attempt at a joke. 'And no football for a month.'

'No football?' said Mrs Pearce. 'I don't watch football.'

'No playing football,' I said. 'Tell the coach that Manchester United will have to manage without you.'

'I've never played football,' said Mrs Pearce. She thought for a moment. 'I used to play hockey when I was at school.'

'OK,' I said, regretting the attempted humour.

'And I'm 87,' she said. 'Why did you think I'd be playing football?'

'Just a joke,' I said. 'You've got the sort of injury footballers get.'

'But I haven't been playing football!'

'No. I understand. Perhaps you twisted it doing something else.'

'I play golf once a week at Ilfracombe. I twisted my leg while playing golf. My ball ended up in one of those sandpits.'

'That would be it,' I said. I hadn't previously seen Mrs Pearce as a golfer. She was not a fast mover. I wondered how early in the morning she had to start in order to finish a round before nightfall.

'What would be what?'

'You twisted your knee playing golf.'

'I just told you that, young man! Are you deaf?' Mrs Pearce glowered at me and shook her head. 'Are you going to give me some tablets for the arthritis?'

I wrote out a prescription for a knee support and made a note to myself to ask Bradshaw, the district nurse, to pop round and show her what to do with it. Left to her own devices Mrs Pearce would probably open a tin of steak, pop in the bandage and try to turn the whole confection into a stew. I don't think she is very far away from dementia and she does eat a lot of stews. I added a few mild painkilling tablets to the prescription.

As she was leaving a second plane zoomed overhead, rattling the chimney pots and shaking the whole surgery.

'Are we at war?' asked Mrs Pearce.

'I don't think so,' I told her. 'Miss Johnson would have told me if we were. Miss Johnson would certainly know if we were at war.'

'Pity,' said Mrs Pearce. 'It's about time we had a good war. People get flabby and complacent if they don't have a good war every so often.'

When I'd finished the morning surgery, and had completed the visits I popped into the Duck and Puddle to see if Frank knew anything about the planes that had flown over that morning. Frank, being the landlord of the only pub in the village, knows about everything that has happened and about most things that are about to happen. Even Miss Johnson gets much of her information from him. Frank was outside the pub watering one of his hanging baskets.

According to Frank, the half of the village that hadn't already lost its hearing and its senses was up in arms about the two jets which had buzzed the village.

Mr Jenkins at Honeydew Farm had apparently reported that eight of his best milking cows had been so startled that he would be surprised if they produced more than a gallon of milk between them. Mr Larchminster had been painting his garage and had fallen off a stepladder. He hadn't broken anything but he had spilt a good deal of paint and the area of rough ground in front of his garage was now painted in 'Creamy Yellow' patches. The hairdresser working at Peter Marshall's new multifaceted emporium had jumped so much that he had snipped off a large chunk of hair belonging to Gerald Merrymore. The hairdresser had had to give Gerald an army haircut in order to disguise the mishap.

As we talked, another jet flew over. This one came over the village so low that we both instinctively ducked. The jet was closely followed by two pursuers.

'We ought to do something about this,' said Frank who often becomes indignant but never actually does anything.

'Can I borrow your telephone?' I asked. 'I'm going to ring the Ministry of Defence to find out what is going on.'

A surprisingly pleasant fellow at the Ministry in London told me that the local RAF station had recently reorganised its route for low flying exercises. 'Your village is on a hill which our pilots are using as a sighting point,' he said merrily.

'Do you mean that this is going to happen often?' I asked.

'Oh yes,' said the man from the Ministry. He didn't seem to think we ought to mind.

'So what are we going to do about it?' asked Thumper that evening.

I had organised an impromptu, unofficial action committee and he, Patsy, Anne (Thumper's common law wife), Patchy, Adrienne, Peter Marshall and I were sitting in the bar at the Duck and Puddle, trying to decide how to deal with this new enemy.

We decided that we would write letters to the Ministry.

I wrote a letter to the Minister of Defence informing him that I intended to take up kite flying and that I thought he ought to know about this new hobby of mine so that he could warn the pilots of his noisy aeroplanes to avoid the area. I said that I didn't want any of his low flying planes getting tangled up with my kite string.

Thumper wrote a letter to the Minister informing him that he had been put in charge of the Bilbury Firework Display Committee and that he would be testing fireworks for the Committee on a regular basis in readiness for the quarterly displays which were being planned.

And Patchy wrote to say that he had become a keen pigeon fancier and that his pigeons would be flying over Bilbury on a regular but unpredictable basis.

Three days later a man came down from the Ministry to see us.

'Are you all serious?' he asked us.

We all nodded and said that we were indeed very serious and that we hoped that our activities did not put his aeroplanes at risk but that we felt sure that he would understand that we were perfectly entitled to fly kites, keep pigeons and set off fireworks.

He had to admit that although he might wish it were otherwise there were no laws forbidding our activities and he went away looking extremely unhappy.

A week after that we each received letters from someone sounding very important who told us that the Ministry had instructed the local RAF aerodrome that, on safety grounds, all future flights should be routed away from Bilbury and Bilbury Hill.

We celebrated our small victory with a modest firework display and six bottles of Polish Champagne which Peter Marshall said was just as good as the French stuff but much better value since it is the bubbles which give champagne it's joie de vivre and the bubbles in Polish Champagne are every bit as good as the bubbles in French Champagne.

The Visitor

I was still in short trousers when I decided that I would like to be a doctor. My reasons then were simple enough.

I had no great urge to cure the world of all its ills and no desire to find a wonderful new cure for a dreadful old disease. There was no grand purpose. I knew nothing of any of those things.

I wanted to be a doctor because, from what I had seen of our rather elderly, definitely old-fashioned family general practitioner, medicine was a rather dignified and respectful profession. Our family doctor helped and respected his patients and they respected him. I believed that practising as a doctor, particularly as a GP, would enable me to help people in a very real, practical way. What better way to earn a living could there possibly be?

To a small boy, it seemed a good way to live.

Ninety per cent of the time one could manage one's work in a fairly methodical fashion and for ten per cent of the time there was enough excitement to keep one on one's toes.

No relatives of mine had ever practised medicine, the nearest we had ever come was an uncle who made false teeth in his spare time, so my view was strictly from the outside. Nevertheless, I don't think my childhood view of medicine was very far from the truth.

Back in the 1950s, a couple of decades ago now, general practitioners were badly organised; they blundered through their days with little more administrative help than a well-thumbed pocket diary.

I thought that sort of life would suit me down to the ground.

Even then I knew that if I had a job in an office, with a desk and a filing cabinet, I would probably keep things in a mess.

The chance to work with people appealed to me enormously. I was not in the slightest put off by the fact that, judging by what I had seen of it, general practice was an unpredictable way to live – organised chaos rather than neat and precise. That was the way that our old family doctor managed his life.

He had two big assets, which made him perfect for the job.

First, he was a kind and well-meaning man.

Second, he was interested in people. He liked to sit and listen. He always had time to listen. He was gentle and full of sympathy, a commodity which he handed out freely and generously. He was far more careful with the pills. He was as wary as his patients were of modern drugs.

When I arrived in Bilbury, just a few years ago, I was pleased and relieved to see that Dr Brownlow was the spitting image (mentally and spiritually as well as physically) of the GP I knew when I was a boy.

Heaven knows what that poor old fellow would make of modern medical practice: the endless gadgets which have been introduced, the filing systems, the appointment systems, the tape recorders, the secretaries, the group practices and so on.

The advances in diagnosis and therapy have been few enough (despite the claims and boasts made by the medical unions and the drug industry) but there have been an abundance of advances in the world of administration. The managers have taken over, and today medical practice is regarded by many as a business. Medicine has been organised and rationalised. The time and motion study experts have cleared away the comfortable old desks, the piles of letters, the dog-eared diaries and the battered filing cabinets. They have replaced the peace, quiet and confidentiality of the consulting room with forms, more forms and yet more forms.

And, of course, doctors in big city practices are now experimenting with computers.

In the big, modern practices everything is organised.

You can be ill from nine to ten but after that you must wait until six unless you telephone the surgery before twelve in which case you can be seen between three and four on Mondays and Wednesdays and four to five on Tuesdays and Thursdays unless you need an appointment for the special vaccination clinic (run by the nurse) or the child clinic (run by another nurse).

If you need a course of treatment and you are looked after in a group practice then you will probably see a different doctor each time you visit the surgery. And if you need to be seen at night you will be seen by someone else.

The continuity has gone out of medicine.

In towns and cities, everything is carefully arranged so that the doctor can take six out of seven evenings off to watch the television in peace. The majority of doctors in city practices have most weekends free of calls.

In most health centres (they don't call them 'surgeries' any more), five, six or even more doctors share ten, twelve or fifteen thousand patients. There is no longer any such thing as 'our doctor'. I know of practices where there are 24 doctors and dozens of receptionists. Doctors in these practices know nothing about their patients and understand nothing about their lives.

My practice is very different. I practise medicine in a very old-fashioned way. I am on call for my patients for 24 hours a day and seven days a week. I am never off duty. I have less than a thousand patients and I have been in just about every house and cottage in Bilbury. I know every family's secrets (some comical and some dark) and I know everyone by name. I happily visit my patients in their homes because many of them, particularly the elderly, do not have their own transport. I often spend a couple of hours a day travelling to visit my patients. But I would rather have my sort of medicine than any other sort.

The old-fashioned doctor used to practice from a room at home.

The dining room was used as a waiting room and when he wanted a break the doctor slipped into the kitchen for a cup of coffee. His wife helped organise the practice. There might be a receptionist but if a patient needed stitches removing or a graze bandaged it would often be the doctor's wife who did the work.

These days, in modern health centres, it is nurses who take blood for the laboratory and it is nurses who syringe the wax out of ears. In the old days, it was the GP himself who did all these things, carefully cementing his relationship with his patients. In the new world, medicine is now practised in purpose built health centres.

In the old days, the doctor's surgery and the waiting room were probably a bit shabby. The magazines were of historic interest. The notices were a bit out-of-date. But it was a real place. There were pictures on the wall, ornaments on the window ledge and souvenirs on the mantelpiece.

Modern doctors tend to practice in concrete, steel and glass shell structures where the doctors go through the motions of being doctors and the patients hardly dare go through the motions of being patients. The doctor is now a technician. He is no longer known by the families he treats, he is no longer loved as one of the family.

Medicine isn't practised any longer, it is just a job. And it pays well if you have things organised properly. If you have a good appointments system, enough special grants and a few efficient secretaries and receptionists you can make a very good living. There are clinics at the hospital to be done, factories which need doctors, immunisation clinics to be staffed and life insurance medicals to fit in during the afternoons. There are lots of ways to make money as long as you don't spend too long with the damned patients.

But what is the point of a life lived like that?

'May you always have enough,' was my grandfather's favourite saying.

But some people don't seem to know when they've had enough. However much they have, they always want more.

My practice is very old-fashioned and would probably appal many 'modern' doctors. I practise at home. Patients who want to see me in my surgery come to Bilbury Grange.

I am, every day, glad I answered Dr Brownlow's advertisement for a young doctor in Bilbury.

When I talk to my friends who are in general practice in towns and cities I feel as if I have come onto the scene fifty years too late. It's rather like arriving at your own funeral.

I don't want to put the clock back to the days when single-handed practitioners all fought heroically to save their patients with leeches, blood-letting and herbal remedies which might or might not prove fatal.

I don't want to go back to the days when the doctor was the local conscience, the respected and respectable pillar of the community.

I just want to be a doctor who practices in a world where it is people who matter. I want to organise my life my own way, make my own mistakes and see my own patients through their problems, their anxieties and their crises.

I was, once again, reminded how lucky I am when a friend of mine from medical school came to stay for a day or two.

'I still don't know how you cope,' said William when he visited Bilbury for the second time. That was almost a year ago. 'Nothing ever changes here,' he said, 'everything always seems the same. Aren't you bored?'

Bored? How could I possibly be bored? There wasn't time to be bored!

William is a GP who works in a large, modern practice near to the town of Wolverhampton, right in the heart of the English midlands. He is probably the brightest person I have ever met. When we talk he always seems to be giving me his full attention, but I can never quite dismiss from my mind the thought that he only needs to use one part of his brain to concentrate fully on our conversation. I am always conscious that while talking to me his brain is dealing with half a dozen other issues at the same time, and that he is giving them his full attention too, in the way that Grand Masters such as Bobby Fischer can play two dozen games of chess simultaneously and, if asked to do so, play them all blindfolded. When William got married I was his best man. It was, I remember, the fourth wedding Patsy and I had attended that year, since many of the students with whom I had studied had chosen to get married at the same time.

When he came back for a third visit, William had changed his attitude a little and seemed pleased to see that things had stayed much the same as they had been on his previous visit.

Indeed, if anything, Bilbury had moved backwards rather than forwards.

For one thing, Peter Marshall had somehow managed to start delivering newspapers which were a day old when they arrived. Actually, I rather enjoyed reading a daily newspaper which was a day out-of-date. There is no point in getting excited about anything in a newspaper which has more in common with history than current affairs.

I did ask Peter what had happened and he muttered something about his distributor having delivery problems but Gilly Parsons at the Duck and Puddle told me that she believed that Peter had done a money saving deal with the wholesaler and was buying day old newspapers as waste and then selling them with some cock and bull story about delivery problems.

I sometimes fear that the big chain retailers probably have a man following Peter's business activities. What happens in Bilbury today will probably happen in London, Paris and New York tomorrow.

'It's a relief to find a bit of England that hasn't succumbed to the modern enthusiasm for needless change,' commented William, as we sat in front of a roaring log fire in the living room at Bilbury Grange.

I love open log fires and tend to have them even in the summer if there is a chill in the air.

It was after lunch and I had done my visits for the day and had no professional commitments until the evening surgery at 5.00 p.m. I had recently begun starting the evening surgery at 5.00 p.m. a couple of evenings a week in order to make it easier for patients who worked in Barnstaple or Taunton to attend. This wasn't an entirely administrative move for I had realised that if I changed the times of the surgery, and made myself more easily accessible, patients would come and tell me about their problems earlier, rather than waiting for things to get worse. As a bonus, I found myself having to do fewer home visits. When you work alone, as I do, and are on call for 24 hours a day and 365 days a year, anything you can do to make life slightly easier for everyone is worth doing.

'Mind you,' William added, 'I've read your books about Bilbury and you certainly have some odd things happening around here. Until I came here and saw for myself I didn't think so many strange things could happen in one place. It's the way you look at things, I suppose. Always on the look-out for the quirky!'

William and I were chatting and talking about our different lifestyles and working days. Patsy and William's wife, Brenda, were in the summerhouse with all the children. Since Thumper put a wood stove into the summerhouse, we have used it far more often. It makes a wonderful hideaway garden room.

Before becoming a general practitioner, William had worked in hospital where he had specialised in general medicine. He had reached far in the hierarchy as a senior registrar but had resigned and moved into general practice when it became clear that he was not likely to obtain a post as a consultant until he was well past his fortieth birthday.

He was tired of the politicisation of the hospital career ladder, weary of still being officially classified as a 'junior hospital doctor', and so with a wife and two small children to look after he decided to jump ship and become a family doctor, albeit an exceptionally well-qualified one.

'I work with seven other partners and two assistants and three nurses,' said William thoughtfully. He leant forward and knocked the dottle from his pipe into the fireplace. He then took a brown leather tobacco pouch from his pocket. He also took out a small, rather clever tool which has gadgets which he can use to poke around both in the bowl and along the stem. It's a sort of Swiss Army penknife for smokers and it looked so much fun that it genuinely made me think of taking up pipe smoking – simply for the joy of having one of those little gadgets in my pocket.

'But I can't remember the last time I actually managed to sit down and discuss clinical problems with anyone,' he continued.

We sat in silence for a while, watching the logs on the fire. They were good apple tree logs, and made excellent burning.

The sight of William's pipe smoker's 'friend' (as those little gadgets are sometimes known) made me reach into my pocket and touch my penknife, for no other reason than to reassure me that it was still there. I don't think I've ever grown up for in addition to the usual coins and keys, my pockets are always stuffed with all manner of useful bits and pieces: pencil stubs, paper clips, rubber bands, a small notebook or possibly two, a piece of string, a prescription pad and other miscellaneous and ever changing bits of stuff. I carry the key to start the car but not for the house because we don't bother to lock the house doors. (Although, I confess, I do lock the cupboard where I keep my stock of drugs such as morphine.)

I have heard it said that with a shilling, a piece of string and a pocket-knife a man is prepared for any emergency. The thought dates from late Victorian days and although the shilling is now probably a little light for serious financial emergencies, I still regard the advice as sound. It is certainly the case that the piece of string and the pocket-knife are indispensable. I never go anywhere without both tucked safely into a pocket. My jackets are all baggy but I believe that pockets are there to be used.

I have a small collection of pocket-knives but, although they are perhaps a little larger and heavier than might be preferred, the Swiss Army knives are without a doubt the most useful. They may wear holes in pocket linings faster than Patsy would like but they are enormously useful and I don't think any country doctor should ever leave the house without one.

My favourite version of the famous red Swiss Army knife, and the one which I usually carry in my pocket, is the one which contains two blades, both types of screwdriver, a pair of scissors, a magnifying glass, a corkscrew, a toothpick, a pair of tweezers and a bodger for making holes in conkers. I keep the main blade as sharp as I can make it, on the grounds that if ever I need a knife in an emergency then I'll probably need one with a blade that cuts tougher stuff than butter.

It is widely assumed that the multifunction pocket-knife is a new invention but Patchy Fogg, antique dealer and lover of all things curious, once explained to me that this is definitely not the case.

He told me that cutlers have been making multi-bladed knives since the early years of the 19th century and the most innovative manufacturers created knives as much to show off their skills and their inventiveness as to attract customers. In 1822, the English firm of Rodgers built an extraordinary knife in order to celebrate their royal appointment by George IV. The knife contained an almost unbelievable 1822 separate blades and the creation was known as the 'Year Knife'. The same Mr Rodgers then produced a rather more practical giant knife containing just 75 tools and blades for the Great Exhibition of 1851. I really would love one of these but I suspect the weight would result in a really large hole appearing in my pocket.

William took tobacco from the pouch and slowly and methodically started to pack the bowl of his pipe. He has a variety of pipes and never travels without three or four. Today he was using one of those curved Sherlock Holmes pipes. It had an absolutely huge bowl. He smokes stuff which he buys from a tobacconist who imports the brand just for him. It smells sweeter than any other tobacco I've ever come across. I did try a pipe full once and found it extremely pleasant.

'But don't you talk to your partners?' I asked him, astonished.

'We have plenty of meetings,' he said, with a sigh. 'But we never seem to talk about anything significant.' He continued to pack down the tobacco in his pipe. Like many other pipe smokers he enjoyed the process of preparing a pipe almost as much as he enjoyed the smoking itself.

'We have a practice meeting every Monday evening,' he said, thoughtfully. He stared at the fire for a while. He lives in a modern house which doesn't have a working fireplace and always enjoys staring into the fire at Bilbury Grange. I cannot imagine why a builder would build a house without a working fireplace. Central heating is all very well but if the boiler breaks down or the electricity supply is interrupted it is good to have an alternative source of heat.

But then, I suppose that power outages are less likely in an urban area than they are in the wilds of North Devon.

'We used to have the meetings in the back room of a local pub but one of the new partners objected and said it wasn't seemly for doctors to discuss practice business in a public house.' He sighed wistfully. 'So now we have our meetings in the practice waiting room. A bloody boring place it is too. And whereas we could have drinks and snacks sent in when we met in the pub, we now have to put up with milky stuff that could be tea or could be coffee. And if we're lucky, someone slips two rich tea biscuits into the saucer.'

'What sort of things do you discuss?' I asked.

I could still remember my own regular meetings with Dr Brownlow, my late predecessor, and the man who had brought me to Bilbury. We had often discussed clinical problems. I always found these meetings enormously helpful and I have no hesitation in saying that I learned more by talking to Dr Brownlow than I learned at medical school. Since Dr Brownlow's death, I had rather envied William the ability to discuss clinical quandaries and dilemmas with a large group of colleagues.

'We discuss administration, finance and employee problems,' he told me, with a weariness which I definitely did not envy. 'We argue about the on call rota, and there will always be someone who claims that they shouldn't be expected to work bank holidays because they're too young or too old or have visitors coming or have children. We have six receptionists and we have to discuss their problems too.'

I stared at him.

'We're running a small business,' he explained, looking rather embarrassed. 'We're actually members of the Federation of Small Businesses! We have to discuss the utility company contract, car parking problems and difficulties with the telephone company and the switching facilities we use.' Not for the first time I gave silent thanks that I worked as a single-handed practitioner and had no partners with whom to discuss things. I felt lucky that my wife, Patsy, and Miss Johnson, my receptionist, dealt with the administration of the practice and made sure that the bills were paid and that there were fresh flowers and magazines in the waiting room. 'Couldn't you have a clinical meeting on another evening?' I asked.

'Not a chance.' said William. 'On Tuesdays we have a meeting with the social workers. They insist that we meet with them in order to discuss social problems. It's always a complete waste of time. I can never understand what they're talking about. Every Wednesday we have a meeting with the health visitors and practice nurses. Those are the meetings when we plan our vaccination programmes. The senior partners are very keen on vaccination programmes because we make a ton of money out of them. On Thursdays we meet with the reception staff who tell us all their problems, anxieties and complaints. And on Fridays we meet the Patients' Consultative Group.'

'What on earth is the Patients' Consultative Group?' I asked him.

'One of the partners read something in a magazine advising doctors to consult their patients more regularly,' said William. 'So now we have a weekly meeting where we discuss practice management issues and listen to complaints and suggestions from the group of largely self-elected patients.'

'What on earth do you find to talk about?' I asked, genuinely curious.

'Oh, all sorts of things,' he said wearily. 'The patients' representatives have been pushing for some time for us to put new curtains up in the waiting room. We agreed that we needed new curtains but no one can agree on the colour. We talk about car parking problems because there is only room for a dozen cars in the practice car park and there is very little parking in the streets around the health centre. And, of course, there are always lots of worries about the appointments system.'

'Ah,' I said. 'You have one of those appointment systems do you!'

William stared at me. 'I'd forgotten you didn't have an appointments system,' he said. 'I'm amazed that you're still holding out. How on earth does that work for you?'

'Very well,' I replied. 'People who want to be seen just totter along to the surgery, give their name to Miss Johnson and sit down in the waiting room. If Miss Johnson is away for any reason, Patsy stands in for her. When one patient leaves Miss Johnson calls out the name of the next patient on the list.'

'But don't patients have to wait for hours?'

'Not usually. And they don't seem to mind if they do have to wait a while. People bring their daily paper or their knitting. If there's a bit of a queue they generally pop along to Peter Marshall's shop and do a few chores there. If they miss their place in the queue then they just fit in a bit later. It works very well and most patients like it because there is none of this business of waiting days or weeks for an appointment. I do a surgery every weekday morning and every evening except Wednesdays and a surgery for emergencies on Saturday mornings. Patients seem to find that the whole thing works quite satisfactorily. And they don't have to waste time and money ringing the surgery to make an appointment. And I don't have to hire extra staff to answer telephone calls from people wanting to make appointments.'

William shook his head. 'I envy you,' he said. 'Believe me, progress isn't always what it's cracked up to be.'

'So you and your colleagues really don't have much time left for discussing clinical problems?' I said.

'None at all,' said William, looking rather sad. He took a box of matches from his jacket pocket and removed a match. He lit it and held the flame against the tobacco in his pipe, puffed and sucked in the way pipe smokers always do when trying to get things going satisfactorily. When he was happy that the pipe was alight, he shook the match from side to side to put out the flame and then threw the dead match into the fire. 'Believe me,' he said quite seriously, 'I envy you the simplicity of a single-handed practice.'

He then went on to tell me that he had heard that the Government and the medical establishment were determined to force all GPs to work in group practices and to introduce appointment systems.

'They'll have a job to do that with people like me,' I said. 'Bilbury is too far away from other towns for a group practice to be able to look after the villagers, and there are nowhere near enough people here to keep a group practice occupied.'

'But you had trouble a year or two ago!' said William.

I agreed that my single-handed practice had been closed down for a while when administrators decided to streamline medical services in the area and to allocate my patients to doctors working in the nearby town of Barnstaple. The residents of Bilbury were not happy about this and there was much delight when the doctors in Barnstaple eventually got tired of driving out to Bilbury on dark and rainy nights and the health authorities were persuaded to relent and to allow me to reopen the practice.

Our conversation was then interrupted by the ringing of the telephone. The caller was Mr Avery-Ware (a bachelor with more than a roving eye who is known to female villagers as 'Hans' – a soubriquet which he finds amusing), asking me to visit his neighbour, Mrs Harborough. Mr Avery-Ware is quite indomitable and as lively as a cricket and looks twenty years younger than he is. When he celebrated his 80th birthday he told me with a glint in one eye (the other had a rather advanced cataract which he refuses to have dealt with) that the best years of his life were yet to come.

Mr Avery-Ware didn't know what was wrong with Mrs Harborough, just that his neighbour had knocked on his door and asked him to ring me and ask me to call round. It was, he believed, her husband who needed help.

Like many people in the village, Mrs Harborough doesn't have a telephone. When those without telephones need something they simply ask someone nearby who has one to make the call for them. There never seems to be any ill-feeling about this. Indeed, villagers whose homes are blessed with telephones usually feel important and indispensable because of their links to their outside world.

'I'm sorry,' I said, when I put down the telephone. 'I have to just pop out. I shouldn't be more than half an hour. Help yourself to whisky! Tell Patsy I've had to pop out to see Mrs Harborough.'

'I wonder,' began William, hesitantly, 'if you'd mind if I sort of tagged along? I'd really like to see a bit of rural medicine in the flesh, so to speak.'

I said I'd be delighted and explained that country medical practice is a little different to town practice in that although it requires the usual mixture of medical knowledge and a supply of common sense, mixed together with a dollop of lateral thinking, it also requires a good deal of local knowledge. Instead of being neatly laid out in logically numbered houses, my patients have a tendency to live in isolated cottages and houses which have names not numbers. The nameplates for most village properties have long ago disappeared. Moreover, their houses can often only be reached by driving five miles along narrow lanes and cart tracks. Since the owner of a cottage knows where he lives and does not usually welcome visitors, most country dwellers live in homes which do not advertise their presence or their identity. Houses in towns often have both names and numbers. Houses in the country may have names but it is rare for there to be a visible sign or a nameplate.

I scribbled a note for Patsy, to explain where we'd gone, and we both climbed into the Rolls.

'I still can't believe you use this for your daily calls,' said William, admiring the wooden dashboard and the magnificent state of the old motor car's interior. 'They don't make cars like this anymore, do they? It's hardly practical though, is it? It must cost you a fortune to run.'

'It has a great liking for petrol,' I admitted, 'and it doesn't fit terribly well into some of thenarrowDevon lanes. But it's a constant joy to drive and I rather think patients prefer to see their doctor turn up in an old, classic motor car than in the sort of fairly ordinary and rather battered old car I used to drive when Dr Brownlow was alive. My patients like to think of the doctor's visit as being something special. I did my calls on a bicycle for a while one summer and I always got the feeling that, although they didn't say anything, patients did sometimes feel uncomfortable about the fact that their doctor had to remove his bicycle clips when he arrived. The Rolls is elegant enough to give them extra confidence and there is a permanence and longevity about it which the folk round here seem to find comforting. It also helps enormously that this was Dr Brownlow's car. They loved him and so a little of his magic rubs off on me now that I drive hisRolls.'

'I understand that,' said William. 'It's well known that a trusted doctor has a healing power, a placebo effect if you prefer, and anything which adds to that power must improve the chances of patients getting better speedily.'

To get to Woodbine Cottage, Mrs Harborough's home, we had to drive through a ford which is often impassable in winter (I keep a pair of waders in the boot of the Rolls Royce for such eventualities) and down a rutted lane which is dusty and bumpy in summer and muddy and glutinous in winter.

(The word 'woodbine' refers not to the brand of cigarette which was exceedingly popular in Britain during the War years but to a variety of 'honeysuckle' for which 'woodbine' is the proper name.

In America, 'woodbine' is, I believe, the name given to Virginia creeper.)

'Do you ever get lost around here?' asked William as the Rolls purred on through the wondrous splendour of an area of North Devon known as the Valley of the Rocks. 'I haven't a clue where we are. Have we crossed any borders? Are we still in England?'

'We're still in Devon,' I assured him. 'I know my way around here pretty well but you can't possibly get lost if you remember that if you aim the hour hand of your watch at the sun, then half way between that and the 12 is the direction of due south.'

I took a turning down a small lane which funnelled into a smaller lane and then into a bridle path.

William looked up at the sky. 'There is no sun,' he said, 'it's too cloudy.'

'Then we just have to hope that the car knows the way home,' I said. 'Dr Brownlow used to have a horse that could find its way home from anywhere in Bilbury. He would fall asleep after making a night call and just let his horse clip clop back home.'

William looked at me disbelievingly.

'It's true,' I said, because it was, and pulled off onto a stretch of fairly wide, fairly flat verge which the Harboroughs, who didn't own a motor car, had mown for the use of those rare visitors who did. I climbed out of the car, plucked my black bag from the back seat and set off for the cottage.

'Aren't you going to lock it?' asked William, still standing by the car and clearly surprised. 'And you've left the key in the ignition.'

'Never lock it,' I said. 'No one round here would steal it, or take anything from it. Dr Brownlow never locked it and neither do I. There is probably a key somewhere for the doors, but I've never bothered to look for it.' I paused. 'I suppose I ought to find the key for when I pop into Barnstaple. I hear that people have been known to steal cars there.'

'Crumbs!' said William. 'If I didn't lock my car and left it for five minutes it wouldn't be there when I got back. Even when it's locked I feel lucky if I get back and don't find the axles balanced on old bricks and the wheels several miles away. And I consider myself very lucky if the hubcaps haven't been nicked.'

Mrs Harborough's cottage is, like many of the properties in Bilbury, quite small. It is what, I believe estate agents like to describe as 'cosy' or, if they like to think of themselves as being 'educated' and are feeling particularly poetic, 'bijou'. There are two reception rooms downstairs: a living room which is used for sitting, eating and sleeping in front of the fire and a small front room which is used only for wedding breakfasts and funeral teas. There is a small kitchen, equipped with an old range which lives on a diet of coal, wood and vegetable peelings and which, as far as I know, has not been out for the best part of half a century, an open fronted dresser which Patchy has been trying to buy off the Harboroughs for as long as I've been in Bilbury, and a Belfast sink equipped with a cold tap which is gravity fed from a small stream which crosses the garden. Hot water, when required, comes from the kettle. Up until around six months ago, the cottage had been lit by oil lamps. But a few months earlier the Harboroughs had, with some considerable reluctance and not a little suspicion, joined the 20th century and agreed to have electricity connected. The electrical supply provided lighting for both main rooms downstairs and both rooms upstairs. Mrs Harborough refused steadfastly to have electricity in her kitchen, readily explaining that she was worried that it might affect her cooking. The man from the electricity company had tried to persuade her that electricity would not curdle her milk and could, indeed, be used to power a modern cooker but Mrs Harborough was a nervous woman and not easily persuaded by any silver-tongued salesman from a company which was, she rightly assumed, anxious to increase the amount of electricity it was selling her.

The privy, or outside lavatory, is, as it is in so many homes in Bilbury, situated a few yards away from the back door. It empties into a cesspit and was still lit by an oil lamp since Mrs Harborough had been as reluctant to have electric lighting in the outside facilities as she had been to have it in the kitchen. Any bathing which was required was done in a battered tin bath in front of the open fire in the living room.

The range, and the open fire, provided the cottage with all its heating and, I have to admit, did so more than adequately. Whatever the season the cottage would not have betrayed any estate agent who took a fancy to describe it as 'cosy'. Not that the Harboroughs were in the market for a buyer. Mrs Harborough had been born in the cottage and was, she was proud to tell me, the first baby Dr

Brownlow ever delivered. As the youngest daughter, she had dutifully and lovingly looked after her parents in their old age. She had, with the agreement of her sisters, all of whom had moved far away and had no use for a small and almost worthless cottage, never doubted that she would remain in the cottage until it was time for her to meet her maker. She had met her husband late in life for she was in her forties when her last remaining parent, her mother, died and she was freed from her responsibilities in that direction.

Mr Wilfred Harborough, a labourer who had worked for Mrs Harborough's parents, had lived in the cottage since their marriage night, and was similarly determined to remain there until he was 'called by God'.

Mrs Harborough had travelled no further than Barnstaple and she had been there only twice in her life. She still talked about those adventures in much the sort of way that an explorer might describe travels to darkest Africa or the Himalayan peaks. Mr Harborough, who considered himself to be exceptionally well-travelled, had been in the army during the Second World War and had, in that capacity, visited camps on Salisbury Plain and in Yorkshire. He had returned from his military service with no medals but his fellow soldiers had rechristened him 'Market' Harborough after the town of that name (which he had, incidentally, never visited) and so had come home to Bilbury with a demob suit and the nickname 'Market'

Upstairs, approached via a staircase which is hidden away in what looks like a cupboard, there are two bedrooms. One contains a huge iron bedstead and a very soggy mattress and the other contains a second-hand divan bed which was installed in the hope of attracting tourists looking for bed and breakfast accommodation and which is, I believe, still waiting for its first occupant.

Mrs Harborough, who is a big woman, almost as broad in the beam as she is tall, met us in the hall. Her Christian name is Blossom. Her parents had nine other girls, all older than Blossom, and every one of them was named after a flower. There was a Rose, a Lily, a Daisy and so on. By the time the enthusiastic anthophilic parents had the tenth girl in their series they had run out of flower names and so the tenth daughter was called Blossom.

I introduced William and explained that he too was a doctor, in general practice elsewhere.

Mrs Harborugh seemed delighted but rather flustered to have two doctors in her home, as though concerned that there might not be enough for two doctors to do. 'I've got some fruit cake ready for you,' she said, 'and the kettle is on. Come on in and I'll find another plate and another cup.'

We followed her into the house.

In the car I had already explained to William that it is quite impossible to enter Mrs Harborough's home without eating at least one slice of homemade cake and drinking two cups of tea.

Early in my career in Bilbury, I had once made the mistake of rushing off without eating the proffered slice of cake, claiming that I had more visits to do and couldn't stay. It had taken nearly two years for Mrs Harborough to forgive me.

'It's the doctor,' Mrs Harborough called to her husband, in a voice that could and does carry across six fields when the sheep or the cows need calling in. 'The doctor has brought another doctor with him,' she added. There was a pause. 'So there are two doctors.'

'It's Wilfred who needs you, doctor,' she explained.

'What's up?' I asked. I always find it important, when visiting one half of a married couple, to get the view of the other half before offering a viewpoint or any recommendations. When a country dwelling couple have been married for ten or more years, and have spent pretty much every day of every week of every month of every year within calling distance of each other, then the chances are very good that they will each know as much about their spouse's weaknesses and strengths, frailties and susceptibilities as it is possible for anyone to know.

'He's gone and bought a mowing machine,' said Mrs Harborough. She announced this as if her husband had purchased a submarine or a locomotive. 'He bought it to cut the grass in the orchard.'

In addition to keeping a few animals, the Harboroughs have an apple and pear orchard which covers well over an acre. They sell the apples and pears their trees produce to a Somerset cider maker. Mr Harborough had, I know, always cut the grass in their orchard with a scythe.

'Oh dear,' I said. I immediately had an awful vision of Mr Harborough putting his hand into the cutters and losing his fingers. 'What's happened?'

'Nothing has happened,' said Mrs Harborough. 'That's the problem. Nothing at all. He can't get it started. They sent instructions but they might as well be in foreign. He's out the back.'

'Then we'd better go and take a look and see if we can help,' I said.

'It's a good job there's the two of you,' said Mrs Harborough. 'Maybe you can make head and tail of the book they sent with it. My Wilf can't make no sense of it. He said the doctor, being a man of learning, would be the man to call.' Mrs Harborough added that a tame pheasant had that morning brought his wife, son and two daughters along to share the food spilt from the bird table and that we were, if possible, to avoid making any sudden movements which might startle the family.

We found Wilfred Harborough in the back yard, scratching his head and staring at a number of parts of what did look like a new mowing machine. There were rollers, a grass collecting box and something that looked like an engine. Mr Harborough had the instruction booklet in his left hand. The five pheasants were standing around looking as though they'd like to help but weren't quite sure how best to be of service.

'Thank heavens you've come, doctor,' said Wilfred, as though I had turned up in the nick of time to deal with a life threatening emergency.

I introduced William. The two nodded and murmured appropriate greetings. I could see that William was a little surprised by the nature of the emergency. I don't think big city doctors spend a lot of time helping patients decipher mowing machine manuals.

'It came in a box in bits and I can't make head nor tail of it,' admitted Wilfred. He handed me the instruction brochure. I could see why Mrs Harborough had called it a book. There were sections in German, Danish, Japanese and Finnish. There was also a section in English but the person who had written the English section did not appear to be a native English speaker.

'Where did you buy it from?' I asked.

'A garden centre in Barnstaple,' replied Wilfred. 'I went there especially.'

Barnstaple is around 10 miles from Bilbury but most of the locals, even the well-travelled Wilfred, regard a journey there to be an expedition requiring maps, compass and a large packet of sandwiches. In the old days, several villagers, both men and women, used to walk to Barnstaple every day to work in the town. At the end of a day's work they would walk back to Bilbury. It was a two and a half hour journey each way and in bad, winter weather it must have required considerable fortitude. These days Bilbury villagers have become more insular than their forebears and, very probably, not so fit.

'But the one in the garden centre was all made up,' continued Wilfred. 'It looked like a mowing machine. This one came in a box, delivered on a lorry.'

'Ah, they do that,' said William. 'We bought a wardrobe two weeks ago. It came packed flat and I had to put the parts together.'

Wilfred stared at him. 'A wardrobe? You bought a wardrobe in bits?'

'Some Swedish company,' said William. 'They sell their stuff in kits. The good thing is that they always give you more than you need. I had tons of screws left over. And a big, spare piece of plywood stuff. Mind you, when I'd finished it, there was a big gap at the back of the wardrobe. I think they probably forgot to send me one bit and sent me two of another bit.' He shrugged and grinned. 'Fortunately, my wife says she'll get someone in to build it if we buy another.'

I bent down and took a look at the bits and pieces of lawn mower. I opened the brochure and found the part that was supposed to be in English. I read the first paragraph out loud: 'For the furtherance of the machine to have been made taking the parts marked D and M on the explosive diagram marked No 1 and with the fastenings provided fasten the part M to the part marked D using the fastenings marked E as provided.'

I examined the 'explosive diagram' which looked as it was the result of dipping a spider's feet in ink and then letting it walk all over a sheet of paper.

I showed the diagram to William who simply frowned and grunted.

I read on.

'After fixating the parts as instructed place part marked B and part marked C in neighbourhood of parts marked E and E and connect together with application of projectiles as entrusted in explosive diagram marked No 2. Important note: do not under circumstances of eventuality of malfunctioning place part C against throttle lever cable adjustment hammer (see page 5) until the cross screw threaded flange divider having been duly fatted with due endeavour is by the eyes tensed.'

I read out the instructions as slowly and carefully as I could. I read them out again. None of us could understand a word of it. The cock pheasant flapped his wings and squawked. His wife and children looked impressed but said nothing.

'I think we might do better forgetting about the brochure and just try to build the mower so that it looks like the mower on the front of the brochure,' suggested William. He took the brochure from me and pointed to a small, two inch square picture of the mower on the cover. We all peered at the picture.

'So that must be the handle,' I said, pointing to a long piece of tubular metal which looked like bicycle handlebars created by one of those fashionable artists who always manages to give his subjects three heads and one leg.

'And that is probably the cable that connects the accelerator lever to the engine,' suggested William. 'And that big bit over there will be the grass box.'

And so we went on, sustained by regular supplies of cake and tea, brought to us by Blossom Harborough.

After a good deal of trial and error, a fair amount of skin, a little blood and all the swear words the landlord of the Duck and Puddle wasn't using at that moment, we eventually succeeded in building something that looked very much like a lawn mower.

'I've got these bits left over,' said Wilfred, holding out a handful of screws and assorted bits of metal.

'Good, they always send spare bits,' said William. 'Keep them somewhere safe in case you ever need them.'

Wilfred put the handful of bits into his overall pocket and William pulled the starter cord several times and then it occurred to me that the mower might need some fuel so Wilfred brought a can of petrol from his outside lavatory and we filled up the tank with the aid of a small funnel Blossom uses when making her cakes. The pheasants, not enamoured of the smell, tottered off up the garden.

Two minutes later we all shook hands when Wilfred, pulled the starter cord and, to our immense surprise, the mower started. Two minutes after that we cheered loudly when Wilfred took the mower into the orchard and showed us that it would, indeed, cut grass.

Attracted by the noise of the cheering and the mower, Blossom came out with more cups of tea and more cake. It was only then that it occurred to me that if we had called Thumper he would have probably been able to build the mower in a tenth of the time. Still, we would have been denied our moment of pride.

'I enjoyed that,' said William, as we drove home in the Rolls. 'I had no idea country practice was so much fun. Do you have many calls like that one?' His suit was ruined, covered in copious amounts of oil and stinking of petrol, and his hands were black with grease and oil. My clothes and hands were no better. On the back seat of the car sat two large tins, each containing one of Blossom's fruit and walnut cakes – one for William and his family and one for Patsy and me.

I drove slowly, trying not to touch too much of the steering wheel. Despite washing them several times, and scrubbing at them with a nailbrush, my hands were still filthy.

'If you ever decide to retire, you must promise to let me know,' said William contentedly. 'I see what you mean about country medicine being a little different to town practice.'

He took his pipe out of his pocket and started to fill it with tobacco. 'If Bilbury is ever looking to find a twin town,' he said drily, 'might I suggest that you put the planet Pluto high on the list of possibles?'

The Accidental Odd Job Man

Patsy and I have always enjoyed reading and between us we get through a vast number of books. We don't watch television very much but usually prefer to spend our evenings sitting by the fire listening to music and reading. As a sole practitioner, I am always liable to be called out in the evening and it is far easier to put a bookmark into a volume to mark the page I am reading, rather than to leave a television programme and then expect Patsy to summarise and explain what I've missed when I returned an hour or so later.

In the summer, of course, the light evenings are usually spent in the garden, sitting by the lake or picking fruit or vegetables. But during the dark evenings of winter we have much more time for reading.

During the dark, cold evenings one winter I spent some time sitting on my side of the fire reading Benjamin Franklin's quite remarkable autobiography and I discovered that, but for a quirk of fate, America's history could have been quite a different one.

Franklin was an excellent swimmer who had enjoyed the sport since he had been a child. He was proud of having studied and practised the techniques described in Thevenot's book *The Art of Swimming* (which had been published in 1696) and was proud to have added some of his own tricks and manoevres. While living in London he had earned some considerable notoriety by swimming 'from near Chelsea to Blackfryar's, performing on the way many fears of activity, both upon and under water, that surprised and pleased those to whom they were novelties' and he had been 'much flattered' by the admiration of the onlookers.

As a result of this display, Franklin was approached by a man called Sir William Wyndham who wanted him to teach his two sons how to swim. Wyndham offered to pay the young American a handsome sum if he would give them lessons.

Unfortunately, for all concerned, Franklin was already planning to return to Pennsylvania and could not accept the invitation but, in his autobiography, he writes that he 'thought it likely that if I were to remain in England and open a swimming-school, I might get a good deal of money; and it struck me so strongly, that, had the overture been sooner made me, probably I should not so soon have returned to America.'

Franklin played such a huge part in America's early development that it is difficult to imagine how things might have turned out if the young printer had not already committed himself to return home and had chosen to remain in England and become a swimming tutor. It always surprises me to realise just how much history is influenced by the little things.

As a country GP, I am constantly reminded how delicately balanced life can be, and how the slightest and most seemingly insignificant incident can have a notable impact.

Consider, for example, the story of how we found an essential member of staff for the Brownlow Country Hotel, our revised version of the hospital we had created out of Dr Brownlow's old home.

The Brownlow Country Hotel had been open for a week when the first patient was admitted.

In order to avoid problems with the local health service administrators, the first patient was, of course, admitted as a 'guest' rather than as a 'patient'. And our rota of volunteer nurses were not known as nurses but could choose to describe themselves as 'housekeepers', 'reception staff', 'chefs' or 'waitresses'.

I was surprised to find that in practical terms the only real difference between running a hospital and running a hotel was the amount of bureaucracy involved. I think if we had attempted to persevere with our plan to open a hospital we would have suffocated under the weight of absurd rules and regulations.

Just three days after our official opening (it had been a very low key affair because we didn't want to attract the attention of the health service bureaucrats by inviting a dignitary to cut a ribbon, unveil a plaque or plant a tree and in any case none of these seemed appropriate now that we were officially running a hotel rather than a hospital) it became clear that although our rota of volunteer nurses could cope very well with looking after the patients (sorry, the guests) we would need someone to help maintain the fabric of the building.

Like all old houses, Dr Brownlow's former home needed constant care and attention. There were always chores to be done.

In what had been the library, a window catch came loose and, as an inevitable consequence, a window wouldn't shut properly and a nasty draught constantly swept through the room. Two light bulbs on a chandelier hanging twelve feet above ground level needed changing. The chimney in the dining room started to smoke and needed sweeping. A tap in one of the bedrooms began to drip and needed attention. A toilet wouldn't flush unless you jiggled the handle up to the left and then down and to the right. The guttering over the back door was leaking, with the result that if it was raining no one could enter or leave the house through that door without having an impromptu shower. The left hand front gate had seized up and needed loosening and oiling. A branch had half fallen off one of the oaks and needed cutting down and, preferably, chopping up into logs. Grass needed cutting, hedges needed trimming and the culvert leading into the lake needed clearing. A broken window pane in the butler's pantry needed replacing.

All these were the sort of relatively minor problems which affect any large house but when the house is very old, the problems become apparent on a daily basis.

As Bradshaw said, 'When you have 36 taps the chances are high that at any one time at least one of them will be dripping.'

Bradshaw couldn't possibly cope with these chores on top of all his other responsibilities and so we needed a full-time maintenance man and gardener: someone capable of turning his hand to pretty well everything practical, someone not too proud to stick his arm into a blocked drain (probably the commonest of common problems in a large country house which has old and complicated drains) and someone prepared to do all this for room, board and a very modest income. I could have asked Thumper to help, and I know he would have done so without a moment's hesitation, but since our problems were likely to occur on a daily basis we need someone living on the premises.

Dr Brownlow had given me a good sum in cash to cover the cost of turning the house into a cottage hospital but a good chunk of the money had already gone on buying hospital beds, linen, towels and other essentials and I knew that the hospital running costs (insurance, rates and so on) would burn up money steadily. I needed to keep the regular expenditure down.

'We need to employ what is, I believe, known in the vernacular as an 'odd job man',' said Bradshaw. He had a natural ability to put inverted commas around certain words and he did it now with the words 'odd job man'. 'We require someone prepared to live in and deal with all these little chores. But how much can we afford to pay?'

'Not much,' I confessed. Bradshaw's salary was being paid by the health authority, since he was officially attached to my practice as my district nurse and we still had money in the bank, but I knew we had to plan for the long term.

'There's a small flat that used to be occupied by the groom,' said Bradshaw. 'It's not been used since he left. But it would tidy up quite nicely. And it gets heat from the stove in the tack room.'

'When did the groom leave?' I asked. I didn't know that Dr Brownlow had employed a groom though I suppose I should have realised that he would have needed someone to look after his horses.

'That would be at the outbreak of World War II,' said Bradshaw drily. 'Dr Brownlow had bought the Rolls Royce by then and we didn't really have anything for the poor fellow to do. He joined the army and in view of his experience as a groom expected to be put to work looking after the horses. Inevitably, of course, he ended up in a tank regiment where he was appointed regimental cook. He didn't know anything about tanks or cooking so I expect the military hierarchy considered him pretty well perfect for the post. I kept in touch with him after the war. By the time the war finished he had risen to the rank of Colonel in the catering corps. He then moved into the hotel trade and became General Manager of one of the large London hotels. Sadly, I then rather lost touch with him.'

I suddenly realised where we could find our odd job man.

I don't know why it took me so long.

But would the man to whom I wanted to offer the post be prepared to consider it?

I realised some years ago, when I was still a young man, that it is often wise to take anything a tramp tells you with a large pinch of salt. I do not mean to suggest by this that they are all malignant liars, deliberately misleading those who take the time to listen to their stories, but, rather, that they tend, rather more than most folk, to select the truths they choose to share with their listeners.

Part of what a tramp tells you will be the truth, the whole truth and nothing but the truth, but some of it will be the truth that he or she wants to share with you, some of it will be the truth that he or she thinks you want to hear and some of it will be the untruth that he or she wants to share or thinks you want to hear. Untangling the truths from the untruths can be a complex and time consuming business.

And, sometimes, tramps are happy with a lifestyle which would not suit other people.

A few years ago, I found a tramp called Colin living under a hedge about a mile away from Bilbury Grange. He refused to tell me his second name and refused my suggestion that he move into the flat which Mr Parfitt had occupied before his marriage. I telephoned the local social services department and, after several hours of pleading, managed to persuade them to offer him a room in a boarding house in Ilfracombe.

To my surprise, Colin turned down the offer.

'That's very kind of you, sir,' he said. 'But if it's all the same to you I'd rather stay in Bilbury.'

'But it's freezing cold!' I pointed out, unnecessarily. 'If you go to Ilfracombe you'll have your own room in a boarding house. You can spend the days out in the open but have somewhere warm and dry to sleep at night.'

But Colin wasn't interested. He preferred sleeping under a hedge.

I was not about to let that frustrating experience stop me from trying to recruit our odd job man.

I drove over to Barnstaple and found Tim sitting exactly where he had been the last time I'd seen him.

'Do you know how to mend a leaky tap?' I asked him.

Clearly puzzled by the question Tim thought for a moment before nodding.

'Could you replace a piece of broken glass?'

Another nod.

'Are you OK with ladders? Can you go up them without getting dizzy?'

'I'm fine with ladders.'

'Would you like a job? The pay isn't much but you get a free flat and free meals.'

Tim stared at me as though not believing what he was hearing.

'Are you serious?' he asked.

'I'm serious. It's in Bilbury, a village a few miles away.'

'I know where Bilbury is. Nice, quiet place with a village green where they play cricket. And a good pub. The Duck and something.'

'Puddle. The Duck and Puddle.'

'Are you offering me a job?'

'I am.'

I suddenly realised that there were tears in Tim's eyes. He stood and picked up the large plastic bag containing his belongings.

I took him to a nearby branch of Marks and Spencer and gave him some of Dr Brownlow's money. 'Buy some clothes,' I told him. 'Whatever you need.'

'There are two charity shops further along,' he said. 'I could buy something second-hand.'

'Buy yourself some new things,' I told him. 'This is a new beginning.'

He looked at me, tears now streaming down his cheeks, and nodded.

The Brownlow Country Hotel had its odd job man.

A Cause for Tears

It is fairly well known in medical circles that things go in runs. If you are woken up at night, then you will probably be woken up for the next three or four nights. If you see a patient complaining of a fairly unusual disease, then the chances are high that you will see another patient with exactly the same symptoms, and precisely the same disease, at the next surgery. I don't know why this should be. But it is just a fact of life.

And so, for example, there was a Tuesday recently when I seemed to see nothing but patients suffering from breast problems.

The first patient I saw was Sharon Bloodwell, a young woman in her mid-thirties who had two young children with her.

Mrs Bloodwell works at home, making cushions for a company based in Exeter and her husband, Norman, works as a labourer on one of the local farms. She's put on a lot of weight in recent years but she used to be very fit and active. She once played netball for the county, and her parent's home is packed with photographs of her and her team mates. The last time I saw her she wanted a pregnancy test because she thought she might 'have caught for another baby'.

I remember that she volunteered the surprising information that she had been having affairs with two other men. 'But there won't be any problems if the baby isn't my husband's,' she told me. 'I only ever have affairs with Norman's relatives – his brothers and two of his cousins.'

I must have looked as puzzled as I felt.

'My Norman, his brothers and the two cousins all have red hair,' she reminded me. 'I won't go with Cecil, the other cousin, because he doesn't have red hair. He's got dark hair.'

It seemed that Mrs Bloodwell had planned her adultery very carefully, doing her best to ensure that any baby that resulted from her illicit affairs would have red hair and look like her husband.

I'd never come across such cold-blooded faithlessness before but Mrs Bloodwell had seemed not in the slightest bit embarrassed by her carefully considered deceit.

Today, Mrs Bloodwell came into the surgery looking very strained and worried.

Some patients prefer to beat about the bush for five or ten minutes before coming to the point, they are too shy or nervous to share their real fears and so they begin by talking about something that might merit a trip to the surgery but which is merely a Trojan horse; an introductory gambit.

If a patient who works as a farm labourer and who hasn't visited the surgery for a decade, comes in to tell me about a graze on a knuckle or a twinge in a toe I would bet the farm that he is about to ask my advice about some more substantial concern.

'Oh, and while I'm here, doctor,' he will say, as he is about to leave, with his hand on the doorknob, 'I've been getting these terrible pains in my chest. I don't suppose they'll be anything to worry about, will they?'

Journalists have noticed the same phenomenon.

A good investigative reporter will keep their mind open after he has closed his notebook.

A good television reporter will have instructed the cameraman to keep his camera switched on even when the interview appears to be over for it is often in that moment that the interviewee will start to talk.

Any professional investigator, doctor, policeman, barrister or journalist, must ask questions but he or she must be first and foremost a good listener, knowing that the most useful answers are the ones which appear by themselves, and not in response to a question.

Mrs Bloodwell, however, could hardly wait to tell me what was worrying her.

She had not come armed with some trivial concern with which to open the proceedings. She got straight to the heart of her concern.

'I'm worried about my breast, doctor,' she said. The words came out in a rush, with a sigh at the end. It was a short sentence but I was sure she had been rehearsing it. 'The right one. It feels swollen and painful and I think I can feel a lump there.'

I looked at her, smiled slightly and nodded slightly encouraging her to tell me more.

She told me that she had noticed the lump the previous day and that she hadn't had a wink of sleep.

'I'm glad you came along so quickly,' I told her. 'Take off your things and let's have a look at it.' I ushered her behind the screen and as jumper, blouse and brassiere were hastily removed and tossed over the top of the screen I tried to comfort her two children who seemed concerned that their mother had disappeared for ever. I know dentists don't approve but I have always followed Dr Brownlow's example and I keep a jar of sweets on my desk. I know of no better way to keep small children happy and quiet.

I examined Mrs Bloodwell carefully and comprehensively and I was quickly sure that she had nothing to worry about.

'You can sleep well tonight,' I assured her, and told her to get dressed again.

The look of relief on her face made it worth getting up that morning.

'What is it, then?' she asked, when she had got dressed.

'The lumps are due to a condition which is known as fibroadenosis or hyperplastic cystic disease,' I told her. 'It's also known as mastitis.'

Mrs Bloodwell nodded. 'I've heard of mastitis. But what is it?'

'It's an inflammation of the breast tissue; probably an infection,' I told her. 'But it will go away quite quickly.'

'Do I need an operation?' she asked.

'Good heavens, no,' I assured her. 'You just need to rest and drink plenty of fluids. I'll give you some antibiotics, in case there's an infection there, and some painkilling tablets which you can take if the pain becomes severe. A warm bath or shower will probably help ease the soreness. And avoid tight fitting clothes. You might find it easier if you leave your bra off for a while. Afterwards, make sure that you don't wear bras that are too tight.'

'Do you mean I shouldn't wear a bra with the wire underneath?' she asked.

'Mastitis can be caused or made worse by bras that are too tight.'

She seemed disappointed. 'I'm big up top,' she said. 'I need support or else they droop down with my nipples aimed at the floor.'

She blushed and then looked down at her breasts. 'You don't think I'm too big, do you?'

'Good heavens, no!'

'Not dangerously big?'

'Not at all.'

Mrs Bloodwell looked relieved. 'That's good,' she said. 'I've always thought they were my best points.' She squeezed her breasts with her hands. 'All the men I know like them,' she said proudly. 'And my best friend, Sheila, says I could have been a barmaid.' She said this as some women might have contemplated missed careers as ballet dancers or ice skaters.

I scribbled out a prescription and told her to come back in a week if the soreness hadn't gone.

The very next patient I saw also had a breast problem though in her case it was not a lump but a rash which affected the centre of her chest and the inner sides of both breasts.

It was beginning to feel like National Breast Week.

Mrs Johnson was not a villager but was staying at the Duck and Puddle for a few days. She and her husband were on a short holiday to celebrate their wedding anniversary.

The rash looked like a fairly standard type of dermatitis or eczematous reaction to an allergen of some kind. It didn't take long to identify it as having been caused by a new perfume which she had bought for the occasion, and had sprayed into her cleavage without doing a test run first.

I explained to her that she should always try out a new perfume on a small area of skin before spraying large amounts onto a bigger area. I then gave her a prescription for some cream that I knew would help clear up the rash quite quickly. I told her to use the cream for five days and to then stop.

'Will I be able to start using the perfume again when the rash had gone?' asked the woman.

'No!' I told her. I explained again that the rash meant that she was allergic to something in the perfume she'd bought and that she must never use that perfume again. I suggested that she should either throw the perfume away or give it to a friend. The suggestion didn't go down well.

The patient with the rash was the last patient in that day's morning surgery and when I'd signed a few repeat prescriptions and dictated a couple of referral letters I set off on the day's visits.

The very first visit after the surgery was to a large house on one of the roads out of the village.

I had never visited the house but I knew that Mrs Utopia Kitteridge, the sole occupant, was a woman in her seventies whose husband had died some years ago.

I parked the car, checked the grounds for dogs, climbed up a steep flight of stone steps guarded by a hugely impressive pair of fierce looking stone lions, and rang the front doorbell.

While I waited for someone to come, I looked around.

The house, which had once been very grand, was in quite a state of despair.

Having spent a good deal of money repairing Bilbury Grange I guessed that the owner had probably let things go because she couldn't afford to repair the rotten window frames and the weather damaged stonework. Weeds were growing out of the cracks in the steps and the driveway, where I had left my car, was overgrown with weeds.

After a minute or two, a thin, grey-haired woman with a pronounced dowager's hump opened the door. Pulling open the heavy oak door seemed to take all her strength. She seemed even older than I knew she was. Some 70-year-olds can easily pass for 50 but Mrs Kitteridge could have played a 90-year-old without any help from clever make-up experts.

'Hullo, doctor,' she said. 'Thank you for coming.'

She was pale and her skin looked paper thin. Her voice was cracked and quiet. She wore a grey, plain dress through which I could see that she was little more than a skeleton decorated with a few pounds of fat.

'I'm sorry to have had to call you out but I don't think I could have made it to the surgery.' She was struggling to open the stiff door so I pushed hard to help open it wide enough for me to enter.

'That's OK,' I told her with a smile. 'How can I help you?'

'I've got a little problem I'd like your help with,' she said.

I closed the door and followed her into a huge reception hall.

'Perhaps you'd be kind enough to examine me?'

I followed her up a staircase that could have been used as a remake for *Gone With the Wind*. She climbed the stairs very slowly, with each step seemingly taking quite a deal of effort.

'Do you live her by yourself?' I asked her when we had eventually reached the landing.

'I do,' nodded Mrs Kitteridge, when she had got her breath back. She held her back and was clearly in some pain. 'Mrs Hilyard from the village collects my pension and Peter Marshall delivers my groceries but I don't see anyone else. They're both very good to me.'

I knew Mrs Hilyard; she was in her 70s herself but she was always running errands for what she called 'her old people'. And although Peter Marshall liked people to think of him as a rather hardhearted businessman he could sometimes be surprisingly gentle and generous. I rather suspected that he probably not only failed to charge Mrs Kitteridge for delivering her groceries but that he charged her considerably less for her groceries than the rest of us paid. He would know that she was, like many of Bilbury's older residents, asset rich but cash poor.

'Don't you get lonely?' I asked. 'Do you ever feel like moving into somewhere smaller, in the village perhaps?'

'Oh, I couldn't leave the house,' she said. 'My husband and I spent our married life here. I have so many memories of our life together.'

I asked her to get undressed and to lie down on the bed so that I could examine her.

'One thing,' she said, 'before you do anything you must promise not to send me into hospital.' She reached out and took my hand. 'No hospital at all. Not of any kind.'

'I don't know…,' I began, hesitantly.

'You must promise,' she insisted.

'I'll do my best not to,' I said.

'That's not enough,' she said. 'You must promise me.'

Mrs Kitteridge was so determined that, perhaps foolishly, I agreed that whatever I found I would not send her into hospital.

She then unbuttoned her blouse.

I have seen a lot of awful things in my life as a doctor but not revealing the shock I had took every ounce of experience.

It was perfectly clear that Mrs Kitteridge had cancer of the breast.

The whole of her left breast had become an ulcerated mass; a solid lump of cancer tissue. When I examined her I found that the cancer had spread widely and there were secondary deposits in several parts of her body. There was clearly nothing anyone could do for her. If she had been a pet animal the vet would have reached into his bag for a syringe and a vial of something fatal.

'You've had this for some time,' I said. It certainly wasn't a question.

'Oh, yes,' said Mrs Kitteridge. 'It's been there a long time.' She paused and thought for a moment. 'Quite a long time,' she confirmed.

'Why didn't you tell anyone?' I asked. I guessed that the cancer must have first become obvious at least a year earlier. Actually, I thought, the cancer had probably shown through the skin more than a year ago. Cancer doesn't have firm rules and is a law unto itself but it usually grows more slowly in older patients.

'I just want to leave in peace,' she said. 'You won't send me into hospital, will you?' She paused and looked straight at me. 'You did promise.'

I wondered what had happened to make her so afraid of hospitals.

And then I remembered that her husband, Gerald, who had been much older than her, had died in a hospital in Exeter some years earlier.

Gerald had gone into hospital for the routine repair of an inguinal hernia, a simple operation that should have been as routine as an oil change, and yet he had died as a result of an infection he had acquired from the hospital staff. Mrs Kitteridge had, not surprisingly, been very upset.

It was not the fact that he had died in hospital that had scarred her so, but the way of his dying. No one ever really recovers from seeing a loved one struggle to survive in an unfriendly, alien environment.

'I can't leave you here,' I said.

'Why not?'

'Well...,' I began. I didn't know where to start. I looked around the bedroom. The walls were covered with framed photographs and pictures in old gilt frames. The furniture was old and well-worn but clearly lovingly tended. The bookcase was crammed full of books, mostly history books and biographies. The mantelpiece was crowded with mementoes.

'Who is going to look after you?' I asked, quietly.

'I don't know,' said Mrs Kitteridge, with tears running down her cheeks. 'But I don't want to die in hospital.'

'Who said anything about dying?' I asked her, and regretted the words the moment they had left my mouth.

Mrs Kitteridge looked at me with a mixture of pity and compassion and reached out to hold my hand. She knew that she was dying, of course. I knew she was dying. There was no little irony in the fact that she was comforting me. We both knew that each other knew, and yet that touch, that simple gesture, told me that the subject was closed.

The young don't worry about dying because they know that they are immortal. As we get older we appreciate life much more (we have had more of it to enjoy and are, therefore, often more reluctant to see the end of it) and so death is usually more of a problem. There are, however, always exceptions and it was clear to me that Mrs Kitteridge was at peace with destiny.

'Have you any relatives?' I asked.

'I've got a niece in London,' said Mrs Kitteridge. 'At least I think she's still in London. I haven't heard from her in years. She does something in advertising. She's extremely important and very busy.' Pride and sadness were combined in her voice.

'I'll fix up for Mr Bradshaw, my nurse, to come in later on today. He'll be in to see you every day,' I promised. 'And I'll come back tomorrow. Nurse Bradshaw will put a dressing on.'

I suspected that I would have had something of a battle with most district nurses for they would have wanted me to send Mrs Kitteridge into the hospital in Barnstaple.

Mr Bradshaw would never suggest such a thing. A qualified nurse, who had been 82-years-old since 1968, he had worked as Dr Brownlow's butler, valet, manservant and factotum for many years and he had nursed the old doctor during his final illness. If I had attempted to move Dr Brownlow into hospital in Barnstaple, Bradshaw would have probably beaten me over the head with a silver tray and then buried me in the garden. Bradshaw was an intensely loyal man who was also gentle, experienced, unshockable and wise.

He also had in abundance the one quality all nurses should have: kindness.

'Thank you,' said Mrs Kitteridge, simply.

'How much pain do you have?'

'Nothing I can't deal with,' she said bravely. 'I have a glass of sherry at night. To help me sleep.' There was a pause. 'A large one,' she added. She smiled at me. 'Do you disapprove?'

'Not at all.'

'Can you see yourself out?'

I said I could.

As I pulled away from the house, out from the driveway and into the road, a large lorry roared past.

The driver, who was driving far too quickly for the lane, hooted imperiously and waved two imperious fingers in my general direction.

Filled with a potent mixture of sadness and anger, I accelerated after the lorry, and caught up with it when it got stuck behind a tractor in Willoughbury Lane. I then pulled onto the other side of the road and drew alongside the lorry. I tooted my horn until the driver looked down at me. Very deliberately, I raised two fingers in rude salute and waved them at him slowly and clearly.

Black-faced, the lorry driver opened his cab door and picked up a heavy piece of wood. He was clearly aiming to come round to my side of my car.

Just then the tractor pulled into a field entrance, leaving a gap.

I may not be blessed with great wisdom but I have, over the years, learned when the most appropriate response to danger is 'flight' rather than 'fight'. I have certainly never been stupid enough to start a fight with a burger fattened lorry driver equipped with a piece of wood the size of a baseball bat. I crossed my fingers, put my trust in the engineers who had built the Rolls and slammed my foot onto the accelerator.

The Rolls Royce 20/25 is not a car that has ever liked being hurried but it does seem to have been equipped with some internal device which enables it to tell when speed is truly of the essence.

We shot forward with commendable haste and left the bad-tempered, well-armed lorry driver enveloped in a cloud of blue exhaust smoke.

As I drove, I rubbed the tears from my eyes with the back of my hand.

Doctors aren't supposed to get upset when patients are dying.

But would anyone really want a doctor who didn't?

The Bonfire

There is something enormously satisfying, albeit primitive and frighteningly powerful, about a garden bonfire.

An editor from a London publishing house, once visited Bilbury Grange in an attempt to persuade me to write a book I really didn't want to write. I am not, of course, the only author to have ever had to put up with editors wanting me to write books that fitted in with their planned marketing programmes. A.A.Milne, the author of the *Winnie the Pooh* books, complained that publishers always wanted him to rewrite the last book that had been successful – whether he or someone else had written it.

While in Bilbury, the London editor berated me for having bonfires, arguing that burning garden rubbish was bad for the atmosphere and for the planet in general.

I disagreed with her then and I still disagree with her.

It is true, of course, that our atmosphere is constantly being polluted. Cars and lorries belch out vast quantities of toxic gases. Buses, trains and aeroplanes all produce serious pollutants. So do factories, of course.

But the damage done by garden bonfires is really very small, the pollutants produced are relatively harmless and the alternatives even worse.

The rather sanctimonious and distinctly self-righteous London editor told me that in the borough where she lived the local council sent a lorry round to collect garden waste. She seemed to think that this was a much better way to deal with the problem. I pointed out that the lorries collecting the garden rubbish were burning up vast amounts of diesel fuel and that once the bags of waste had been collected they still had to be dealt with – usually by burning them at a council run waste site of some kind.

I also pointed out that the amount of garden waste produced by a small urban garden was far less than the amount produced in a large country garden. And I explained that if invasive plants aren't dug up and burned then their seeds will spread and soon take over the countryside.

She hadn't thought about any of these things.

'If I had to bag up all our garden rubbish I would need dozens of bags,' I explained, 'and I would spend hours cramming the weeds and other dead material into the bags. I would then need a lorry of my own to take away the bags.'

I pointed out that a bonfire is the only sensible way to get rid of the diseased prunings, the seed heads of invasive plants such as the Giant Hogweed and the dead, woody material that really won't compost very well. I also pointed out that a bonfire is a good way to dispose of weeds that, if they are not destroyed, will survive very happily in a compost heap.

And I explained that bonfires produce ash which is rich in plant nutrients and which can be used to restore the quality of the soil, as well as producing quantities of charcoal which can be used for making potting compost.

'All things considered,' I concluded, 'a bonfire is the only environmentally sound way to deal with garden rubbish.'

I remembered the London editor as I put another forkful of dead material onto the huge bonfire that I was building with our gardener, Mr Parfitt.

It was autumn and we had collected together an enormous amount of material which needed to be burnt. We had put as much stuff as we could onto the compost heaps (we have three of them) and we had cut up the dead branches that had been brought down into kindling shaped lengths. The stuff we couldn't do something with was going onto the bonfire.

The bonfire was already about ten feet across and nearly six feet high. I was really looking forward to putting a match to it; watching the flames, listening to the crackle of the fire and bathing in its warmth: simple pleasures designed to bring out the primitive man in me.

Suddenly, I heard Patsy's voice.

I turned and saw my wife walking down the garden towards me. She was holding a piece of notepaper which had, I immediately recognised, been torn from the notepad which I keep next to the telephone on my surgery desk.

'Who is it?' I asked. A city doctor would have probably asked 'What is it?' but as a country doctor, working in a small village, I know the names of the villagers, my potential patients, and I know most of their ailments, illnesses and weaknesses.

'Mrs Jackson rang and wondered if you could call round,' said Patsy. 'I've written down her phone number in case you want to ring her before you go.'

'No, I'll just go and see what she wants,' I said.

Rosie Jackson, is married to Colin, a local farmer, and she never rings unless she really needs help. She has a weak heart and a troublesome chest and suffers from irritable bowel syndrome.

'I've got decrepit cardiacs, grumpy intestinals and hissy bronchials,' she once complained with a throaty laugh.

I remembered that I had seen her four days earlier when I had prescribed antibiotics for a urinary tract infection.

'I'll finish building the bonfire,' said Mr Parfitt. 'You leave it to me, doctor.'

Although we had been working together for some years, Mr Parfitt and I were still not on first name terms. Country folk are sometimes like that in Devon. Frank Parsons, the landlord of the Duck and Puddle, once told me that he was still not on first name terms with some of the customers who had been drinking at his pub for twenty years. It is, I suppose, just a question of respect.

Mr Parfitt has been with Patsy and me since we bought Bilbury Grange.

Soon after we had purchased the house and moved in, he arrived at our door asking for a job. He asked for £5 a week and somewhere to sleep and so we made rough but comfortable living accommodation for him in the loft above one of the unused stables.

He later married Miss Hargreaves, the elderly spinster who ran the village school, and although the pair now lived together in her cottage, Mr Parfitt still looks after our garden. We pay him a little more than the original £5 a week and we give him and Mrs Parfitt as much fruit and as many vegetables as they required. Mr Parfitt also gets all the kindling he can use free from the Bilbury Grange garden.

And we share the profits we make from selling excess garden produce to local hotels, restaurants and public houses. Mr Parfitt has the proverbial green fingers and our small market garden has proved surprisingly successful, though to be honest I never really understand just how we manage to do so well for whenever I see him, Mr Parfitt seemed to be resting and 'contemplating nature'.

In the winter, he sits in the potting shed drinking tea laced with whisky. 'This is the time of the year to let the garden breathe', he once told me. 'Besides, it is too cold and muddy to be out there doing things.'

In the spring and summer, he does a little digging and some planting and spends a good part of each day sitting in the potting shed drinking tea laced with whisky. At the busiest times he has two men from the village to help him with the digging and with chores such as mowing and hedge trimming but he insists on doing the planting himself.

'Any fool can dig,' he once told me, 'but it takes a gardener to know how to sow.'

He never wastes time on weeding.

'There's no such thing as an unwanted weed in this garden,' he told me. 'The bees and the butterflies need the wild flowers to do their pollinating. Without the bees and the butterflies we'd have no apples or pears.'

It was Mr Parfitt who told me that dandelions are an excellent early source of pollen for bees. Our bee colonies were certainly doing well and our aviary produced quite a good deal of honey.

'It's too hot to be doing much,' he told me one August day. He was sitting in the shade of the potting shed, drinking tea that was probably laced with whisky. 'It's too hot and there's too many of them damned horseflies about.'

In the autumn he would cut back the dead wood, help take up the dead plants and, of course, build up the compost heaps and the regular bonfires which I so enjoyed.

I left Mr Parfitt to the bonfire, changed my trousers, put on shoes instead of boots, washed my hands and climbed into the car.

The Jackson's farm is some miles away, with wonderful views over the Bristol Channel. The only snag with it is that it can only be approached along a long, very bumpy farm track which passes through half a dozen fields and, inevitably, half a dozen gates. Every time you drive through a gate you have to stop the car, open the gate, drive through, stop the car, close the gate and then continue to the next one. Even with modern cars this would be tricky. With the elderly and slightly temperamental Rolls Royce 20/25 which I inherited from my predecessor, Dr Brownlow, it was rather more than tricky since the vehicle has a tendency to stall when it is left unattended.

And, to make things more complicated, and to slow things down even more, each time the visitor stops he has to be careful where he treads because Colin Jackson keeps cattle and sheep and his fields are, inevitably, well decorated with the inevitable consequences.

I have on several occasions trodden in large, soft cowpats and I am painfully aware that the stickiness and the smell are difficult to remove from a shoe and even more impossible to remove from the floor of a motor car.

(To do all this on a rainy night, in the dark, as I had once done, is considerably more wearing – especially since, when the journey is being undertaken at night, the chances are high that there is a good deal of urgency about the whole affair. On the second time when I had been asked to visit the Jackson's at night I had given instructions that a farmhand who lived in the house put on a coat and hat, arm himself with a bicycle and a torch and open each gate as I approached it.)

'Oh, thank you for coming,' said Rosie, when I finally arrived at their farmhouse. 'I feel really silly but I've got myself into a bit of a tizzy with those pills you gave me for the water troubles. I was in such a state I had a twinkle right up my spine, the way you do, you know.'

I wasn't sure that I've ever had a twinkle go right up my spine but I nodded and smiled.

I had prescribed an antibiotic to be taken four times a day and Rosie explained that she couldn't remember how many she had taken and whether or not she was due to take another capsule. 'You did say it was important not to miss any,' she reminded me.

'When did you start the course?' I asked.

'Last Monday,' she said, without hesitation. 'I took one when I got home and another one last thing at night.'

'And it's Thursday today, isn't it?'

She looked at the calendar on the kitchen wall and confirmed that it was, indeed, Thursday.

'Did you take all your capsules yesterday and Tuesday?'

She said she had.

'You started with 28 capsules,' I said, 'and you took two on Monday and four each on Tuesday and Wednesday. That means that you've taken ten so there should have been 18 capsules left when you got up this morning.'

Mrs Jackson looked very confused. 'If you say so, doctor.'

'How many have you got left?'

She produced the packet. I counted the remaining capsules. 'You've got 17 capsules left so you've only taken one today.'

'I suppose I have,' she agreed.

'What time did you get up?'

'Five minutes to six. I took the pill when I'd made Colin his cup of tea. He likes a cup of tea before he goes out to do the cows. Then while he does the cows I make his breakfast.'

'But it's a quarter past two now and you should have taken one at twelve o'clock,' I told her.

'Is it all right for me to take it now?' she asked.

'It's fine,' I told her. 'Take one now, and then take the next one at six this evening and today's last one at midnight.'

'I set the clock for that one,' said Mrs Jackson. 'We go to bed at half past ten regular because of Colin having to get up to do the cows of a morning. So I put the alarm clock on for twelve and get up and take it. I keep the pills and a glass of water by the bedside. Colin is a sound sleeper because of his deafness so I don't trouble him.'

She took her antibiotic capsule and I wrote a little chart on the back of an envelope for her to keep. I listed the days vertically and the four times of the day when she was due to take capsules horizontally. I then drew lines down and across to make little boxes. I put ticks in the boxes to denote when she had already taken capsules and told her to put a tick in the appropriate box every time she took another capsule.

'That's wonderful, doctor,' she said. She seemed genuinely grateful, even awestruck at my mathematical and logistical brilliance.

Dealing with Mrs Jackson's problem, and drawing her simple pill-taking plan, took less than ten minutes but eating the seed cake she insisted I ate, and drinking the cup of tea she insisted I drink, and opening and closing all the gates took a lot longer. I was away from Bilbury Grange for over an hour and a half – probably nearer two hours.

As I drove home I realised that I could have easily dealt with the whole problem over the telephone. But, I had a smile on my face as I approached Bilbury Grange. I was looking forward to setting light to my bonfire.

However, when I got out of the car and walked round the side of Bilbury Grange I could smell the unmistakable odour of a well-established bonfire. Patsy claims that I can smell a decent bonfire from five miles away – further if the bonfire is upwind.

And, moreover, there was a thin plume of smoke rising from the part of the garden where the bonfire had been built.

'I thought I'd get on with it,' said Mr Parfitt when he saw me approach. 'I finished building the bonfire and set it alight for you'

I looked at the huge pile of smoking ash that was pretty well all that remained of the bonfire. I felt like crying out of disappointment.

'We can just leave that to cool down for a few days,' said Mr Parfitt. 'And then we can spread the ash around the garden.'

I felt cheated.

Only another bonfire enthusiast could quite understand the feeling. I had been looking forward to that particular bonfire, by far the biggest of our autumn bonfire season, for over a week.

'Thanks,' I said to Mr Parfitt. 'Thank you very much. You've been very helpful.'

I was proud of the fact that I think I managed to sound genuinely grateful.

I turned and headed back up to the house.

As I did so Ben, who had been asleep, came bouncing down the garden to greet me. The tablets he was taking for his arthritis were really helping. Behind him came our three cats, Emily and Sophie and Jeremy. At dusk all animals, whatever the species and whatever the age, like to run around and get rid of their excess energy. The four animals walked back up to the house with me.

Not a bad life, I reflected. And there will be other bonfires.

The Confidence Trickster

Thumper and I had to pop into Barnstaple to fetch some beds we needed for the new hospital. We had purchased 12 single beds and three double beds, sight unseen, from a hotel sale. The beds had been left unsold at the end of the sale, held the previous day, and the auctioneer, a friend of Thumper's, had asked if we wanted to buy them for the proverbial 'song'. (We paid £5 for the lot because, as the auctioneer explained, if we hadn't bought them the hotel's creditors would have had to pay to have the beds taken away and dumped.)

We travelled in Thumpers truck, towing a trailer we borrowed from Patsy's father, and after we'd loaded up the truck and the trailer, we managed to find enough space to leave the truck in a public car park near to the bus station. We both needed to go to the bank to get out some cash, and I had to pop into the pet food shop to buy some tins of food that Ben is particularly fond of but which Peter Marshall cannot obtain from his wholesaler.

We were walking away from the truck when we were approached by a man in his mid-twenties. He was carrying a brown paper parcel neatly tied with string and he seemed to be very upset. I noticed that there were no stamps on the parcel.

'I'm terribly sorry to bother you,' he said, 'and I assure you that I wouldn't normally approach strangers in this way, but I've had some terribly bad fortune this morning. I live in Ilfracombe and came into town on the bus this morning because I needed to see my solicitors. I had to talk to them about my mother's estate – she died just a few weeks ago.'

'I'm sorry to hear that,' I said, sympathetically.

'She was ill for quite a while,' said the young man. 'Heart trouble was the underlying problem but she had a cancer too. Lung.'

'So what happened to you after you'd got into town?' asked Thumper.

'After I'd seen the solicitor I popped into the Post Office to post a parcel to my sister who lives in Scotland,' said the young man. 'She's the other beneficiary of the estate and to be frank with you she really needs her half of the estate. She has two small children, one of whom suffers with cystic fibrosis, and although she managed to get down for the funeral, she had to go back up North after a few days. Her husband works on the fishing boats and she has to cope with the children by herself most of the time. It's the little boy's birthday in two days, the one with the cystic fibrosis, and I've got his present wrapped and ready to go. I'm his godfather as well as his uncle. While I was queuing in the Post Office I lost my wallet – every penny I had on me.' The young man paused and shook his head sadly. 'Actually, I didn't lose it,' he said. 'It was stolen. It was my own fault. I know it's a stupid thing to do but I put the wallet into my hip pocket. They say you should never do that because it makes it too easy for pickpockets but,' he shrugged and shook his head sadly, 'with everything on my mind I'm afraid I simply stuffed the wallet into that pocket without thinking.'

'So what...' I began.

'I'm not asking you to give me money,' said the young man, interrupting me. 'Not to give me money. Good heavens no. But if I don't get this parcel posted off today there isn't much of a chance that it will reach my godson in time for his birthday. And without my wallet I can't possibly get home tonight.' He paused. 'If one of you could just give me a loan, for the postage and the bus fare, and give me your name and address I'll put a cheque into the post just as soon as I get home.'

I was reaching inside my jacket, about to pull out my wallet, when Thumper spoke.

'A decent try,' he said, 'though I think you over embellished the story with all that stuff about your sister's husband and her sick kid. If you make the story too complicated it stops being believable.'

'What the hell are you suggesting?' demanded the young man, rather angrily.

I confess that I too was rather shocked.

'It's a good variation on a very old story,' said Thumper, ignoring the young man, 'but you made two mistakes. First, the only bus from Ilfracombe arrives in Barnstaple at 1.45 p.m. I know this because my wife's aunt lives in Ilfracombe and she's always complaining that if she gets the bus into town she only has an hour before the bus leaves to go back to Ilfracombe.' Thumper looked at his watch and showed the time to the young man. 'It's 1.37 p.m. at the moment,' he said. 'And that bus stops at every bus stop between here and Ilfracombe. It is never early. So if you came into Barnstaple from Ilfracombe, and you travelled by bus, you couldn't possibly have gone to see your solicitor and gone to the Post Office.'

The young man didn't say anything but started to back away. Suddenly he stopped. 'What was the other mistake?' he asked softly.

'If you've got a solicitor in Barnstaple and your mother has just left you a sum of money why not go and ask him for a small cash loan? That's what a normal, honest person would do.'

'Hmm,' said the young man. 'I see what you mean.'

'Does this scam usually work for you?' asked Thumper.

'Oh yes, it usually works like a charm.'

'Do you have a sister in Scotland?'

The young man hesitated.

'I'm just interested,' said Thumper. 'I'm not going to dob you in to the police.'

'I've got a sister but she lives in Dawlish. She works for Tesco.'

'Children?'

He shook his head.

'And your mother?'

'She lives in Barnstaple. I live with her and my Dad.'

'How did you get into Barnstaple? Motorbike?'

'Yes. How did you know?' He frowned. 'Did you see me on the bike?'

'You have mud splashes on your trousers. You could have got them on a pushbike if you'd ridden fast enough but you're not someone who pedals anywhere are you?

He grinned and shook his head.

'What's in the parcel?'

'Oh just a couple of old books I found in a cupboard. My Gran used to be a bit of a reader. The parcel needs to be heavy so that it looks as if it will cost a bit to post.'

'Of course it does. Undo the parcel. Show me.'

The young man untied the string, unwrapped the parcel and showed us the books. They were both hardbacks. One was a copy of an old copy of a long out of date *Home Doctor* book. The other was a novel called *Brighton Rock* by Graham Greene. The book still had its dust wrapper.'

'May I look?' I said.

The young man handed me the two books. I opened the Greene and looked inside. 'I haven't read this,' I said. 'How much do you want for it?'

'You can have them both for 50 pence,' said the young man brightly.

'That's just what I was going to charge you for the consultation and the advice,' said Thumper.

'No, no, it's OK,' I said. 'I'll give you 50 pence for the two books.' I took some change from my pocket and handed 50 pence to the young man. He seemed grateful.

'Now bugger off, go home and start thinking about getting a proper job,' said Thumper. 'You're a bloody awful con man. You're lucky to have got away with it for this long.'

The young man, mumbled something and shuffled away.

We both knew Thumper was wasting his breath. This was, without a doubt, a young man who would never work for a living. He was a trickster through and through.

'You shouldn't have given him 50 pence for the books,' said Thumper. 'I'd have got you them for nothing. In fact I was thinking of making him buy us our car park ticket – just to teach him a lesson.'

I handed him the *Home Doctor* book. 'You can have this one,' I said. 'But I'll keep the other one. It'll pay for the beds we bought for the new hospital. And it'll pay for a good few other bits of furniture as well.'

Puzzled, Thumper looked at me. 'How do you make that out?'

'The Graham Greene is a first edition. *Brighton Rock* is one of the most difficult of his books to find – especially in a dust wrapper.'

'What's it worth?'

I thought for a moment and looked at the book. It really was in excellent condition. It looked as if it had been read just the once. 'Between £300 and £500,' I replied.

Thumper stared at me for a moment and then burst out laughing.

The Taxman Calls

During the night an unexpected, blustery south westerly gale had blown the felt from the roof of an elderly garden shed which we use to store bits and pieces of equipment. I was up a ladder, equipped with a hammer and a pocket full of tacks, attempting to repair the damage, when Patsy appeared. She looked rather flustered.

'The taxman is here,' she said.

I looked down and frowned. 'What on earth for?' I had not yet had my breakfast and surgery was due to start in fifteen minutes time.

'He says he wrote to you and told you he was coming.'

I racked my brains and suddenly remembered that I had received a letter marked Inland Revenue and that there had been something in it about an enquiry or an investigation. I had filed the letter and tried so hard to forget about it that I had pretty well succeeded.

I have, over the years, received more than my fair share of correspondence from the various departments of the Office of Tax Obfuscation (which has, generally speaking, done a magnificent job of making income tax entirely incomprehensible to the average taxpayer) and these days I find it difficult to have any respect for its officials.

Many of those with whom I have corresponded have been rude and unnecessarily aggressive and it seems to me quite unfair that this should be the case. I know I am old-fashioned but it seems to me that taxpaying citizens have the right to be treated as innocent until proved guilty, and to be treated with a modicum of respect.

Moreover, it seems to me that most of the tax officials with whom I have had dealings have very little understanding of how the real world actually works.

When I published my own books and sold them through the post, one tax inspector had completely misunderstood the way my small business worked.

'You had 2,000 books printed,' he reminded me, 'and paid £3,000 to the printer. The price printed on the jacket of each book is £10 so you owe us tax on £20,000, the retail value of all the books, minus £3,000 which is £17,000.'

It took me hours to convince him that many of the books were still unsold, stored in one of our barns, and that he could hardly expect me to pay tax on money I had not received. I also pointed out that I was entitled to claim the cost of buying stamps and packaging for the books. The taxman found this a difficult concept to understand and so I had tried to explain how things worked by using another example.

'If a café owner buys a bag of 50 teabags for £1 and can make one cup of tea from each bag and charges 50 pence for a cup of tea, will you expect him to pay tax on 50 cups of tea the minute he takes delivery of the teabags?'

This puzzled the taxman.

'Are you now going to start selling cups of tea?' he demanded sternly. 'How many tea bags have you bought? You have not previously declared this business.'

I climbed down from the ladder, put the hammer down on the ground and walked back to the house alongside Patsy. Suddenly she put a hand on my arm and stopped me. 'What on earth has happened to your waistcoat?' she asked.

I looked down. 'Nothing, as far as I can tell.'

'That button, second from the bottom!'

I looked down. 'It's exactly the same as all the other buttons.'

'Yes, I can see it is. But it's sewn on with green cotton and all the other buttons are sewn on with black cotton.'

'Ah yes, I was pretty pleased with myself about that,' I said. 'The button came off yesterday after dinner – I think it was that second helping of apple and blackberry pie that was responsible – and you were busy with the little ones and I didn't want to bother you so I thought I'd sew it on myself. After all, I thought, if I can sew up people I can surely sew on a button.' I looked down at the waistcoat.

'I'm sure the button is sewn on very nicely,' Patsy agreed. 'But why on earth did you use green cotton?'

'Oh, I couldn't find the black stuff. So I thought green would do fine. Actually I used some suture material I'd got in the surgery.'

'You can't see the taxman with a button on your waistcoat sewn on with green cotton!' she said, aghast. 'Whatever will he think?'

'I don't care what he thinks about my waistcoat button. I hope he enjoys my accounts but I don't much care a jot what he thinks about my sewing.'

But Patsy was not so easily appeased. She was determined that the button must come off and be put back on again with black cotton. Suddenly I had a brain wave. 'Go on ahead,' I told her. 'When I catch up with you in a hundred yards or so the button will be sewn on with black cotton.'

Patsy looked at me very doubtfully but hurried on ahead. Three minutes later I caught up with her. 'There you are! Now look at it!'

Patsy inspected the button. And then she bent closer and examined it more carefully. 'How on earth did you do that?' she demanded. 'It's now sewn on with black cotton!'

'Just a magical medical trick,' I told her.

Patsy looked at me very doubtfully. 'I don't know how you did that,' she murmured. I don't think I had ever seen her look quite so puzzled. 'How on earth did you do that? Is that the same waistcoat?'

'Ah!' I said, with a smile. 'Pure magic. I'm not allowed to tell you how it was done.'

I found a small and very officious man waiting for me in the waiting room. He looked to be in his forties but had shaved his head to try to hide the fact that he was going bald, so in fact he looked older and had a five o'clock shadow on the top of his head. He had grown a small, old-fashioned toothbrush moustache and although I suspect he had grown it hoping that it would give him a jaunty, film star air, in reality it made him look like a very untrustworthy car salesman. It was more Adolf Hitler than Errol Flynn or Ronald Colman. I wouldn't have bought a set of tyres from him, let alone a whole motor car.

I confess that at that moment, at the sight of this wretched man who had come to inspect my accounts and doubtless pick holes in them, I felt rather sorry for myself.

It had been a strangely annoying month or two.

First, I had written a thoughtful, reasoned article for a medical journal suggesting that high levels of stress might produce raised blood pressure, and had been astonished that the response from the medical establishment had been universal condemnation. One professor from Nottingham University had announced that I should be struck off the medical register for daring to suggest such a thing.

Second, I had received a good deal of abuse for having written a paper criticising the over-prescribing of benzodiazepine tranquillisers. I had suggested that patients who were given the drugs for long periods of time were becoming addicted, and this suggestion had not gone down well with the drug companies.

It seemed that everything I wrote about medicine caused controversy. A medical journal article suggesting that the over-prescribing of antibiotics would result in the development of stronger and more lethal infections, had been the subject of sneering laughter from a group of doctors who were, I suspected, encouraged by the drug companies making antibiotics. I was acquiring quite a number of enemies within the medical establishment.

As the 1970s progressed, it seemed that anything which made people think produced abuse rather than debate and I had a feeling that things were not going to improve. I had recently made the decision to give up writing papers and articles for the journals. I really needed a rest from the world.

And now the taxman had arrived and I wasn't thrilled by his presence.

'My name is Merriment, Mr Merriment,' said the taxman, instantly making it abundantly clear that this was not going to be a convivial conversation conducted on first name terms and involving lots of merriment and good humoured banter. 'I have need of sight of your receipts for the fiscal year ending last April.'

He had managed to confuse me with his very first sentence.

'Fiscal year?' I said. 'I'm not sure I understand…'

'I need to see your accounts for the financial year ending last April and for that purpose I will require full, unfettered sight of your receipts and account books.'

He sounded like a cross between the speaking clock and a Government propaganda broadcast. I wondered if he always spoke in such a stilted, formal way or if it was something he reserved for taxpayers under investigation. I imagined him arriving home for tea. 'Good evening, Mrs Merriment. I am home for the evening and now require approved sustenance to be provided in accordance with our nuptial agreement. I see that you have been to the hairdressers. The appearance is satisfactory.' I tried to resist the temptation to reconstruct a honeymoon confrontation.

'I've got everything in a cardboard box in the stable,' I told him. 'All the paperwork is there. If you'd like to take a seat in the living room I'll bring you the box. Would you like a cup of tea? Can I get you anything to eat?'

'It is not my custom to accept comestibles in any form from inquiry subjects,' he told me. 'But I will accept a glass of water taken from the domestic water supply.'

I fetched the box and put it down on a small table in the living room. It would have been better to able to put the box on the dining room table but the dining room was serving its secondary purpose as the practice waiting room and was, in that role, full of patients. I then gave the taxman a glass of tap water. He sat down, opened the box and started to remove the contents. There wasn't much in the box and I felt that he was rather disappointed. There was a large, used brown envelope full of receipts, a similarly sized brown envelope full of pay slips, royalty statements and so on and a small, red, sixpenny notebook purchased from a branch of F.W.Woolworth years earlier. The notebook still had the faded sticker on the front, showing that it had been purchased prior to decimalisation.

'What's this?' he demanded, holding up the sixpenny notebook.

'That's my accounts,' I told him.

'I thought I had made it acceptably clear,' he said, speaking to me as though to a child of three or four years of age, 'that I required sight of your full accounts.'

'That's all there is, I'm afraid,' I confessed, now wishing that I hadn't been quite so mean and had bought the one shilling notebook.

Mr Merriment opened the pages of the small notebook as though he were examining a valuable piece of evidence in a multiple murder case. 'This is all there is?' he asked, clearly finding it difficult to believe that I wasn't hiding more accounts in another box somewhere.

'That's all there is, I'm afraid,' I said. I leant over and pointed to the pages of the notebook that he was examining. If you look on the left you'll see the details of the money I've spent, and if you look on the right you'll see details of the money I've been paid. The receipts and so on for the money I've spent are all in the big brown envelope marked 'Receipts' and the bits of paper relating to my income are all in the big brown envelope marked 'Income'.'

Mr Merriment looked very disappointed; and he reminded me of a child who has unwrapped an attractive looking Christmas parcel and has found that it contains a hand knitted scarf and a pair of matching hand knitted gloves carefully packed into a cardboard box marked 'Toys'. He made a snorting sound that reminded me of one of Colin Jackson's Gloucester Old Spot pigs snuffling its way through a new delivery of turnip heads.

'Do you mind if I leave you for a while?' I asked. 'I'm a bit busy just at the moment.' This was true but I also didn't fancy standing behind the tax collector as he worked his way through my six penny notebook and the accompanying brown envelopes.

Mr Merriment looked up and glared at me as though he were a hangman and I were his next victim. 'As long as you remain available for me to question when I have completed my preliminary enquiries,' he said.

'Well I might have to pop out if there's an emergency,' I said. I looked at my watch. 'And I was due to start morning surgery twenty minutes ago.'

Mr Merriment glowered disapprovingly, said nothing more and turned back to my accounts. There wasn't much charm available and absolutely no bonhomie.

I left and went into the consulting room to start the morning's surgery.

It was, inevitably, a busy day. There were already twelve patients sitting patiently waiting for me.

I put Mr Merriment out of my mind, forgot the shed roof and concentrated on other people's problems for a while.

The first patient, 'Amelia' Rate (whose real first name is Phillippa but who is known to everyone as Amelia), wanted to know if I could recommend an organisation that would help her with her addiction to television soap operas which, she confessed, were now taking up most of her waking life. Mrs Rate, who suffers from advanced and probably irreversible steatopygia and is married to a tree surgeon who runs a small, local firm called 'Special Branch', is a regular visitor to the surgery and she nearly always manages to be first in the queue. She is addicted to therapy and attends all the addiction groups she can find. She goes to Alcoholics Anonymous and Gamblers

Anonymous, of course, and is also a keen member of a group for chocoholics. She loves talking about herself and the minute there is an organisation for people who are addicted to organisations for addicts I will happily refer her to them. Meanwhile, she comes to my surgery several times a month. 'I just want to find myself,' she once told me.

The second patient, Miss Tomkins, complained that she constantly felt as though insects were crawling over her skin. I could find nothing wrong with her. There were no signs of any scabies or other beasties and when I gave her the all-clear she told me that she had suspected that there weren't really any insects on her skin but that she had hoped that there would be so that she would know that she wasn't going mad.

'You aren't going mad,' I assured her, 'your problem is formication.'

Miss Tomkins is in her early 50s and given her age and medical history, I thought it possible that the condition might have been brought on by the onset of the menopause. This is a common and harmless cause of formication.

I was about to continue by explaining that there are a number of causes of this condition and that before reaching a diagnosis I would need to get some tests done, when Miss Tomkins stood up, pushed back her chair and told me that she had never been so insulted in her life.

'I am a maiden lady,' she told me proudly. 'I have never had relations with any man.' She actually shuddered at the thought.

'Ah, no, formication,' I said. 'It's spelt with an 'm'. It has nothing to do with 'fornication'.

'Oh,' said Miss Tomkins. She now seemed rather embarrassed and sat down again.

I told her that I would arrange for some tests to be done at the hospital in Barnstaple.

The next patient, a man in his early 70s who is called Paddy Fields, came in coughing badly and complaining that he had bronchitis. He's had bronchitis often enough to be able to make his own diagnosis now.

Mr Fields, is a former denture repair salesman who is famous locally for wearing bright red trousers and a green waistcoat, gets bronchitis several times a year but refuses to give up smoking. He claims that he smokes only one or two packs a day but judging by the nicotine stains on his fingers, and the condition of his heart and lungs, I would guess that he gets through one or two packs an hour rather than a day. I have tried hard to persuade him to cut down but I never seem to be able to get anywhere with him.

Paddy walks like a rodeo rider after an exceptionally hard day at the office. His legs are so bandy that you could drive a team of Shetland ponies through the gap between his legs without touching his inner thighs. He likes people to think that he is bandy legged because of the size of his nuptial equipment but his secret is that he has a huge swelling, a hydrocele, which has developed in a sac around his left testicle. Paddy refuses to see a surgeon and since the hydrocele is no threat to his life, I have never felt able to push him into doing so.

Paddy supplements a probably inadequate pension by delivering logs. I have no idea where he gets them from, for he lived in a tiny terraced cottage on the road to Lynton, but his logs are the best in the county – always reliably aged and all selected for their good burning qualities.

Those who do not understand the wonders of the log fire may find this an odd thing to say but it is important to have the right type of wood if you're planning a log fire. Ash, beech, apple, hazel, holly, hornbeam and juniper, rowan, yew, hawthorn and cedar all burn exceeding well, and with pleasant aromas as a bonus. For me the best smelling woods are apple, pear and cherry, all of which give off an extremely pleasant, sweet smell, though lilac is also very pleasantly fragrant.

Conifers burn fast, produce a spicy scent and make good kindling but if used as logs they tend to produce a lot of sparks and the resultant firework display can be a little disturbing if you simply want to sit in front of a warming fire with a good book and don't want to spend the evening jumping up and down to put out the smouldering fireside rug.

Alder makes poor firewood, as does elm unless it is at least two-years-old. Lime is very poor. Sycamore also needs to be two-years-old, as does wood from the willow, which tends to smoulder and produce more smoke than heat.

All firewood burns best when it is seasoned, preferably at least a year old, but Paddy would not dream of giving alder, elm, lime, sycamore or willow to his customers.

At Christmas, Paddy always brings us half a dozen yule logs. These are monstrous, heavy and usually consist of well-matured oak. Oak is another smouldering wood though if it is thoroughly dried it burns quite well and it does make an excellent yule log. One end is placed in the fire with the other sticking out into the room. As the wood burns the log is pushed into the fire. A good yule log will last for hours.

'I'm not going to give up my fags and booze so that I can live for another three months in a shared bedroom in a grotty council run nursing home in Ilfracombe,' Paddy told me when I tried yet again to persuade him to cut down his consumption of cigarettes. I found it difficult to think of an argument that would convince him otherwise.

I gave him a prescription for an antibiotic.

And so it went on.

By the time I had finished, I had seen 18 patients altogether; a light surgery for a city based GP with a list of 3,000 patients but a fairly heavy surgery for me. Like all doctors who work in rural areas, I spent most of my time doing home visits because it took me much longer to travel to my patients. A city GP can visit three or four patients an hour if they all live in neatly numbered houses. I often found myself spending an hour or two visiting just one patient.

The stream of patients at least succeeded in distracting me from the thought of the taxman in the living room.

The final patient was a young man who demanded a sick note.

Kevin McMurray is a pushy, cockalorum who was born at the paddling end of the national gene pool and who works in Taunton doing something with motor cars. He always gives the impression that he is a mechanic or a salesman but Patchy, who goes to auctions in Taunton once a month, says he has seen him washing cars on a garage forecourt.

Although he is hardly ever at home in Bilbury, Kevin has, probably through laziness rather than loyalty or respect for my medical skills or bedside manner, remained on my list of patients.

He always wears jeans and a denim jacket with lots of safety pins and badges in the lapels and I put this down to the fact that he lives in the market town of Taunton – which is, to those of us in Bilbury, a big city. I think the population is around 45,000. I once asked Kevin why he had so many safety pins on his person, assuming that there might be some practical explanation. He told me that they were decorative and that his girlfriend had a safety pin fixed through her nose. He said he found this very attractive.

Teenagers sometimes complain that old people all look the same to them but I'm beginning to reach the age where all youngsters look the same.

Kevin told me that he needed a sick note because he had backache. I was not at all convinced that he had any back trouble at all (he seemed perfectly able to walk and to sit) and I suspected that he wanted time off to attend a football match. I tried to resist his demands but when a patient insists that he has back pain it is impossible to prove that he doesn't. So, in the end, I signed a sick note and wrote 'plumbi oscillans' in the space where I was expected to write the nature of his illness.

'What's this?' demanded Kevin, peering at the diagnosis.

'It's the Latin name for your illness,' I told him.

'Oh,' he said, satisfied and impressed.

He left clutching his sick note as though it were a ten pound note.

I was glad he didn't push me for a translation because plumbi oscillans is the Latin for 'lead swinging', an ancient euphemism for malingering.

Exhausted by the morning I walked into the kitchen, gave Patsy a hug, fell into an easy chair and let out a huge sigh. 'Food,' I said. 'I need food and drink.'

Miss Johnson had, during the morning surgery, brought me two cups of black coffee and a couple of digestive biscuits but in my view two cups of coffee and two biscuits are not enough to keep body and soul glued together.

'I hate to be the one to have to tell you this,' said Patsy, 'but Mr Merriment is still in the living room. He asked me to tell you that he wants to see you. Actually, I think what he actually said was that he had 'unearthed a serious accounting misreckoning' and was 'desirous of further communication with you'. I don't know who writes his dialogue.'

I groaned and looked at her. 'Oh bugger,' I said. 'They probably have a special phrase book. Actually, they probably go on miscommunication courses.' I pulled myself up out of the chair and wandered to the living room.

'Ah, doctor,' said Mr Merriment. 'I'm so delighted that you could spare me a little of your valuable time.'

I wasn't in a mood to put up with the taxman's sarcasm. 'I have been rather busy,' I told him. I was tempted to tell him that there was an outbreak of smallpox in the village, in the hope that this might send him scurrying back to Barnstaple, but I bravely resisted the temptation.

The taxman listened to me without blinking. I now decided that he looked like a lizard, contemplating his prey. I examined him carefully, searching for any signs of a forked tongue snapping out to catch me unawares.

He took from the table, and held up, items which he clearly regarded as forensic evidence: in his left hand he had several pieces of paper and in his right hand he held my sixpenny notebook.

'You have included in your expenses claims for five electricity bills,' he said, waving the pieces of paper at me as though producing the blood-stained knife with which I had murdered the little princes. There was an unpleasant element of triumph in his voice. This was, I thought, a man who, if he ever watched a football match, would cheer not because one side had won but because the other side had lost.

I stared at him, uncomprehending.

'There are only four quarters in a year, doctor,' he said. He was really pleased with himself. 'But you have claimed for five quarterly bills.'

I reached out a hand. 'May I look?'

He handed me the pieces of paper he was holding. There were, as he said, five electricity bills.

'But I put them into the accounts because they all arrived in the same year,' I explained. 'And if there were five in this set of accounts then there will be three in another year's accounts.'

'I am going to disallow the last of these five bills,' said Mr Merriment, ignoring my explanation. 'You will receive a demand for the tax owed and for interest payable. If you do not pay within 30 days you will be subject to penalties.'

I opened my mouth to protest, then decided there was no point. It wasn't worth the time. And I was hungry. 'OK,' I said. 'Would you like another glass of water before you go?'

'No thank you. But I would very strongly suggest that you keep your accounts in a more appropriate way in future.' He looked at the cardboard box, the two brown envelopes and the sixpenny notebook with undisguised contempt.

'What do you suggest?' I asked.

'Have you considered employing the services of an accountant?'

'I did have one of those,' I said. 'But he retired and I never got round to finding a replacement.' I looked at the items on the table. 'I'll buy a bigger notebook for next year's accounts,' I promised.

Mr Withymooor did not look impressed by this. He made another snorting sound, reminding me once more of Colin Jackson's Gloucester Old Spot pig, and headed for the door. I followed him out. 'Would you please telephone for a taxi,' he said. 'I will be heading back to the Inland Revenue offices in Barnstaple.'

I had not realised that he hadn't come in his own car. I said I would be happy to call him a taxi.

'If you submit a claim for the cost of the telephone call I will deal with it appropriately,' he told me.

'No need for that,' I told him. 'Let's just put it down as a small bribe, shall we?'

He went very red.

'Would you like to wait in the living room? The taxi will be a few minutes. I'll ring one of the local chaps because it will take nearly an hour for a taxi to come out from Barnstaple.'

'I will wait by the roadside,' he said. I wondered if he had his hair shirts washed or just wore them until they fell apart.

He left.

I telephoned for a taxi to come and pick him up and then headed for the kitchen.

'Would you like breakfast or lunch?' asked Patsy.

I looked at the clock. 'Both,' I told her. 'I'll have both. Breakfast first, and then lunch. But in that order, of course.'

'Has Mr Merriment gone?'

'He's standing in the lane waiting for a taxi to arrive,' I told her. 'He's standing next to the sign that Thumper and Patchy put up when I started practising again.'

(When the local authorities had allowed me to reopen my surgery my good friends had erected a very smart sign which read: 'No Wart Too Small, No Rash Too Faint'. I had never bothered to move the sign, partly through laziness and partly because I rather liked it.)

'Who did you call?' asked Patsy.

'Samuel Houghton,' I said, putting two slices of bread into the toaster.

Patsy, who was bending over the oven, stood up and looked at me. She was frowning. 'But Samuel Houghton doesn't have a taxi,' she said. 'As far as I know he doesn't even have a car.'

Samuel Houghton is a local farmer. He was in his seventies several years ago and if time serves him as it serves the rest of us, he must now be in his eighties. He wears a tweed jacket which he bought when he was 25 and holds up his trousers with baler twine. He has pretty well retired from farming but has the local authority contract for clearing snow from the lanes. He drives a huge, red tractor which can do nearly four miles an hour when travelling downhill.

'He's got a tractor,' I reminded Patsy. 'And when I last saw him he told me he was setting up a taxi service.'

'But the tractor has only got one seat?'

'Ah, but when he uses his tractor as a taxi, Samuel tows a trailer behind. And he puts a bale of straw on the trailer as a seat.'

Patsy started to giggle. 'It'll take hours for him to get to Barnstaple!'

'Samuel doesn't mind,' I said. 'And I told him that his passenger is a taxman who wants to see a bit of the countryside on his way back to town. Sam said he'll go via Combe Martin, Berrynarbour, West Down and Braunton. I told him he can charge the guy whatever he likes.'

'They'll be lucky to be back in Barnstaple before dark!'

'That's no problem. Samuel has had lights fitted on the tractor and he says he's going to stay over with his nephew in Prixford, and then do some shopping in Barnstaple tomorrow. It's a long time since he saw the big city lights.'

'The big city lights in Barnstaple?' said Patsy incredulously.

'There are at least three sets of traffic lights in the town!' I reminded her.

The toast popped up. I reached for a slice, put it onto a plate and unscrewed the top off the marmalade.

Just then there was a knock on the door. It was the taxman.

'I told you to call me a taxi,' he said. 'What do you mean by arranging for this man to bring his tractor?' He pointed at Samuel, whose tractor was chugging in the lane outside.

'I'm afraid we don't have any formal taxi services in Bilbury,' I told him. 'As a service to the community Samuel has agreed to help out when required. He'll get you back to Barnstaple.'

The taxman glowered.

'I'd take you back myself,' I told him. 'But my insurance doesn't allow me to take paying passengers and since I don't have to go into Barnstaple on business I wouldn't be able to claim the cost of my petrol.' I shrugged and attempted to look frustrated. 'The rules must be obeyed,' I added. I then waved to Samuel, and said goodbye to Mr Merriment, surely the most inappropriately named civil servant in the history of the civil service.

'Now you can tell me how you managed to re-sew that button on so quickly,' said Patsy. 'If you can really sew buttons on that fast then you should be in the next Sewing Olympics! And where did you find the black cotton.'

'Trade secret,' I said, smearing liberal quantities of marmalade onto my toast. I either have butter or marmalade – never both.

Patsy came up behind me and niftily removed my plate. 'How?' she demanded.

Faced with the loss of my toast I had no choice. I took a black felt tip pen out of my inside pocket and showed it to her. 'I just covered the green cotton with black ink,' I explained.

'You are impossible!' cried Patsy.

But she gave me back my toast.

The Forger

Like most ancient English villages, Bilbury stands at and around the top of a fairly large hill. Early settlers liked living on top of a hill because it made them feel safer from invaders, wild animals and from floods.

It's much easier to repel attackers if you're higher than they are because then you're firing arrows and throwing stones downhill whereas the enemy, wretched souls, are having to trudge uphill while firing their arrows, and they are throwing their stones up instead of down.

And, of course, those who dwell on the top of hills are far less likely to get their feet wet if they haven't finished building your arks when the floods come.

(The name Bilbury, incidentally, comes from the prefix Bil- which means promontory or ridge and the word 'bury' which has nothing to do with dead bodies but which is a corruption of the word 'burh' which originally meant a fort. So, Bilbury was originally a fort on a ridge of high ground. The nearby town of Barnstaple also has a military history. In Saxon times, Barnstaple was the principal business centre in North Devon but it was also a stronghold built to withstand attacks from Danish invaders and the name literally means 'post of the battleaxe' – a meeting place with a battleaxe as its identifying symbol.)

Apart from the obvious advantage of being safe from invaders and biblical style floodings, there are other good things about living on a hill.

Most notably the views tend to be spectacular. And so, for example, although Bilbury stands a mile or two from the North Devon coast we can see the Bristol Channel from several of our bedrooms at Bilbury Grange. On a very clear day we can see Wales.

The only bad thing I can think of is that living on the top of a hill means that you are far more likely to suffer when the winds are strong. And in the south west of England the winds are sometimes very strong indeed. Strong winds mean that most villagers tend to lose a few roof tiles or slates every winter and bits and pieces of houses and cottages which aren't fastened on tightly, such as rusty guttering and aged downpipes, tend to end up somewhere other than where they are supposed to be.

(To those locals who live in what might be politely termed 'an insurance based economy' this really is more of a benefit than a problem. There are, I'm slightly embarrassed to admit, not a few villagers who rely on the insurance claims resulting from winter gales to subsidise their modest incomes and to enable them to keep their bodies and souls within hailing distance of each other.)

After yet another day and night of gales, our garden was littered with tree branches which had been blown down. Even healthy trees shed branches occasionally and in any large garden there will always be one or two trees which are old, creaky and liable to lose branches in a high wind.

I always cut up the decent sized branches for firewood. Bigger branches can be sawn into logs and smaller branches can be turned into kindling. But there are always lots of small twigs which are too small to be useful in the fireplace and they go onto the bonfire. As a confirmed garden pyromaniac, I don't mind this one bit.

But, of course, lighting bonfires when the wind is still blowing can be a difficult, not to say hazardous, activity and I had recently decided to buy myself an incinerator so that I could light a bonfire whatever the weather; without having to worry about glowing embers blowing into a part of the garden where I didn't want a fire starting. We have also had rather a lot of trouble with the badgers raking over our bonfire site looking for something to eat. The result has been that bits and pieces of half burnt rubbish have ended up fifty yards away. I rather hoped that the incinerator would help put an end to that.

Thumper came round this morning as I was putting the damned thing together.

It seems that these days you can't even buy an incinerator which is entirely readymade. This one needed to have four feet fixed onto the bottom, to keep the base of the incinerator off the ground. I was struggling to do this when Thumper appeared.

'Brilliant idea!' said my friend. 'You can provide your patients with a complete service now.'

I looked at him, puzzled.

'You can cremate the ones who die!' said Thumper with a grin. 'We'll make you a new sign: 'Bilbury's Family Doctor: Cradle to Grave and Beyond'.'

I threw the screwdriver I was holding in his direction but he ducked and I missed by yards.

'Mel asked me to ask you to pop in and see him,' said Thumper, picking up the screwdriver, gently moving me aside and fixing the foot I'd been trying to fix in a tenth of the time it would have taken me. 'I went out there to fetch a couple of his pictures for Patchy to put in his gallery. A bloke from London bought the last two.'

'The chap who bought the old railway station?' I asked. I couldn't think of anyone else in the village whom Thumper would describe as 'a bloke from London'. Besides, I remembered that Hardley-Fitzwalter had boasted of buying cheap pictures in the village.

'That's the one,' replied Thumper. 'A complete pillock.' He laughed. 'He probably thought he'd managed to pull the wool over Patchy's eyes.' He said this as though it were an utterly absurd idea.

'How did the bloke in London get to see them?' I asked smiling at the idea of anyone pulling wool over Patchy's eyes.

'Patchy had them in his new gallery.'

'In his gallery?' I didn't know Patchy had anything that could be properly described as a gallery. He keeps most of his stock in his garages.

'Well, they were in what was his garden shed. Patchy now calls it his gallery. I think he got the idea from Peter.' Peter Marshall had recently converted his garden shed into a multi-purpose commercial site which was proving very successful. 'The bloke bought them and paid cash.' I wasn't surprised that it had been a cash transaction. Patchy will write cheques happily enough but he won't accept them.

Mel is Mel Bourne, an artist who lives in an old woodman's cottage in the middle of a wood in the middle of absolutely nowhere. He has no electricity, no running water and no telephone. His real name is Cyril or Nigel or Claude or something similar but everyone in Bilbury calls him 'Mel' because he comes from Australia, though to be honest he hails from Sydney and not Melbourne. Still, there wouldn't be any point in calling him Sid Bourne, would there?

Mel lives with a sequence of 20-year-old girls whom he refers to as his au pairs. He calls them all Mabel and for some inexplicable reason they all seem happy enough to put up with this.

Although he lives simply, I suspect that Mel earns a good living as a professional painter. He is an excellent artist and could easily produce works of art of his own but, sadly, it is apparently difficult for a painter to make a living these days unless he is prepared to create an outlandish public persona for himself. The artists who do well under their own names tend to wear large bow ties, get drunk in public, appear on television and get involved in carefully orchestrated rows with selected members of the art establishment. Mel is far too shy to do any of those things and so he follows a well-trodden route and produces paintings which are, to put it politely, 'eerily reminiscent' of the works of other artists. He does lots of stuff which looks as if it was painted by Renoir, Manet, Monet, Picasso and Chagall. He prefers doing Chagalls because he says Chagall is the easiest to imitate. (People like Mel never use the word 'forge', preferring words such as 'homage', 'tribute' and so on.) When he's creating a Chagal lookalike painting, Mel simply puts in a moon, a badly drawn woman, a cow and a chicken and use a lot of blue paint.

Mel sells most of his paintings at auction houses up and down the country and always puts a sticky label on the back making it clear that the painting has been done 'in the style of' or 'after Chagall'. He gets a couple of hundred pounds apiece for them and they always sell well. He says he knows that the buyers are usually antique shop owners who peel off the stickers, put the paintings into their shops and then pretend not to know what it is that they are selling. Browsers see what looks like a Chagall or a Renoir and they are blinded by the sound of cash pouring into their pockets. If names are mentioned, the antique shop owner pretends not to have heard of Chagall and says he thought that a fellow called Renoir used to play for Manchester United.

The antique shop owner then sells the picture on for five hundred pounds and makes a good profit. Up until that point, no one in the chain of deceit has done anything illegal.

The buyer who purchases the picture from the antique dealer then either hangs the picture on his wall, and gloats about how little he paid for it, or else he flogs it to a London dealer as an original but unsigned painting.

It is, I'm told, surprising how many famous artists never bothered to sign their work, particularly the stuff they did when they were young, unknown and penniless. Why would a young artist bother to sign his name to his painting if his name wasn't going to mean anything to prospective buyers? According to Patchy there are now four times as many paintings attributed to Marc Chagall as the great man ever produced in his lifetime. Not all those were produced by Mel Bourne, of course, but his share of the total is almost certainly greater than anyone else's.

Thumper fixed the next and final foot to the base of the incinerator with an ease which I envied. If you gave Thumper a large box full of old motor car parts he would build you a motor car in a day – and have absolutely no bits left over. And if you gave Patchy Fogg a large box full of old motor car parts he would sell the bits as souvenirs, paperweights and bits of modern sculpture. My skills, such as they are, seem simple and rather primitive in comparison.

I thanked Thumper and drove out to Mel's cottage.

This is something much easier to say or to write than it is to do, since the last part of the track through the wood is so rough, so rutted and so strewn with fallen branches that I had to park the Rolls Royce on a bed of pine needles and walk the final quarter of a mile.

The current Mabel, a lovely Dutch girl who dotes on Mel and regards him as a genius, met me at the cottage door, insisted that I accept a large glass of wine and took me in to the room which doubled as a bedroom and an art studio. Mel was lying on a huge double bed. Mabel, who had clearly been crying, stayed with us, settling down onto a large bean bag in a corner of the room.

Mel Bourne is an unusual fellow in every possible respect. He has small black eyes, which sit like solitary, sinking currants in a double handful of uncooked dough, a mean cook's interpretation of the currant bun, and thin, pale lips which had clearly long ago run out of smiles. These are situated a couple of inches above the finest collection of chins I had seen for a long while. The chins are well worth numbering and categorising. Some people collect stamps, some collect old typewriters. Mel looks as though he collects chins and had been very successful at it.

Although born in Australia he is now a staunch Englishman; the sort of fellow who is proud enough of his country to believe that the newspaper headline *Storm in Channel –Continent Isolated* makes absolute good sense. He speaks in a slow, stentorian voice which made him sound like the fellows NASA employed to talk to the astronauts on America's early adventures in space.

I've always found voices fascinating.

I once knew a fellow who was a very successful disc jockey on the wireless. He worked on pirate radio and then moved to Radio 1 when the BBC realised, rather belatedly, that there was a market for popular music. I first met him when he was doing a programme in which short interviews with guests were slotted in between the records. I remember that he interviewed me about a book of mine called *Bodypower*. I was so fascinated by the famous, voice that I had difficulty in answering any of his questions. Every time he opened his mouth it sounded as if he were about to introduce the very latest single from the Rolling Stones. Years later, when I knew him well, I still found myself in awe of the voice. If he asked me if I wanted another cup of coffee I would find myself sitting waiting for the next record to start playing before I answered.

'What's up?' I asked Mel, carefully moving a few magazines onto the floor and sitting down on the edge of the bed. I put the glass of wine which Mabel had given me down onto the floor beside the magazines.

'I'm buggered,' said Mel. He had no teeth at all. I didn't remember him being edentulous. 'Totally worn out and obviously dying. You'll have to give me a jab to put me out of Mabel's misery. I've left her the cottage and a dozen paintings – they'll last her until she finds a new boyfriend.'

There was a sob and a protest from the corner of the room.

Mel nodded towards the wine I'd put down. 'You'll like that,' he said, 'it's a Saint Emilion Grand Cru, 1954. Costs a fortune but very drinkable. I was going to drink all the good stuff before I popped my clogs but I won't manage it now. Ask Mabel to give you half a dozen bottles to take home with you. And take a couple of bottles for Thumper.' I noticed that his false teeth, an upper set and a lower set, were sitting on the wooden cabinet beside the bed.

Unless there are exceptional circumstances I don't usually drink before lunchtime but this seemed an exceptional circumstance so I picked up the wine glass and took a sip. It was like drinking velvet; blood red, heavy bodied, light-headed, rich as Croesus velvet. I had never tasted a wine quite like it nor, I suspected, half as expensive. I took a bigger sip.

'In what particular way are you buggered?' I asked.

'It's been coming on for a while,' said Mel sadly but stoically. 'Some time ago I reached the age where I always needed to take an antacid before I ate anything, just as a precaution'. He paused, enjoying half-forgotten memories of meals enjoyed and now mourned. 'But,' he continued with a forced and gummy grin, 'until recently I always told myself that however old and knackered I became my best years were still ahead of me. And I damned well intended to go ahead and prove it.' He sighed and moved awkwardly as though in pain. 'But that was then and this is now. I'm as weak as a kitten and I've started to get pains that I really don't like.' He sighed. 'The end is nigh, doctor. It's time to give me the jab.'

'The jab?' I said.

'The stuff you give people to send them on their way,' said Mel, with a debonair wave of a hand. 'Mabel kisses me. You say goodbye. You both say I'm very brave and you'll never forget me. I tell you I want to be cremated and to have my ashes strewn in the woods – which I do incidentally – then you bung a needle in my bum and shoot me full of arsenic or cyanide, or whatever it is you medics use these days.' He tried to raise himself up off the bed but failed. 'If you leave here without giving me the jab I'll just cut my wrists!' he told me. He produced an old-fashioned cut throat razor from underneath his pillow. Mabel sobbed loudly.

I stared at him. It took me a moment or two to realise that he was deadly serious.

Under normal circumstances Mel is one of those individuals who goes through life apparently unconcerned about things going on around him. I have always envied him his laissez faire attitude.

It has always been my experience that the things which go wrong are invariably the things we haven't thought about, and therefore do not worry about, and I long ago concluded that there are two ways to try to deal with this problem.

The first way is to think more, and worry more, in the hope that you will eventually spot the potential problem before it rears its doubtless very ugly head.

The people who follow this path tiptoe nervously through life. One minute they are looking over their shoulders for the madman who is lurking in the shadows and about to leap out and wrap his bony fingers around their neck, and the next minute they are looking up into the sky for the unexpected scaffolding pole or roof tile that is about to come plummeting down and crush their skulls. Around every corner there is always a new disaster waiting.

Some of those who fall into this category are incorrigible.

I once tried to teach a patient how to relax by using his imagination to visualise the peaceful delights of a walk in the country. He lay on the couch while I painted a word picture of a beautiful walk along a sunlight lane. Suddenly, he leapt up screaming. 'What on earth is the matter?' I asked. 'There's a body in the ditch at the side of the lane!' he cried, his face etched with horror and agony.

Sadly, the chronic worriers usually find that their thinking and worrying is of very little value because there is always something they miss. In between looking out for the mad mugger and watching for the falling roof tile, they are mown down by a runaway lorry or an out of control cyclist. Moreover, their constant worrying makes them ill and they invariably suffer from one or more items chosen by a Higher Authority from an a la carte menu of a wide variety of stress related disorders – heart disease, high blood pressure, stomach ulcers, asthma, cancer and so on.

The second solution is to think less and to worry not at all; thinking of yourself as a shore upon which the waves will constantly break and over which you cannot possibly have any control.

Mel fell firmly into this category.

The people who follow this philosophy are very slightly more likely to find themselves facing serious and unexpected problems. Occasionally they will get their feet damp, and from time to time they will be washed away to sea.

But they are far less likely to suffer from stress related diseases.

They tend to saunter through life, taking each new vicissitude with an aplomb which is envied by their more nervous neighbours. They eat, drink and smoke whatever they like, without a thought for the consequences. They shrug off all thoughts of falling tiles and lurking murderers and wander freely through life, with enviable nonchalance. Insouciance is their watchword and equanimity their guide. They are calm and untroubled by the terrors of the world. Insurance is, for them, something other people take out.

The trouble is that their sense of fatalism is likely to encourage them to give up too soon when illness strikes.

Mel is settled resolutely into the second category of individual.

He regards worry as an unnecessary luxury; as pointless as a battery operated back scratcher or diamond studded collar for a goldfish.

Worry has always been something he was quite happy to go through life without. He has always been happy to accept whatever life throws at him. And now that he was convinced that he was dying he didn't want to fight. Instead, he wanted to get the whole damned thing over as quickly as possible.

'Tell me what symptoms you've got,' I told him. I took another sip of the wine. It really was very good. I felt slightly guilty for drinking at such an early hour. And I had to drive the car back home.

'Everything's gone stiff,' said Mel. 'I think it's probably the rigor mortis setting in a bit early.'

'What do you mean by 'everything'?'

'Well, not the bit I'd like to be stiff,' said Mel with a laugh as hollow as a chocolate Easter egg. There was a half-stifled sob from Mabel. 'My neck is stiff, my shoulders are stiff and my hips are stiff. My hips and thighs are so stiff that I can hardly get out of bed. And my shoulders are so painful and stiff that I can hardly lift a bloody paint brush.'

'How long has it been coming on?' I asked him.

'A few days,' said Mel. 'No more than a week.'

'Does anything make it worse?'

He thought for a moment. 'The stiffness and pain are worse in the morning,' he said. 'They're terrible when I wake up. By the end of the day the pain and stiffness are no worse than awful.' He thought for a moment and sighed. 'I feel as weak as a kitten and I just know I'm dying.'

'Anything else?' I asked.

'Isn't that enough?' he demanded.

'You seem depressed,' I said.

'Of course I'm bloody depressed! I'm only 57 and I'm dying because my body has worn out! I should be able to get a rebate. I thought we were supposed to have a guarantee of three score and ten!' He tried to move but winced. He lay quietly for a few moments. 'I'm not ready to die,' he said, 'but when your time has come there's no point in whingeing about it, is there?' Tears appeared in the corners of both eyes and slowly ran down his cheeks.

I finished off the wine and put my glass down.

'Is there no hope, doctor?' asked Mabel. 'Can you get him into hospital? Are there some tests you could do?'

'I'm not going into a damned hospital!' cried Mel. 'I hate hospitals.'

It is surprising how many people are terrified of going into hospital – probably because they know people who've been made worse, caught infections or had the wrong leg chopped off. In this respect, little has changed from the Middle Ages when patients would fight to stay out of hospitals because they knew that once they went in they would only leave in a coffin. I was contemplating this sad truth when suddenly, in a flash, I realised what was wrong with Mel and I knew that he wasn't dying. I'd seen a patient with these symptoms before. Experience and intuition can be a potent combination on the rare occasion when they work together. Instinct, intuition, call it what you will is unconscious logic and while I'd been thinking about something else my mind had been whirring and had dug out the answer.

Mel looked at the empty glass I was still holding and told Mabel to pour me more wine.

The more I thought about it the more certain I was that Mel had a disease called polymyalgia rheumatic – a relatively uncommon disorder which seems to exclusively affect people over the age of 55.

As with so many diseases, no one knows what causes polymyalgia rheumatic. Indeed, no one knows much about it at all except that it seems to involve an inflammation of the lining of the large joints and that this inflammation causes severe stiffness and pain in the muscles of the hips, the shoulders and the neck. The symptoms tend to be worse in the morning and they are so distressing that patients feel generally unwell, miserable and often depressed.

There are blood tests which can be done but if I took blood samples immediately I wouldn't get the results back for several days, probably a week. The erythrocyte sedimentation rate (ESR) is raised dramatically in patients with polymyalgia rheumatic but I didn't think I had a few days. Mel was so depressed that he would almost certainly kill himself if he had to suffer for another week.

I could try to persuade him to go into hospital. But would he go? No. I knew he wouldn't. I could probably obtain a legal order forcing him to go into hospital but that would take time I didn't have. And I feared that the minute I left Mel and returned home to start the legal processes he would cut his wrists. And even if Mel agreed to go into hospital there would be the problem of getting him out of the cottage and into an ambulance. He would have to be carried for a quarter of a mile at least. The pains and stiffness in his big joints would make the whole operation unbearably uncomfortable for him.

Suddenly, I made a decision. I took a gulp of the beautiful wine Mabel had put into my glass and opened my drug bag. Maybe the wine gave me the courage to take action.

'I think I can mend you,' I told Mel. I finished off the wine.

He stared at me, disbelievingly.

'I think I know what's wrong,' I said. 'If I'm right I can get rid of the pains and the stiffness.'

I rummaged around in my drug bag until I found what I needed. Although doctors don't know what causes polymyalgia rheumatic, and certainly don't have a cure, it is known that the symptoms can be banished with the aid of corticosteroids' these seem to block the actions of the chemicals which produce the inflammation causing the pain and stiffness.

I took out a small bottle of steroid tablets and asked Mabel to fetch a glass of water. When she returned, I told her to give the glass of water to Mel. I then shook three tablets out into his hand. 'Swallow those,' I instructed him.

'Are these going to kill me or cure me?' he asked. I wasn't sure he cared which.

'They won't kill you,' I told him. 'They will cure you.'

In truth, I should have said that I hoped that they would cure him but I needed all the help I could find. I needed Mel to believe in the treatment I was giving him.

I watched Mel take the pills and then turned to Mabel. 'Make sure Mel takes another three tablets tomorrow morning. There won't be any improvement tomorrow but I'll come back in 48 hours and the pain and the stiffness will be easing off by then.'

Mel would have to take the steroid for a year or two. And he'd need to be certain not to miss any. But if his symptoms started to disappear I didn't think I'd have any problem persuading him to keep taking the tablets.

I made Mel promise that he would not cut his wrists before I returned and then I left, hoping and praying that my diagnosis was right.

I worried all the rest of that day, all that night and all the next day. I had been trained to do tests and investigations before making a diagnosis of a serious disease such as polymyalgia rheumatic. But here I was just handing out steroid tablets in the belief that I was right.

I wanted to go back to see Mel the next morning but I knew that the steroids would not have had time to work. I would merely have to repeat my confident assurance that the pills would cure him. Another visit before there had been any change might reduce Mel's confidence and, therefore, do more harm than good. I thought it best to wait 48 hours in the hope that by the time I returned to the cottage there would be a real improvement.

And so I waited.

And I finally returned to the cottage 48 hours after I'd left.

As I walked along the rutted, branch-strewn track from where I had left the Rolls Royce, I found myself murmuring a prayer that I'd been right and that Mel would have made at least some improvement. If he wasn't any better, then I really didn't know what else I could do.

I could try to persuade him to persevere with the tablets for another 24 hours. But would he wait that long before cutting his wrists? Rarely have I been more anxious to see the outcome of a treatment programme.

Mel and Mabel had heard me coming and when I got closer to their cottage I could see that they were standing in the doorway. They had their arms around each other and they were both crying.

Mel's symptoms hadn't entirely disappeared.

He was still a little stiff and he still had some pain. But he was, he said, so much better that he had, that morning, been able to do a little painting. He was no longer depressed. He was alive again and as full of ambition, hope and good cheer as I had ever seen him.

I told him again that he had to take the tablets every day and that he would need to persevere with them for some time. 'You must not suddenly stop them,' I told him firmly. 'If you do then you will be ill again.'

'I'll make sure he takes them,' promised Mabel; who has far more common sense in her little finger than Mel has in his whole body.

'You forgot your wine,' said Mel, pointing to a full crate of Saint Emilion claret.

I protested that the offer of the wine had been made when he thought he was dying. I also pointed out that he had originally promised me just six bottles.

'If you don't take it then I won't take the pills,' said Mel, who looked as if he were about to stamp his feet and have a tantrum. 'And besides, two bottles are for Thumper. Remember?'

And so I had little choice. I picked up the crate of wine.

'Oh, and we wanted to give you something else,' said Mabel. She darted back into the cottage and reappeared a moment later carrying two paintings.

'Which would you prefer?' she asked. 'A late Chagall or an early Monet?'

I looked at the two paintings. They were amazingly good.

'I did the Chagall and half the Monet last night and finished the Monet this morning,' said Mel.

'I can't...,' I began, trying to refuse the paintings without giving offence.

'Take them both,' insisted Mel. 'If it hadn't been for you, I'd be pushing up daisies.' Once again he wouldn't allow me to refuse.

Since I was carrying the wine, Mabel carried the two paintings to the car.

'Be careful with the Monet,' called Mel as we disappeared off up the track. 'Remember, I only finished it this morning and the paint is still a bit tacky.'

I put the crate of wine on the back seat of the Rolls and Mabel lay the two paintings down on the boot floor.

I then drove home singing.

When things go well there is no better job in the world than being a country GP.

The Man in the Yellow Anorak

The Rolls Royce 20/25 is a magnificent motor car. Built in an era when all motor cars had style, individuality and presence, the 20/25 was one of the first Rolls Royce cars built to cater for the growing number of owner-drivers; customers who were happy to drive their cars themselves (either because they couldn't afford a chauffeur or because they enjoyed driving too much to pay someone else to do it for them).

When Dr Brownlow died he left me his Rolls Royce 20/25; it was and is quite possibly the most absurdly inappropriate vehicle for a country doctor to use. I find it quite impossible to think of anything more absurdly unsuited to driving around in the Devon lanes.

The car is too wide, too long and difficult to steer; it has brakes which need to be applied a good five minutes before the driver wishes to stop and although it consumes fuel at the sort of rate which might be associated with an ocean going liner it accelerates (in comparison with a relatively small, modern family saloon such as an Austin Allegro, Honda Civic or Volkswagen Passat) with stately dignity rather than startling speed. As Patchy Fogg once put it, the Rolls Royce 20/25 was built for travelling rather than arriving.

But few cars have the panache and style of an elderly Rolls Royce motor car and although I had been tempted by the idea of selling the car and purchasing in its stead a more practical vehicle, my affection for Dr Brownlow, and my determination to continue to practise in a way of which I thought he might approve, meant that I had resisted the temptation with great ease. Patsy, I am pleased to say, agreed with me that we should keep the Rolls Royce and say bugger to convenience and practicality. Since the car was not fitted with seat belts (and I had absolutely no intention of having them fitted) she and the babies invariably travelled in the back when we went out en famille and she would, on occasion, wave to pedestrians in a distinctly regal manner. She swears that on one occasion a middle aged woman in South Molton actually curtseyed as we drove past.

Thumper is looking out for a small regal-looking pennant and suitable fixing pole which I can have affixed to the bonnet.

Dr Brownlow's motor car, a spacious limousine, had first seen the light of day in 1930 and, as with all the other vehicles known as 20/25s, only the chassis, six litre engine, gearbox and other mechanical parts had been made by the Rolls Royce company. Dr Brownlow had bought the car second-hand from the widow of a Harley Street consultant with whom he had trained. The consultant had worked himself to death and the widow had decided to sell everything and to move to Monte Carlo for the weather, the social life and the lack of taxation. She had decided that she did not want to be set off on her new life encumbered by a black limousine. The car was less than two-years-old when Dr Brownlow became the owner and in Rolls Royce terms it had barely been run in.

The bodywork for the car had been made ('built' is a more appropriate word) by a firm of coachbuilders known as Thrupp and Maberly. The vehicle had originally been designed to reach a top speed of 75 mph but as they mature, cars – like people – become a little less frisky and I had never managed to take the car above 65 mph. Despite its age, however, the car handled easily and smoothly and was a delight to drive. The steering was an absolute joy, finger light to the touch, and the car had all the mod cons of the day – including a rear fog light, a reversing light, a heater (complete with fan) and windscreen wipers which could, with the aid of two silver knobs, be parked away from the screen when not in use. The dashboard was made of mahogany with black lacquer highlighting. Tolstoy's, the Bilbury garage, had looked after the car when it belonged to Dr Brownlow and they continued to look after it (and even clean it) when I took over ownership.

All that more than made up for the fact that the size of the car, and the rather large turning circle, made it entirely unsuitable for driving around the narrow lanes of Devon. However, spending so much time in close proximity to the Devon hedges did encourage me to learn more about how they had come into being.

Having been brought up in the suburbs of a town in the English midlands I knew very little about the countryside when I first arrived in Bilbury.

As far as I knew, a ditch was just a gulley at the side of the road, dug to cope with excess rainwater, while a hedge was something which existed to mark a minor boundary and to keep animals from straying.

But as time went by, I learnt that things aren't quite as simple as I had once thought.

Boundaries, whatever form they may take, are terribly important to everyone and especially so in the country. Even a farmer who has several hundred acres will worry enormously if he thinks he is losing a foot of land or, just as importantly, someone else is gaining a foot. I also discovered that ditches and hedges are often more than they might appear to be.

Back in Roman times, when the Romans conquered Britain, the entire population of Britain was probably considerably less than half a million and you might have thought that there would be plenty of land to go around. But even back in those simpler days, farmers were protective of their land and guarded their boundaries as jealously as any modern landowner, and with the same dogged determination.

In early Devon, as in the rest of England, the standard unit of cultivation was a piece of land known as the strip. A full strip of land would be 220 yards long and 22 yards wide (the original acre) but most farmers had strips of half an acre or a third of an acre. A bundle or a parcel of strips for cultivation were known as a furlong and a 'campus' or a 'field' was made up of scores of furlongs (and, therefore, several hundred strips) of many different sizes and shapes. The area of land enclosed by ditches and hedges was known as a park and it would be subdivided, by further hedges and ditches, into smaller parcels in order to make it easier to control animals and their grazing.

When a landowner died his estate would, of course, have to be divided up so that it could be shared between the heirs. Each heir had to be given a fair share of every sort of land available – garden, orchard, meadow, woodland, pastureland and heathland – and the result was that land had to be divided into very small fields, some of them no more than half an acre in size. This would, inevitably, mean that the new landowners would need to get digging ditches and building banks and hedges in order to make their boundaries clear.

Today, ditches and hedges mark thousands of boundaries, many of which have been lost. An ordinary looking ditch may mark the boundary line of a former royal manor and there are ditches, hedges, banks and lanes in the county of Devon which are well over a thousand years old.

The village of Combe Martin, just a few miles from Bilbury, originated as a small valley village about a mile inland and only gradually spread down to the valley to the sea as the centuries wandered effortlessly by. Today, Combe Martin still has many mediaeval hedges: boundaries which have been in place since they were grown to mark off individual strips of land.

Bilbury itself, like nearly every village which can be found on a map of England, existed long before William the Conqueror ordered the creation of the Domesday Book in the eleventh century.

Walk along a narrow track, hardly wide enough for a horse drawn cart, and you might imagine that you are merely following in the footsteps, or wheel tracks, of a long forgotten farmer who used that route to pass from one field to another, to move animals, feed or crops from his farmhouse or barns to a distant pasture.

But things aren't that simple.

There are tracks in Bilbury, known to historians and archeologists as 'hollow ways', which were already ancient in the tenth century. However, these 'false' tracks weren't built as tracks or lanes at all but were originally created by two landowners digging out ditches to mark their boundaries.

As they dug, the two landowners or their ditch digging employees, threw up the earth they had moved and built up continuous banks on their side of their ditch. Ditches were customarily expected to be four feet wide and four feet deep and since two ditches were dug side by side this explains why so many tracks and lanes in Devon are just eight or so feet wide.

There was four feet of ditch for landowner A on the left hand side of the lane, and four feet of contiguous ditch for landowner B on the right hand side.

The two mounds of earth produced with the soil taken from the ditches were then planted with a hedge of hazel, oak, maple or ash or, more likely, a mixture of all of these. A good number of hawthorn bushes would be thrown in to the mix to make the hedge tighter, thornier and more impenetrable.

There might be an occasional elm too but the sycamore, now so common, was not introduced into England until the end of the 16th century.

By planting their hedges with what are called 'coppice woods', suitable for providing branches which could be used for fencing and firewood, the landowners could give themselves a constant and useful crop of wood, while maintaining their hedgerow boundaries.

The other advantage of these huge banks and hedges was that animals would be able to shelter from wind and rain. And a pleasant side effect was that the hedges would provide homes for huge numbers of birds.

As the years went by the broad, eight foot wide ditch would need clearing out from time to time, and the soil removed would be thrown onto the top of the bank, building up to the sort of height which can be seen today. What now appears to be a track was originally merely the confluence of two ditches and the track might be wide enough for a man on horseback or even for a cart is merely a convenient coincidence. Look carefully and you will see that these narrow tracks (which can be seen all over Devon, and not just in Bilbury) are several feet below the level of the fields on either side.

Even a man well over six feet tall will, if he walks along a fairly ordinary Devon track, be unable to peer over the top of the earth bank, let alone through the hedge on top of it (which may, itself, have now become a hedge of towering trees), and see into the fields on either side.

Today these banks are now widely known as 'traditional Devon banks' and local planning departments, not understanding their origins or purpose, sometimes insist that builders surround new housing estates with mounds of earth in an attempt to preserve the Devon bank tradition. Sadly, the modern builders usually build the banks out of discarded rubble and rubbish and cover them with a thin layer of clay and stony earth. The result is invariably a sad, weed encrusted earth wall with bits of broken pipe poking out amidst the dandelions, dock and nettles.

It is no wonder that ditch digging and hedge building and layering were for centuries two of the most common forms of employment in the English countryside. And the topography of today's countryside is a direct result of all that digging and layering. The narrow lanes along which people drive in Devon are confined and winding because they follow the tracks and ditches which lie between the banks built to define the extent of each landowner's domain. Since moving huge boulders or trees would take an inordinate amount of effort, the landowners usually wriggled around them – and hence many of these tracks seem to wander hither and thither in a very irregular way.

There are some who might say that driving one of the largest cars on the road in an area of the country with the narrowest lanes is close to lunacy.

I prefer to think of it as driving one of the most beautiful cars ever made in a part of the country with the most beautiful lanes and hedgerows.

Nevertheless, despite this optimistic viewpoint, I have to admit that a huge, old Rolls Royce is not the most sensible vehicle for a country doctor to drive in Devon.

As I travelled around on my daily visits, I was constantly trying to avoid bushes, branches and brambles in narrow lanes which had originally been nothing more than ditches, which had then developed into tracks for driving sheep from field to field, which had been used by farmers on horseback and which had eventually been commandeered by the occasional, wealthy individual with a trap and a pony.

I had become unusually adept at reversing (most of the local lanes were far too narrow to allow cars to pass one another and if two vehicles met, one would invariably have to reverse and find a gateway or field entrance) but I had found, to my surprise, that most other drivers would quickly start to reverse when they saw the Rolls approaching. Even farmers would reverse their tractors to allow the Rolls to pass by.

Locals in and around Bilbury always know how far they have to reverse to reach the last passing place or gateway and when two locals meet in a narrow lane the customary practice is for the one closest to a gate or passing place to do the reversing.

Visiting motorists are, however, rather different. They usually panic when they come face to face with another vehicle in a lane so narrow that there is grass growing in the middle of the road and both of their vehicle's wing mirrors are brushing along in the hedges.

And so, even though my vehicle is longer and wider than most other cars on the road I end up reversing more often than not.

While I was out on my late morning calls one rainy day, I found myself bonnet to bonnet with a dark blue saloon car.

I think it may have been an Austin 1800 but I am ashamed to admit that a lot of modern cars look the same to me and it could well have been a Hillman or a Ford of some kind.

The blue car was towing a caravan and I realised immediately that even though the saloon car driver had a passing space less than twenty yards behind him, I would be the one going backwards. The driver had a look of combined fury and terror on his face and to be honest I'm not surprised. His caravan was about two feet wider than the lane he was in and branches and brambles were scratching along both sides. I remembered that a visitor from Leeds once had to have his caravan unhooked from his car and pulled out with a tractor when it got stuck in the particularly narrow piece of a lane which goes alongside Softly's Bottom. The caravan sides were peeled back by blackthorn and hawthorn branches and the caravan was a write-off when it was finally extricated.

And so I started to reverse the Rolls, trying to remember where there was a passing place behind me and how narrow the lane would get before it widened out again.

It was summer at the time but you wouldn't have known it from the weather.

It had been raining for a week and the rain was bucketing down as though the manufacturer of the stuff had a vast quantity of surplus stock, and was trying to get rid of it because the storage space was needed for hail, snow and other forthcoming meteorological goodies.

As I looked over my shoulder and reversed down the lane, I first saw something orange and then saw something yellow on the other side of the hedge.

The hedge was thick at that point, mainly beech and hawthorn, and even though I was moving very slowly it was difficult to see clearly. When the something yellow moved, I realised that I had spotted a human being in a brightly coloured anorak. He or she was lying on the ground but moving about from side to side. There was a dark shape beside it but it was raining so hard that I couldn't make out what it was: a child or an animal of some kind perhaps.

As I drove backwards, trying to avoid the hedges and peering through the rain, it slowly became clear from the shape that the something orange was a small tent; one of those tiny little things just big enough to provide space for one person who doesn't suffer from claustrophobia, and accompanied by nothing more cumbersome than a thin sleeping bag, a pair of boots and a torch. It was one of those little tents which are light enough, when rolled up, to be carried on top of a rucksack or on the back of a bicycle.

Suddenly the hedge became thinner and I could see through it more easily. But the figure in yellow didn't look right. And what was the small child doing next to the figure in yellow? Was it a child? There was something about the way the individual was moving that concerned me and so I stopped my car and wound down my window. I could then clearly tell that the person in the anorak was in trouble. The rain was pouring down; bucketing down as the Devonians sometimes say.

I speeded up a little and continued to reverse the Rolls as quickly as I could until I came to a gateway. There still wasn't space for the blue saloon and its caravan to pass but there was room for me to open my door and get out of the car. And, just as important, I could get into the field to see what was wrong with the person in yellow.

I jumped out of the car, pulled on my raincoat, grabbed my bag from the back seat, opened the gate and hurried into the field. As I did so, the driver of the blue car pressed his horn impatiently. One of those imperious and irritating toot toots that always make it clear that the person doing the tooting is far more important than everyone else around and must be obeyed immediately. Maybe he thought I had decided to pop out into a wet field to enjoy an impromptu picnic.

I ignored the unhappy motorist and his hooting and hurried over to the figure in yellow. It turned out to be a male; a fellow in his late forties or early fifties I guessed from his face, hair and beard. Although he was moving, writhing would be the most appropriate word, he appeared to be unconscious. He was groaning loudly and crying out in pain.

As I approached the man in the yellow anorak, I could see that there was no child beside him but that two dogs, one large and one small, were crouched over him.

Although I could not, at first, see what was happening it was quickly obvious that the dogs weren't playing with him. Something far more sinister was going on. I shouted loudly to attract their attention and the two dogs duly lifted their heads.

It was raining so heavily that it was difficult to see what breed they were but the big dog appeared to be a Doberman Pinscher and the small dog looked like a Jack Russell terrier. The dogs were, inevitably, soaked. Their fur was flattened as if they had been swimming in the sea.

Only when I was no more than five or six feet away could I see that their mouths were red with blood. I realised with horror that they were eating the man on the ground.

It was absolutely no consolation to see that I had been right about the breeds; the big dog was a Doberman and the small one was a Jack Russell. I knew that there was someone in the village who had two such dogs but for the moment I couldn't for the life of me remember who it was.

I spoke quietly to the dogs, trying to avoid looking directly at them. I kept still, holding my arms by my sides and trying not to look threatening. I talked to them, gently trying all the usual commands I could think of: 'sit', 'lie down' and so on.

But the dogs had tasted blood and they were too excited to be calmed down in such a tepid way.

And so, I hit out at the bigger dog with the only weapon I had – my heavy black, leather medical bag – and caught him a glancing blow on the side of his head. He looked up, growled, snarled and then carried on biting and chewing. The poor man in the yellow anorak was being eaten alive. I swung my medical bag again and this time managed to catch the Doberman a really good blow. He staggered, moved away from the man on the ground and came towards me. I knew that I had to stay upright. If the Doberman managed to get me onto the ground then both I and the camper would be beyond hope.

I love animals in general and dogs in particular and our collie Ben is one of my very best friends but I had never before seen anything quite so menacing as this Doberman.

I swung the bag again and then suddenly realised that the damned Jack Russell terrier was biting my calf. As the Doberman backed away a few feet I swung the bag round as hard as I could and caught the Jack Russell soundly on his chest. The smaller dog backed away whimpering and the lock on my case broke open.

It didn't matter a damn at that moment but I remembered where I had seen a Doberman Pinscher and a Jack Russell together.

The snooty charity executive and his snooty Home Office wife, the couple who had bought the old Bilbury Halt railway station and who had a daughter with alleged asthma, had a Doberman and a Jack Russell.

And their holiday home was only a couple of miles away across the fields.

The man had boasted that he let his dogs run wild and roam across the countryside. These were their damned dogs.

The rain was, if anything, now heavier than ever and the water pouring down from my hair meant that I had to brush my eyes with the back of my hand so that I could see anything at all. It was summer but the rain was colder than I'd expected. I found myself shivering, though I was not sure whether this was because of the cold or through simple fear.

The camper in the yellow anorak was groaning but was now quite still. Arterial blood was spurting from two bites. I knew that if I didn't manage to get to him soon he would definitely be dead. I desperately wanted to attend to the man but I couldn't do that until I had dealt with the dogs.

What had set out to be a fairly ordinary day's morning visits had suddenly become a fight for my life.

Behind me, back in the lane, I could hear the damned driver of the blue car impatiently banging on his horn. I continued to ignore him and risked a look at the man in the yellow anorak. There were huge, ragged tears in his blue jeans and in his anorak and through these I could see that the dogs had bitten great chunks out of him. They had attacked his face too and there was blood streaming down his left cheek. His nose had been half bitten off and it looked as though one ear was missing.

I looked at the unfortunate camper for too long and suddenly found that the Doberman was moving forwards and staring at me and growling. I am not ashamed to admit that I was terrified. I had seen what the dogs had done to the man in the yellow anorak. I was still holding my now open medical bag and I looked down at it and realised that as a weapon it was pretty well useless. I glanced inside. There were syringes and drugs within my reach and if I had time I could inject the bigger dog with a large dose of something suitable.

A good shot of morphine would do the trick. But the dog wasn't going to give me time to take the wrapping off a syringe, let alone break open an ampoule of morphine. I dropped the bag, thanked the heavens that I had not bothered to fasten my raincoat and reached into my jacket pocket. It took just a couple of seconds to open the largest blade on my Swiss Army penknife.

When the Doberman prepared to leap at me, I knew that I didn't have many more chances.

I knew that if I did not make the first slash with the knife count, then I would end up lying alongside the badly bitten and mauled camper; I would be the rest of lunch.

I felt the Jack Russell biting again at my calf and made the mistake of half turning as I tried to shake it off. It occurred to me too late that the dogs were probably operating as a team. The Doberman chose that moment to hurl itself at me. As it was in the air, I waited for what seemed like hours and then stabbed my knife at the animal's neck. I was hoping to stab the dog somewhere in or near its carotid artery. The jugular vein would do. Anything major would be acceptable; any blood vessel at all.

I had never had to fight for my life before.

And I knew that even if I didn't die I could lose a leg or an arm.

Even the loss of a hand would mean the end of my career as a GP in Bilbury. How many one-handed country GPs can there be?

Either the dog was too fast or I was too slow but the knife blade dug fairly harmlessly into the beast's flank, irritating it enough for it to howl with outrage but not disabling it. Nevertheless I managed to sidestep the dog as it leapt.

The animal's claws scratched through my raincoat and the dog finally landed on the grass. I looked around, desperate for another weapon of some kind. There didn't seem to be anything I could use. And then I glimpsed a dead branch on the ground a few feet to my right. The branch was about three feet long and as thick as a rolling pin. I lunged for the piece of wood, picked it up and had it in my hand as the Doberman leapt again. Its mouth was open, its eyes staring madly, angrily and hungrily. Its teeth were bared.

'Don't those bloody people feed their damned dog!' I remember thinking, utterly inconsequentially. My only other thought was the hope that the stick wasn't rotten and wouldn't break up the moment I tried to use it.

I thrust the stick deep into the dog's open mouth and as the dog kept coming I kept pushing until a foot, eighteen inches, two feet of the stick had gone down into the creature's throat. His eyes bulged as he fought for breath. The Jack Russell terrier, seeing the Doberman disabled, backed away for an instant and then came for me again, sinking its teeth into my leg. Using my free leg, I stamped down onto its head as hard as I could and so unbalanced myself that the two of us toppled over. The dog still wouldn't release its hold on my calf. The pain was excruciating. I put my hands around the dog's throat and squeezed and squeezed until it went unconscious. Even then I didn't stop squeezing. The two dogs were going to die anyway. After the way they had behaved they were doomed. I didn't want the Jack Russell attacking the man on the ground. And I didn't want it attacking me as I tried to help him. Only when the small dog went limp did I release my hold on its neck.

I looked around at the Doberman. It was struggling unsuccessfully to remove the stick from its throat and it too was now dying. I looked for a stone with which to finish it off but couldn't see one and so I left it to its fate. The man on the ground needed help now. I had to staunch the bleeding if he was going to have any chance at all.

I have seen some awful things in my life but this was by far the worst. This was the stuff of nightmares. The man was moaning, drifting in and out of consciousness, and I couldn't begin to count the number of wounds which were pouring blood. I had to stop all, or at least most of, the bleeding and I had to do it very quickly. Out here in the field the rain was so heavy that I could still hardly see. There was no telephone for miles around and even if I could ring for help it would be the best part of an hour before an ambulance could reach us. I was on my own. If I could act fast enough, and do enough, then I could probably save him.

But I needed to get him indoors, out of the rain, so that I could assess his wounds and deal with them.

Just then the man in the blue saloon beeped his horn again. He had probably been beeping it constantly but I hadn't heard it. And I remembered that behind the car there was a caravan.

I found my bag, took out a syringe and a vial of morphine and gave the camper a hefty injection to knock him out. I then grabbed some bandages and my suture kit from my black bag and stuffed them into my raincoat pocket before picking up the camper and carrying him out of the field and back to where my Rolls and the blue saloon were still parked bonnet to bonnet. He was, fortunately, a small and light man. Equally fortunately I'm well over six foot tall.

'What the hell is going on? Where have you been? What do you mean by running off and leaving us blocked in?'

The questions came thick and fast from the driver of the blue saloon. He still hadn't left his vehicle but had wound down his window. His engine was still running. It was, I suppose, fortunate that if it had occurred to him to try to reverse his car and caravan out of the way he had decided not to put the thought into practice.

The angry driver, a neat looking man who wore a pink sweater, didn't seem to notice the man I was carrying, let alone the fact that he was unconscious and dripping blood from a dozen major wounds.

It was his wife who noticed.

'What's happened to that man?' she asked.

Looking at her I noticed for the first time that there were two children in the back of the car; a boy and a girl. They both looked to be about twelve or thirteen-years-old. The boy was ashen-faced and looked as though he might be sick. The girl looked fascinated, as though she were watching an exciting film or television drama.

I explained that the man I was carrying had been attacked and bitten by two dogs. I also told them that I was the local GP and that I had to try to stop the bleeding.

'Can we help?' she asked.

'I need to lie him down somewhere flat so that I can try to stop the bleeding. My car isn't big enough. Would you open your caravan so that I can lie him down on the floor? It will be easier to see what needs to be done inside and out of the rain.'

'He's bleeding!' complained the man. 'He's pouring blood. He'll ruin our carpet.'

'Jeffrey!' cried his wife, more upset than angry. 'Don't be awful. The man needs help. Give me the caravan key.'

'But you know how difficult it is to get blood out of a carpet…' protested the driver.

'Jeffrey!' said the woman. 'Give me the caravan key. Now!'

Jeffrey took a key out of his trouser pocket and handed it to the woman. She got out of the car, opened the caravan and helped me lay the camper down on the floor. I half expected her to faint for the man was in a terrible state.

'I've got a first aid kit,' she said, 'I did a course at work. I'm quite good with bandages.'

'Have you got a sharp knife?' I asked. My Swiss Army penknife was still stuck in the side of the Doberman.

'My God!' she said. 'You don't have to amputate anything do you?'

'No, I need to cut off his jeans and his anorak. I need to find all the bleeding points.'

I cut through the man's clothing with a steak knife the woman took from the caravan's cutlery drawer.

The bleeding was worst from his right leg and his right arm. One of the dogs, presumably the Doberman, had bitten deeply into the lower part of the man's leg and into his arm. His leg, in particular, was a terrible mess with great chunks of flesh completely missing, and presumably inside the dogs. Both sites were bleeding so badly that although I managed to suture some of the wounds I had to tie tourniquets round both the thigh and the upper arm. The woman's first aid kit was sadly inadequate but I used my tie for the man's thigh and one of the caravan owner's ties for the man's arm. I then made two pads from folded bandages, put one on the man's ear and another on his nose, both of which were pouring blood, and told the woman to keep them firmly pressed into place. Within five minutes we had temporarily staunched the worst of the bleeding. There was little else to do for the moment.

'Will he live?' asked the woman.

'There's a chance but only if we get him to hospital quickly,' I told her. 'He needs proper care quickly. These wounds need cleaning out and sewing up and he needs penicillin. Can you stay in here with him while your husband follows me to the hospital in Barnstaple? It'll be quicker to drive there than to find a telephone and wait for an ambulance.'

I couldn't stay in the caravan with the man in what was left of the yellow anorak because I had to reverse my car down the lane and then show the driver of the blue saloon the route to Barnstaple.

'Of course I will,' said the woman, who had turned out to be what folk used to call a 'real trouper'. Heaven knows what she was doing being married to the awful little man driving their motor car.

'Release the tourniquets every fifteen minutes for a minute or so at most,' I told her. 'And then retie them tight enough to stop him losing too much blood.'

The woman nodded. 'They taught us that,' she said. 'If you leave tourniquets tied for too long the part of the body deprived of blood and oxygen will die.'

I climbed out of the caravan and hurried along to the driver. It was still pouring down and the sky was black. If I hadn't known better I would have said it was eight or nine o'clock at night. The driver had wound his window up and I had to tap on the glass with my knuckles to persuade him to lower the glass. Even then he only opened it a couple of inches, presumably to make sure that he didn't let too much rain into his car.

'Your wife is staying in the caravan to help stop the bleeding,' I told him. 'I'm going to reverse my car. You follow me and then, when I've found a place where I can turn round, you follow me to Barnstaple.'

'I don't think it's legal for anyone to travel in the caravan while it's in motion,' said the driver, as though that settled the matter. 'And we were going to Taunton for the day since it's raining,' he added. I really don't know what he was planning to do with the badly injured man lying on the floor in his caravan and being tended to by his wife. Perhaps he expected me to put the injured man back into the field. Or maybe he wanted to take the bleeding man toTaunton, leave him in the caravan while they wandered around the shops, and then drop him off at a hospital later that evening.

'Follow me!' I told him. 'Follow me or I'll have you arrested for contributory manslaughter.'

This was, needless to say, an offence which I had made up on the spur of the moment, but the driver of the car was convinced, or at least he wasn't convinced that I was talking nonsense, and so my small deceit did the job. I had guessed correctly. The man, who had seemed to me to be one of those fussy little rule lovers who never dares do anything which might get him into any sort of trouble with any form of authority, grumbled and mumbled but agreed to do as I had told him. When I got into the Rolls and started to reverse, he followed me, and when, three hundred yards later, I found a junction where I could turn round he continued to follow me.

It took less than 40 minutes for our small convoy of two to reach the hospital in Barnstaple, and the journey in a speeding, swaying, unstable caravan must have been an absolute nightmare for the woman nursing the still bleeding and unconscious man.

At the hospital, we enlisted the help of two porters to carry the man into the casualty department. I had given him a decent dose of morphine and he was still too drowsy to talk but he was moaning a good deal and was obviously in a terrible state. I found one of the doctors and explained what had happened. While we were talking a nurse came over to us and asked me if I knew that my left leg was dripping blood. I pulled up my torn trouser leg and saw that the Jack Russell terrier had managed to take two big bites out of my calf muscle. There was so much adrenalin in my blood stream that I had completely forgotten that I had been bitten and I hadn't noticed the pain until the wounds had been pointed out to me. One of the other doctors on call cleaned up my wounds, put in a dozen stitches and gave me a tetanus injection. I told him I didn't think either of the dogs had rabies.

Finally the caravanner's wife and I walked back to where her husband had parked his vehicle and its attendant caravan.

'The carpet in our caravan is ruined!' complained the man, clambering out of his blue saloon, the minute he saw me approaching. My leg was now quite sore and I was limping. 'It's soaking wet with rainwater and blood and it will have to be replaced.'

'I'm sorry about that,' I said, 'will your insurance company cover the cost of a new carpet?'

He made a sort of huffing noise. At his request I followed him across to the caravan. The sides of the caravan were badly scarred and scratched from branches and brambles in the lane but that really wasn't my fault. However, I realised that it did all seem a bit rough on the poor fellow. He had taken his family out for a drive in the Devon countryside and had ended up having his beautiful caravan commandeered and used as a field hospital.

The man said that if he claimed on his insurance he would lose his no claims bonus and have to pay the first £50 of the cost. 'You commandeered my caravan,' he said, 'you should pay for a new carpet.'

I told him that I knew the name and address of the owners of the dogs which had attacked the camper and suggested that he demand compensation from them. The whole awful incident was, after all, entirely their fault. I wrote all the details down on a prescription pad (the only available piece of paper I could find) and, having looked at my watch, pointed out that it still wasn't too late for him to take his family to Taunton so that they could spend an hour or two looking around the shops. He said, however, that the day was ruined and that he was, therefore, going to find a campsite where he could park, rip out the blood soaked carpet and dowse his caravan floor with a strong antiseptic solution.

I thanked him and his wife (the latter with slightly more enthusiasm) and drove back home via the field where it had all happened so that I could collect my medical bag. I also packed up the camper's tent and a few belongings and stuffed them into the boot of the Rolls.

I didn't get round to finishing the calls I had set out to do until several hours later.

I don't know whether Jeffrey, the unhappy caravan owner, ever received any compensation from the Hardley-Fitzwalters but I was never offered any compensation for my badly damaged leg and the ruined pair of trousers – though, indeed, I never asked for any. I was too relieved to have escaped from the confrontation alive and with my limbs intact to want to spend time reliving the experience any more than I had to.

I was still waking up with nightmares a month after the event. Gradually the awful experience began to fade and the nightmares became less violent and less frequent.

When the Hardley-Fitzwalters discovered that their two dogs had been killed their initial reaction was to complain to the police, and to demand that I be arrested, imprisoned, fined and forced to pay compensation. But when they themselves were threatened with prosecution for allowing two dangerous dogs to roam free they scurried back to London and were never again seen in Bilbury.

The couple put the former railway station into the hands of a local estate agent and told him to sell it as quickly as possible for the best possible price.

There are quite a few folk who have properties in Bilbury which they visit only at weekends or for holidays and most of them fit in well; adapting to our slower pace of life with enthusiasm for it is precisely that quality which attracted them to Bilbury in the first place.

But the Hardley-Fitzwalters never fitted in at all. They made it clear that they considered themselves superior in every conceivable way and treated everyone with whom they came into contact with condescension and arrogance. They will not be missed.

The best bit of the story is that the camper, the man in the yellow anorak, made a complete recovery.

He spent several days in hospital in Barnstaple and then had to be transferred to a specialist unit at a hospital in Bristol where his wounds could be treated and he could be provided with the extensive plastic surgery he needed. His nose and ear required a good deal of reconstruction work and altogether he was in hospital for nearly six months.

When he was released from hospital, the camper, whose name turned out to be Norbert, came back to Bilbury to say 'thank you', which I thought was very good of him. Considering everything he had been through I thought it was brave of him too. Lots of people would, after an experience of that kind, have been determined never to set foot in North Devon again.

Norbert told me that he used to be a school master in a boys' preparatory school but that he had given up teaching in order to become, as he put it, 'a wandering minstrel'.

He said he played the violin in shopping centres and on beaches and lived on the coins he collected from members of the public. He insisted on performing what he called a 'concert' at the Brownlow Country Hotel as a 'thank you'. We had five in-patients at the time and it seemed a nice idea. Sadly, however, it turned out that he was an absolutely terrible violinist. Someone, I forget who, commented that the people who gave him money probably did so out of pity or, perhaps, in the hope that he would either go to a pub and buy himself a pint. Someone else, I think it was Thumper Robinson, said he hoped Norbert used some of his takings to pay for violin lessons.

Still, Norbert was a nice enough bloke and it was good to see him looking so well. The plastic surgeon had done a fantastic job on his face. We all thanked him very much and Patsy made a lovely coffee and walnut cake to celebrate the occasion.

Norbert said he had thought about suing the Hardley-Fitzwalters but that he had decided he really just wanted to forget about the incident and get on with his life. He told me that the woman who'd nursed him in the caravan had visited him several times in the hospital after reading where he was in a newspaper article that had been written about his narrow escape.

He said they corresponded regularly and that he had spoken to her once or twice on the telephone. I got the impression that he hoped that their relationship might develop into something more.

He showed me a copy of the article that had been written about him. The headline was *The Man Who Escaped from the Hounds of Hell*. There was a photograph of the man sitting up in bed, with his face half hidden by bandages and alongside it, the art editor had placed a stock picture of a Rottweiler. Someone in the art department had put what was supposed to look like blood dripping from his fangs. I assume the newspaper either got the breed of dog wrong or else the person who had put together the page didn't know the difference between a Doberman and a Rottweiler.

I offered Norbert his tent and the stuff I'd collected from the field but he said that he'd bought a new tent and that I could throw the old stuff away. He explained that he had been paid a fee by the newspaper which had run the article about him and that since he'd been in hospital he hadn't had any living expenses for quite a while.

It's always nice when a potentially tragic story has a happy ending.

The Woman Who Dared To Feed The Birds

When I wandered into the kitchen to have my breakfast, I found Patsy already there. She had a brush and some tiny pots of paint and was using the former to apply the contents of the latter to the side of one of the kitchen cupboards.

'You'll need a lot of those little tins of paint if you're going to do the whole kitchen,' I told her.

Patsy looked at me in the way she favours when she wants to tell me, silently of course, that the joke would have been acceptable if I'd been seven-years-old.

I apologised, cut two slices of bread and popped them into the toaster. Patsy doesn't eat breakfast.

'The kitchen needs decorating,' she explained, 'it's a disgrace.'

I didn't think it merited the word 'disgrace', but then when I was a medical student I lived in a flat which hadn't been decorated since before the First World War and I never saw any need to rush out and buy brushes and pots of paint. I always thought that peeling paint gave a building history and gravitas.

I allow Patsy, who does all these things much better than I ever could, to take all decisions relating to interior and exterior decorating. If she wants to have the windows painted purple and the soffits picked out in bright yellow that's absolutely fine with me. I try to limit myself to moving and carrying stuff that isn't breakable, spillable or valuable. Or exceptionally heavy, of course.

'What do you think of this one?' asked Patsy, showing me a sheet of paint colours and pointing to one that looked like mud.

'Very nice,' I said.

I always say 'very nice' when asked to make comments on things of this nature. I find that in the long run it is the best way.

'Or do you prefer the 'Dead Trout'?'

I looked at her and raised an eyebrow.

'This one,' she said, pointing to another patch of colour on the chart.

'That's very nice too,' I said, sticking to my well-established script.

I know from past experience that choosing colours for bathrooms, kitchen cupboards and dining room walls is a long, arduous and sometimes painful process which can last a considerable amount of time and involve many changes of mind and direction. I find that I need to pace myself by avoiding too early a commitment.

'I really don't know what to go for,' said Patsy who was clearly still in the early stages of indecision. 'The one called 'Squirrel's Breath' is rather good.' She paused and thought for a while. 'But I also like 'Churlish Brown' and 'Drying Plaster''.

I don't know where the paint companies find the names they give their products but I sometimes think they're just taking the mickey. In the space of the next two minutes Patsy showed me paint colours named 'Tiger's Breath', 'Hilltop Mist', 'Old Slipper Green', 'Peppermint Tea', 'Mole's Back', 'Downpipe White', 'Ethel's Blush' and 'Old Arsenic'.

What on earth is any sensible person to make of such nonsense? Whatever happened to 'Blue', 'Red' and 'Green'.

Or, if you want to be fussier, 'Dark Blue', 'Light Blue', 'Dark Red', 'Light Red', 'Dark Green' and 'Light Green'?

'And which white do you think for the ceiling?' asked Patsy.

'Which white? How can there be a choice? Surely white is white unless it's dirty.'

Patsy looked at me as though I needed help and filled the kettle.

I drank my coffee, ate my toast, ripped through the morning mail (most of which was advertising material from drug companies which went straight into the rubbish bin) and wandered into my consulting room in good time to start the morning surgery. When you work from home it is difficult to excuse a late start and so, unless I am out dealing with an emergency, I always try to start seeing patients bang on nine o'clock.

The surgery passed without any exceptional incidents.

Mrs Swingsby came in for the eighth or ninth time to ask if her cataracts were ripe enough for surgery (they still weren't) and Mr Popplethwaite proudly showed me the biggest bunch of haemorrhoids I'd seen since the last blackberry picking season.

I told Mrs Swingsby to pop back in another three months and promised to refer Mr Popplethwaite to a surgeon at the hospital in Barnstaple.

When Miss Johnson brought in my coffee and two digestive biscuits at eleven she brought with her a paint chart with circles and question marks around two colours entitled 'Camelia's Curls' and 'Breakfast Brown'. I wrote 'very nice' alongside both 'Camelia's Curls' and 'Breakfast Brown'. Miss Johnson said she thought the 'Breakfast Brown' to be particularly attractive and so I added an exclamation mark against the 'very nice' I'd written alongside that one, but spent the next half an hour regretting the addition.

The last patient was a real joy to see.

Mrs Evadne Deverell, was not a Bilbury local but was passing through the village on her travels around the country in a small, motorised camper van. She came to see me as what is called a 'temporary resident' and wanted help because she had suddenly noticed that the hearing in both her ears was deteriorating. She said she thought the right ear was the worst affected.

While I looked inside her ears she told me a remarkable story.

She reported that she had visited her GP eighteen months earlier complaining of pain and unusual menstrual bleeding. Her GP had, after a brief examination, referred her to a consultant gynaecologist and after an excruciating wait of five months she had eventually been seen by a specialist at a local hospital.

Few things annoy me more than the fact that patients often have to wait extraordinary lengths of time to find out whether or not they have a serious disorder such as cancer – and to start whatever treatment may be considered appropriate. I found it particularly appalling that Mrs Deverell's GP had apparently made no attempt to speed up the process.

The consultant, who was running an hour late, gave Mrs Deverell very little of his attention and rushed through the whole examination in no more than five minutes. He examined her, took a swab and told her that he or his secretary would be in touch.

Two weeks later, Mrs Deverell had a telephone call from the gynaecologist's secretary who told her bluntly that she had cancer and would need major surgery. She was told that there would be a fairly lengthy wait for surgery, partly because the gynaecologist had a long waiting list and partly because one of the other doctors was going on a sabbatical for three months and was not being replaced. The secretary did not know where the cancer was, what sort it was, what the prognosis was, or whether the long delay would dramatically alter the outcome.

When Mrs Deverell asked if she could see the gynaecologist again to discuss her situation in person, she was told that her GP would have to write another referral letter and that there would be a wait of up to six months.

'So it's really not worth bothering,' said the secretary. 'You'll probably be called for your operation before you see him again. He's very busy.' Mrs Deverell told me that the underlying message was that she would probably be dead by then so what was the point.

Mrs Deverell did not bother going back to her GP.

She surprised herself, she said, by how calm she was. She thought she was going to die and that there was absolutely no point in making a fuss or wasting what few months, weeks or days she had left sitting around waiting for the gynaecologist to see her.

Nor, she decided, did she want to take pills which would, if the rumours she had heard were to be believed, make her sick and result in all her hair falling out.

Mrs Deverell had no one with whom to share her remaining time on earth. Her husband had died several years earlier and they had no children. She had no living relatives and no real friends.

Instead of simply waiting for what she saw as the inevitable, she resigned from her job in the local planning department, sold her small house and bought a Dormobile. She put the money left over from the sale of her house into her current account and decided that she would travel until she was too ill to do so and then she would deal with things by, as she put it, 'driving the Dormobile off a cliff somewhere quiet and remote'.

She had decided originally to go abroad and to see the places she'd seen on television. Paris, Venice, Vienna, Rome and Amsterdam were top of her list. But then she thought about it some more and decided that she would rather spend whatever time she had left seeing Britain. She decided that she would drive around the coast and turn her final days into an unending seaside holiday.

It was now over a year since she had received the telephone call from the consultant's secretary and Mrs Deverell was, to her considerable surprise, feeling quite well. The symptoms which had originally taken her to the doctor had disappeared as mysteriously as they had appeared.

She had come into my surgery merely because she had noticed that her hearing had deteriorated. The story of her mistreatment at the hands of a particularly uncaring part of the health service came out only when I talked to her.

'Do you think they made a mistake?' she asked, when I had removed a good deal of wax from her eternal auditory canals. Her deafness was simply due to a build up of wax.

Few procedures are as quick to do, or as satisfying for both the patient and the doctor, as flushing wax out of ear canals.

My friend William, who is a GP in a large, modern practice, tells me that where he works the nurses do the syringing, since the procedure is considered to be rather beneath the skills of a medical practitioner. I think this is a mistake, for squirting warm water into ears is a very easy way to establish a good rapport between doctor and patient.

I asked Mrs Deverell if she would like me to examine her, to see if there were any signs of the cancer.

She said she would be grateful if I would do so.

Thirty minutes later, after a fairly comprehensive examination, I told her that I had found absolutely no signs of cancer.

'I could send you along to the hospital to have some blood tests and X-rays,' I told her. 'It's the only way to be sure.'

She laughed. 'Thank you for the offer,' she said, 'but I think I'll pass. I'm feeling fine.'

'What are you going to do?' I asked her. 'Are you going to continue with your travels?'

'I certainly am,' she said. 'This has been the best year of my life. I'm going to send that consultant a postcard thanking him for helping to change my life. I hated that damned office where I spent the best years of my life. I should have run away ages ago but I know I never would have done it at all if I hadn't thought I was dying.'

She left with a smile and a cheery wave.

At the end of the surgery there were just three home visits to do.

Two of the visits were routine, involving elderly patients who found it difficult to get to the surgery and who I visited at home once a month or so just to check that all was well.

But the third visit was to Mrs Entwhistle, a lively 67-year-old who has high blood pressure and early signs of Parkinson's Disease but who is, otherwise, as fit as most 40-year-olds I know.

There is no sign of a Mr Entwhistle and Mrs Entwhistle has never mentioned him.

Mrs Entwhistle spent all her life in the military. She was brought up on the Continent and she speaks both French and German fluently and during the Second World War she was parachuted into France to help the French Resistance. After the War she was transferred to the intelligence services and although I know she worked for MI6 I have no idea what she did.

These days, top spies don't always seem to feel the need to remain secret. It will doubtless not be long before they are writing books about their experiences, and wandering around the country giving talks at Women's Institutes about how to make invisible ink out of pigeon droppings.

But Mrs Entwhistle is old school.

She never talks about her life as a spy and has never once told me why she has burn scars on her chest or scars on her back that were clearly made by bullets. Her medical records contain no entries between the ages of 18 (when she had glandular fever) and the day she arrived in Bilbury just a few years ago. When I asked her why this might be she explained that she thought her medical records for the intervening years were probably regarded as 'sensitive' and were, in consequence, probably stored deep in a vault at the Secret Intelligence Service's offices in London.

The request that came in to the surgery that morning was not to visit Mrs Entwhistle at her home but at the police station in Barnstaple where she had, apparently, been incarcerated overnight.

I drove to Barnstaple as quickly as I could, wondering what strange circumstances could have led Mrs Entwhistle to a police station.

'I'm so sorry to trouble you,' said Mrs Entwhistle, who was sitting in a small, stark cell which I would have found intolerably confining, cold and frightening. She seemed quite calm and at peace.

I asked her what on earth had happened.

'I've been arrested,' she told me in the same way that she might have reported the discovery of a corn or a small bunion, 'and I have to appear in court this morning.'

Mrs Entwhistle is not a woman who gives anything away. In fact, though I like her and respect her I've always thought her to be very reserved; a rather cold sort of fish.

'Unfortunately, I don't have my blood pressure tablets with me,' she said, 'I came into Barnstaple to visit the optician and had intended to be back home yesterday evening.'

I had my black bag with me but I didn't have any of the tablets which I know she normally takes so I wrote out a prescription, wandered out to the nearest town centre pharmacy, and hurried back to the police station.

Having taken her tablets, Mrs Entwhistle then explained what had happened.

'I bought a sandwich from a little shop near the Post Office,' she told me. 'They do very nice salad sandwiches there and since I had a two hour wait for the bus to Lynton I sat on a bench by one of the churches to have a little picnic. It's always quiet there and there are always birds and squirrels to watch.'

(I should explain that the bus service to Bilbury is virtually non-existent and so villagers without their own transport have to catch the bus to Lynton, get off the bus at Blackmoor Gate and then walk two miles to the village.)

Mrs Entwhistle explained that when she sat down to eat her sandwich a couple of sparrows and two or three pigeons gathered around her waiting for any crumbs which fell to the ground.

'They seemed so hungry,' she said, 'that when I'd eaten all I wanted I crumbled up the last few bits of bread and gave them to the birds.'

I nodded and waited, wondering what else had happened.

'A policeman who was walking by saw what I'd done and came over and arrested me.'

I frowned, finding it difficult to believe what I had heard.

'What did he arrest you for?' I asked.

'For feeding the birds.'

I stared at her, probably rudely and definitely in disbelief. 'You were arrested for feeding the birds?'

'Apparently there is a by-law against it.'

'A law against feeding the birds?'

'Apparently so.'

'That's…,' I stumbled for a moment, unable to think of an adequate word. 'Madness!' I eventually managed. It was a woefully inadequate word for what I felt.

'But there isn't any evidence!' I said. 'The birds ate all the crumbs which you dropped!'

For a second it seemed to me to be a brilliant defence.

Mrs Entwhistle smiled. 'Sadly they wouldn't accept that argument,' she said. 'I'm told that as far as the court is concerned, the policeman's word is considered quite adequate.'

'But feeding the birds is a traditional thing to do,' I said, 'and it's well-known that when people look after wild creatures they feel better and their health improves.'

Mrs Entwhistle shook her head. 'I don't think that will get me very far.'

I racked my brains, trying to think of some other defence.

'Thank you for getting me the tablets,' said Mrs Entwhistle with a smile. She reached out and patted me on the arm. 'I mustn't keep you any longer. If they let me go with just a fine I can catch the bus back later this afternoon.'

'I'm staying at the station with you,' I told her. 'And I'll take you home afterwards.' It was, I know, what my predecessor Dr Brownlow would have done. And I always try to conduct my practice in a way of which he would approve.

When Dr Brownlow, had died he had bequeathed me his practice, his house, which I had decided to turn into a hospital where the sick, the frail and the dying could be nursed, £50,000 in cash, which I earmarked to help run the hospital and, of course, his 1930 black Rolls Royce 20/25. But Dr Brownlow's most valuable legacy could not be measured in money, bricks or horsepower.

His most valuable legacy, the gift I cherished most, was the knowledge he had given me; the wisdom which it had taken him a lifetime to acquire.

When I had first started in general practice, just a few years earlier, I had been extraordinarily naïve and woefully ignorant.

I didn't realise that, of course.

Like all young men and women who have spent many years studying at university I was under the impression that graduation had miraculously completed my education.

Indeed, I confess with shame that I had thought myself superior in knowledge to those doctors who had qualified decades earlier, before the introduction of antibiotics, oral contraceptives and sophisticated X-ray technology.

After twenty years at school (primary school, grammar school and medical school) I had acquired a medical diploma and unfettered access to the arrogance of youth.

For about a day after I qualified, I thought I knew everything a doctor could ever need to know.

And then, slowly, I started to learn about life, about patients, about medicine and about the many, many things that doctors do wrong.

Gradually, by working alongside Dr Brownlow, I began to understand that the most important lessons a doctor learns are found not in textbooks but through real-life, practical experience.

Lectures and textbooks are good enough for providing background knowledge. I had acquired a basic understanding of human anatomy and physiology. I knew the names of the small bones in the wrist, the way the liver works, the marvellous things that white blood cells can do and the many ways in which things can go wrong. But it was only after I qualified that I learned that the stuff that is taught in classrooms is of far less value than the things which are learned by the patient's bedside.

Dr Brownlow's greatest legacy to me was a vast reservoir of knowledge and wisdom distilled from decades of practical experience and a deep understanding of the human condition. Dr Brownlow knew that medicine is one third science, one third craft and one third art and he taught me that the more we look, the more we see and the more we see the more we realise that we really don't know anything very much. He taught me the importance of listening.

The wiser we become the more we realise the extent of our ignorance; this is doubtless why only teenagers and young doctors, unsullied by wisdom and experience and not yet weighed down by knowledge and understanding, are the only truly omniscient beings in our world.

My only contribution was to have acquired enough humility to realise that if I listened to Dr Brownlow, and tried to absorb some of his knowledge and understanding, I would be able to cut short the learning process and add his accumulated wisdom to my own modest supply.

Six months after Dr Brownlow had died, I still missed him terribly and I knew that I would always miss him.

One of the most important things he taught me was to try to look at problems, dilemmas and clinical puzzles from all possible angles. 'If you're stuck with a diagnosis, try to look at the problem from another direction,' he told me. 'It won't always lead to a solution. But it will dramatically increase your chances of finding an answer.'

Something else he taught me was to treat all my patients as members of my extended family.

'Always treat every patient as you would like your loved ones to be treated, or as you would like to be treated yourself,' he told me.

Those thoughts stuck with me and there wasn't a day when I didn't remember his advice.

Looking at Mrs Entwhistle, sitting patiently in her cell, I knew that if Patsy were in this situation I would want to be with her. And I knew that if I were locked in a cell I would appreciate having a friend to stand beside me.

I also hoped that by using Dr Brownlow's advice, and looking at Mrs Entwhistle's problem from all angles, I might be able to find a solution.

And when Mrs Entwhistle's case came to court a few hours later, it was Dr Brownlow's piece of essential advice (to think from other directions, from outside the constraints of orthodox thinking) that enabled me to find a way to help my patient to victory in her small battle against the local establishment.

Once I had convinced Mrs Entwhistle that, whatever she said, I was going to stay with her, I asked the station sergeant if I could use a telephone to tell Patsy where I was. He pointed me in the direction of a payphone and once I had found a kindly constable prepared to sell me some change for the telephone, I rang Bilbury Grange and told Patsy where to reach me if she needed me.

When Mrs Entwhistle's case came to court, a snooty and very self-important policeman stood up to give evidence for the prosecution. He was, predictably, an unbearably officious fellow, one of those policemen other policemen can't abide or trust, and clearly destined to rise to great heights within his chosen trade. I wasn't in the slightest bit surprised. What sort of human being would arrest an old woman for giving crumbs to a few sparrows and pigeons?

Mrs Entwhistle refused to say anything in her defence and so suddenly, having had a flash of inspiration, I stood up.

'Yes?' said the chairman of the three magistrates, a stern looking woman in a twinset and skirt of some hairy looking material that looked as if it were probably hedge and bomb proof. She had huge dangly earrings and a solid looking necklace around her neck. 'Who are you and what do you want?'

'I'm Mrs Entwhistle's doctor and I have evidence which the court should hear,' I said, when I had introduced myself.

I had, I thought, hit upon a possible defence. It was, I knew, a trifle bizarre but then the whole idea of arresting a pensioner for feeding the birds seemed pretty bizarre.

The three magistrates muttered among themselves and called the advice of the clerk. It was eventually decided that I could be allowed to give evidence in the witness box.

'Mrs Entwhistle has early Parkinson's Disease,' I told them. 'The symptoms of this disease include, as I expect you know, a tremor or shaking in the hands. If Mrs Entwhistle was eating a sandwich then her hands would shake and some crumbs would fall to the ground. It seems to me that no harm has been done since the birds who were present ate up the crumbs.'

'Mrs Entwhistle was seen rolling bits of bread into small balls,' said the woman in the tweeds and pearls.

One of the other magistrates, the one in the middle of the trio, and the one who was clearly the chairman, looked at me and smiled, unexpectedly. I recognised him. I'd seen him at one or two medical meetings. He was a well-respected and widely liked consultant at the local hospital, though I couldn't remember what his speciality was.

'Does Mrs Entwhistle have the characteristic pill rolling tremor associated with Parkinson's Disease?' he asked me.

'She does!' I replied instantly, realising that this magistrate was on our side.

'The pill rolling movement is a well-known characteristic of Parkinson's Disease,' I explained to the other magistrates. 'The patient rubs their thumb and forefinger together. The movement is known as 'pill rolling' because it is the sort of movement apothecaries would have made when they were making hand rolled pills.'

'So the police officer might have assumed that Mrs Entwhistle was rolling the small pieces of bread into round balls when in fact he was seeing the pathognomonic signs of her illness?' said the medically qualified magistrate.

'She would,' I agreed eagerly.

'I can see no reason to continue with this case,' said the medical magistrate, leaning back. 'Mrs Entwhistle has clearly been wrongly arrested.'

The woman in the twinset, the chairman of the trio, looked desperate to interfere but although she opened her mouth she didn't say anything – clearly unwilling to interfere in a matter on which two doctors had already expressed a single opinion. She closed her mouth again and gave an excellent impression of a woman sucking an acid drop for a moment. 'The court admonishes the unnecessarily officious police officer who arrested this woman,' she said at last, 'and apologies profusely to Mrs Entwhistle.'

I then took Mrs Entwhistle back to her cottage.

When I dropped her off, she smiled and kissed me on the cheek. 'Thank you,' she whispered. 'You're a good egg.'

I could not have been prouder if I'd been given a knighthood.

The 'good guys' don't often win battles against the rule followers and the niggly, pettifogging, small-minded bureaucrats who seem determined to stamp out joy and individualism. But it seemed to me that this was a victory worth celebrating. On my way back to Bilbury Grange I stopped off at Peter Marshall's emporium and purchased two bottles of his very best Polish champagne and a large box of almost fresh jammy doughnuts.

No one can ever accuse me of not knowing how to make whoopee.

Afterword

There will, I know, be those who will dismiss the memories in this book as nothing more than shameless nostalgia.

There are many people in our society who are ardently committed to change at any price, and who consequently regard nostalgia as something rather sinful. They believe that all change is progress which should be applauded and accepted until it, in turn, is replaced and becomes tomorrow's nostalgia.

We should, they believe (and preach), be forever marching forward, putting aside our past in the same way that a child puts away his toys when he grows up; without regret and without ever looking back.

This attitude, surprisingly prevalent these days, assumes that everything that is new is essentially good and that everything that is old must inevitably be bad.

And it is an attitude which I find it quite impossible to accept.

There is, of course, much about the past which is bad and which deserves to be buried and forgotten.

No one can feel nostalgic for open sewers, wash tubs or tenement buildings.

No one remembers child labour, racism, discrimination or enforced servitude with pride.

Pea soup fog you could cut into cubes with a knife may look good on screen in Victorian melodramas but it wasn't much fun for those who tried to breathe it.

But the fact that we may justly condemn the less savoury aspects of our past does not mean that we must automatically shudder at the memory of such almost forgotten moral principles as honour, privacy and respect. Nor do we need to sneer at the memory of horse drawn ploughs, maypole dancing and the smell of bread toasting over an apple log fire.

Our lives are faster now but are they better?

Our motor cars may (in theory, at least) enable us to travel from A to B more speedily than ever before but is B always a better place to be?

What value should we put upon the quality of the journey?

Is today's production motor car better looking and in every way superior to the motor cars of yesterday?

Is modern medical practice always better than medicine as it was practiced nearly half a century ago?

When considering these questions we must, of course, also ask ourselves how much our admiration of the past is coloured by the hue of our spectacles.

And that brings us neatly back to Bilbury.

How much of it is real? How much is imagined? And how much is wishful thinking? Were things ever that good? Do these questions matter? Are the answers important?

One reader pointed out to me that Bilbury must be real because on the original hardback version of Bilbury Grange the cover photograph is credited to a certain Thumper Robinson.

Good point.

An unintentional hint in the direction of the truth, perhaps.

All I can tell you is that in our hearts, my wife and I live in Bilbury. And Thumper and Anne, Patchy and Adrienne, Peter, Frank and Gilly are our very good friends.

Whether or not you believe that Bilbury exists is entirely up to you.

But why wouldn't you?

Appendix 1

While my GP friend William and his family were staying with us at Bilbury Grange, William and I compiled a list of our favourite, obscure medical words.

He and I have always been fascinated by words – especially medical words and quasi medical words – and when we were students together we would waste rare evenings in the local pub looking up and memorising examples of obscure medical terminology.

As far as we were concerned the more obscure the word the more we liked it. William had a Victorian dictionary which we scoured for new examples. And since I am a bibliotaph I have, over the years, acquired an embarrassingly large collection of dictionaries, books of quotations and thesauruses.

Over several evenings (and a few bottles of port) we took it in turns to try to outfox each other with bizarre words.

The first rule was that although the words which we selected had to be heard or read only rarely they had to be quite real – proper words rather than made-up words.

The second rule was that a word would not count unless the person offering it could both spell it and pronounce it.

Here is the list we came up with:

Abulia – an abnormal inability to make decisions
Adipsia- not drinking for a long time
Adust – looking sunburned or tanned
Agerasia – a youthful appearance in an old person
Anophelosis – a morbid state due to extreme frustration
Anosmia – the loss of the sense of smell
Bantingism – losing weight by not eating sweets
Bariatrics – medical speciality dealing with obesity
Bathukolpian – large breasted
Bibliolatry – the worship of books to an unnatural degree

Bibliotaph – Someone who hoards books is a bilblitaph

Borborygmus – a rumbling sound caused by too much wind in the intestine

Brannigan – a drinking binge

Callimastian – having beautiful breasts

Callipygean – having beautiful buttocks

Civestism – the habit of dressing only in the clothes of one's own sex

Cogniscent – being aware of something

Confabulation – the unintentional production of distorted memories

Coryza – common cold

Crapulous – If you feel ill as a result of eating and drinking too much then you are crapulous.

Curmuring – The low, rumbling sound sometimes heard coming from within the bowels is known to educated gastroenterologists as curmuring.

Cyanthropy – a condition in which the sufferer believes himself or herself to be a dog

Cyesis – pregnancy

Cystoureteropyelonephritis – an inflammation of the bladder, ureters and kidney

Dactylonomy – the habit of counting on one's fingers

Daymare – an anxiety attack

Deipnosophist – This isn't, strictly speaking, a medical word but it is such a delight that William and I had to include it in our list. It means someone skilled in making dinner table conversation.

Diurnation – habit of sleeping during the day instead of at night

Dormition – a peaceful and painless death

Dysmorphosteopalinklasy – the re-fracturing of a bone which has healed with a deformity

Edacious – voracious eating

Ejaculatorium – room in which sperm bank donations are made

Emboinpoint – a woman's bosom

Encephalomyeloradiculoneuritis – disease caused by a virus and associated with encephalitis

Euneirophrenia – a peaceful state of mind after a pleasant dream

Evancalous – pleasant to embrace

Feuterer – an individual who keeps a dog

Gargalesthesia – the feeling resulting from tickling
Girouettism – constantly altering personal opinions to follow other people's views
Glossospasm – moving the tongue in and out very quickly
Haematoma – a posh word for bruise
Heterogamosis – marriage between individuals who are entirely unsuitable for each other
Hypnopedia – learning while asleep (usually by listening to a tape or disk)
Iatrogenic – a disease caused by doctors
Idiopathic – a disease for which the cause is unknown
Idiopathic cyesis – a pregnancy of unknown cause or origin
Illeism – referring to oneself in the third person
Infavoidance – disguising one's inferiority complex
Jen – love of everything and everyone
Kathisomania – an irresistible compulsion to sit down
Lapidation – stoning someone to death
Macarism – making other people happy by praising them
Macrophallus – an exceptionally large penis
Malneirophrenia – anxiety after a nightmare
Matutinal – anything that happens in the morning
Melorrhoea – an irresistible urge to write excessively long musical works
Meteorism – uncontrollable passing of wind
Metrona – a young grandmother
Micromastia – exceptionally small breasts
Microphallus – abnormally small penis
Nomogamosis – marriage between individuals who are highly suitable for each other
Omnistrain – the stresses and strains of modern day living
Omphaloskepsis – contemplating one's own navel
Onchyophagy – fingernail biting
Pneumoencephalographically – taking pictures of the brain after injecting air into the ventricles
Pneumonoultramicroscopicsilicovolcanoconiosis – miner's lung disease (caused by inhaling fine dust)
Pogonophile – an individual who has a fetish for beards
Polyandry – when a woman legally takes several husbands
Polydactyl – having more than five fingers or toes

Polygyny – when a man legally takes several wives
Priapism – a disorder in which the penis is permanently erect
Prosopagnosis – an inability to remember faces
Pygalgia – sore buttocks
Quadragenerian – someone between the ages of 40 and 50
Remontado – an individual who runs away to the mountains
Scrofulous – corrupt or morally degenerate
Sialagogue – anything which promotes salivation
Snurp – to become shrivelled and wrinkled
Sockdolger – a definitive answer that ends a dispute
Steatopygia – having an unusually large, fatty bottom
Suigenederism – tendency of a child to spend time with other children of the same sex
Syngenesiotransplantation – a graft of tissue which takes place between closely related individuals
Tachyphagia – eating very quickly
Tenterbelly – a glutton
Trilemma – one more lemma than a dilemma
Ultracrepidarianism – the habit of giving opinions and advice on matters which are outside the speaker's knowledge (common among politicians and callers to radio phone in programmes)
Valetudinarian – someone over concerned with his or her health
Verbigeration – the frequent use of much loved words
Wederognomonia – using aches and pains to predict the weather
Xenomania – having an excessive interest in foreign customs
Yaffling – eating noisily and greedily
Yatter – to make idle chit chat or gossip
Yerk – to hit someone with vigour
Zaftig – having a pleasingly plump figure

I'm including our list here because I hope that readers might have a little fun by introducing as many of these words as possible into their daily conversation.

So, for example, Mrs Carruthers might say: 'Good morning Mrs Carstairs, I do apologies for the curmuring and for my borborygmi. I'm feeling crapulous this morning and I've got a bad attack of meteorism.'

And Mrs Carstairs might reply: 'Don't worry about it, Mrs Carruthers. My anosmia is playing up. But I'm afraid I can't stop and yatter this morning for according to my wederognomonia, it's going to rain and I have to get the washing in.'

Note from the author:

If you have enjoyed this book I would be genuinely grateful if you would leave a short, positive review on the Amazon product page.